Faith and Hope in Midlife

Faith and Hope in Midlife

Reflecting on Churchgoers' Experiences

Anne Shave

Philip
Garside
Publishing Ltd.

Paperback International edition 2022:
ISBN 9781991027092

Also available

Paperback New Zealand: ISBN 9781991027108
Paperback print-on-demand USA: ISBN 9798807984838

PDF: ISBN 9781991027061
ePub: ISBN 9781991027078

Philip Garside Publishing Ltd
PO Box 17160
Wellington 6147
New Zealand

books@pgpl.co.nz — www.pgpl.co.nz

Cover photograph:

Close-Up Abstract Details of Blue and Green
Stained Glass Vertical

Photo 169043525 © Robert St Pierre | Dreamstime.com

Contents

Introduction

All spiritual experience, all Christian belief and practice, is rooted in our common humanity. Sit and listen to anyone telling you the story of their days, and you will find yourself listening to the common story that binds us all: a story that contains love and hurt and pain, loneliness and belonging, desire and disappointment, anger and guilt, the need to forgive and to be forgiven, that are implicit in the costly business of living and loving. The story of any one of us is also, in a profound sense, the story of us all.

Michael Mayne, former Dean of Westminster[1]

As I embarked on writing this book I asked one middle-aged churchgoer, whom I shall call Jane, what she would like to read about in a book about midlife and Christian faith. She replied, "Stories are good because they either trigger off things you haven't thought about, or they are helpful because you realise 'it's not just me'." So, for Jane, and for all who find stories a helpful entry point for personal reflection and learning, this book is full of stories. They are true stories of people's experiences of midlife, of church and of faith, told by New Zealand churchgoers, ministers and priests from Presbyterian, Anglican and Catholic[2] churches, and spiritual directors from these and other denominations.

By way of introduction, it is perhaps appropriate that I share a little of my own story as far as church involvement and midlife is concerned. I am a member of the Presbyterian Church of Aotearoa New Zealand, but I have (in various ways) been actively involved in all three of the denominations from which interviewees for this book were selected. My upbringing within the Presbyterian Church and involvement in it throughout my life has shaped my understanding of Christianity and undoubtedly colours my perception of other church traditions and particular spiritual practices. Having also sung in Catholic choirs for nearly 30 years, and having attended spiritual direction and retreats led by Catholic directors over a similar period, I have some experience of Catholic practices and teaching. In 2019 I trained in retreat direction and spiritual guidance at St Beuno's Jesuit Spirituality Centre in North Wales. In my 30s, the liturgy of Evensong and Choral Night Prayer attracted me to the Anglican Church. I continue to attend those services regularly and I am a member of a small group within an Anglican parish.

Some personal factors prompted my interest in midlife spirituality. I am a "Gen-Xer" (I was born between 1965 and 1980). My mid-to-late 40s were punctuated by a number of significant life events which included choosing to leave a rewarding career as a high school teacher, the loss of both my parents, and a period of ill-health. Major earthquakes in Canterbury, and their aftermath, also impacted upon my experience of midlife. On the plus side, during this period of significant change I was able to spend a lot of time with my family, to enjoy the company and support of friends, and to think deeply about my Christian faith as I studied theology through the University of Otago.

In my late 40s it became very apparent to me that many people of about my own age were dealing with significant transitions and challenges and embracing new opportunities, some of which related to their age and stage of life and some of which did not. I am single. I was aware that married friends and family members were adjusting to changes in family dynamics and in their marriages as their children moved into their teens or left home. Some friends who had been at home with children were enjoying moving into the paid workforce. A number were coping with challenges in their own health or in the health of those close to them. For us all, attendance at funerals was becoming a more frequent occurrence. Associated with these events and transitions were subtle shifts in attitudes, values, beliefs and spiritual practices, which intrigued me. These things stimulated my interest in the complexity of midlife.

I became interested in the connection between the cluster of issues that seem to arise for many people in midlife, the internal shifts that seem to occur naturally, and Christian faith. I wondered how clergy and congregations were responding to the challenges and transitions that middle-aged parishioners might be coping with, and how attentive they were to the spiritual needs connected to the issues arising in this stage of life. Having attended church since childhood, I had frequently observed the needs of people in other age groups being taken into account but I had never heard any discussion about midlife spirituality. Yet it seemed to me that midlife, with all its complexity, could be a part of life during which people might be particularly open to spiritual matters.

It was out of these experiences, observations and questions that my desire to complete a doctorate in theology arose. My thesis, *Your Strength in Our Hearts: New Zealand Churchgoers in Midlife*, which is available in the public domain,[3] explored the experiences and spiritual practices of middle-aged churchgoers and the role of the church in supporting people in this stage of life. This book draws upon that research and upon many additional conversations and interviews conducted since the completion of my studies, and is intended to be broader in scope. I hope that it will be both accessible and useful to a wide readership.

As I have mentioned, the people who contributed to my research were almost all from Anglican, Catholic and Presbyterian churches. Although there are some obvious differences in theology and ecclesiology between these three churches this book affirms the commonality of faith experience shared by people across these denominations. But within each of these denominations there exists a variety of church types. In my selection of interviewees I endeavoured to ensure that this diversity was reflected. Among my interviewees were those who described themselves or their faith communities as evangelical, liberal, charismatic, contemporary and contemplative. Some of the people I spoke to felt most comfortable worshipping in very traditional liturgical contexts whereas others were accustomed to relatively informal church services, including services which occurred in environments other than traditional church buildings. The parishes the interviewees came from also varied greatly in size, with Sunday attendances ranging from around 30 to over a thousand. A number of the people I spoke to regularly attended services at more than one church. I hope, therefore, that the stories shared within this book may resonate with readers from a variety of church types.

This book is for Christians in midlife who:

❖ would like to have some theoretical understanding of midlife issues

❖ would like to read about the experiences of other Christians in a similar stage of life to themselves

❖ have found a place of belonging in the church OR are finding that church is currently feeling a little less like home

❖ hope to build their awareness and understanding of spiritual practices which may be helpful to them now or in the future.

It is also for clergy, church leaders and congregations who would like to be able to offer more intentional support to parishioners in midlife. Very little has been published about the experiences or needs of middle-aged churchgoers in the New Zealand context. This may be partly due to the fact that in many congregations in this country people in midlife are conspicuous by their absence. It is therefore understandable that exploring the needs and experiences of middle-aged Christians who *do* attend church has for some time seemed less urgent than trying to work out why many people in this age group *do not* (or no longer) attend.[4] These are, of course, related issues. Listening to the stories of those who (mostly!) appreciate being involved in a church community can help us learn a lot about what might attract or help others of a similar age to come or to remain connected. The priests and ministers I interviewed were disarmingly frank in acknowledging that, in their experience, the needs of Christians in midlife are often overlooked in the church. They were interested in reflecting on this issue and several suggested that they and their colleagues would find reading about this topic valuable. I hope that they may find this book useful.

Spiritual directors and those contemplating or undergoing training in spiritual direction are likely also to find it interesting to reflect on stories and opinions shared by interviewees, including, of course, comments made by other spiritual directors. For those readers who are not familiar with spiritual direction, a straightforward explanation of this ministry is that it is a one-to-one conversation, similar in some ways to counselling, in which a person seeks to answer the question, "What is spiritual growth and how do I foster it in my life?"[5] The combination of directees' willingness to attend regular appointments to devote time and attention to the spiritual life, the nature of the questions that are posed in spiritual direction, and the fact that spiritual direction is conducted on a one-to-one basis in a context within which confidentiality is assured, means that issues of real import can be discussed. Some of the matters that are raised in spiritual direction may never be shared elsewhere, even – and sometimes, particularly – within churches. As expected, interviews with the spiritual directors shed light on aspects of Christians' midlife experience which other people did not mention, as well as reinforcing themes which emerged from interviews with churchgoers and clergy.

As well as having obvious appeal to Christians in midlife, clergy and spiritual directors, I hope that other readers will also find that certain stories and reflections shared here will resonate with them. When I have spoken about midlife spirituality to mixed-age audiences and congregations, older people have told me that the material was of interest to them because it not only reminded them of experiences that they themselves had been through but alerted them to issues that their adult children were dealing with that had simply not arisen for them, or their acquaintances, two or three decades earlier. For younger adults, particularly those approaching midlife, reading about a stage of life which they are yet to enter may also be helpful. There is a predictable quality about certain midlife experiences but for many people they can come as a surprise. As we shall see, having some awareness of common midlife experiences, particularly those that relate to faith, can go a long way toward alleviating anxiety or bewilderment if or when they occur.

International research on midlife has gathered some momentum in recent years through the work of The John D. and Catherine T. MacArthur Foundation Research Network on Successful Midlife Development,[6] studies conducted by Margie E Lachman and others involved in the Lifespan Developmental Psychology Lab at Brandeis University and the Brandeis University Lifespan Initiative on Healthy Aging, the work of Oliver Robinson and team members at the Department of Psychology, Social Work and Counselling at the University of Greenwich, and others. Despite this upsurge in interest in midlife, the link between midlife, human development and Christian spirituality has not received much attention. The 1980s and 1990s produced a number of publications on this theme as Christian writers grappled with the significance of theories of adult development which had been published and popularized in the latter half of the 20th century. While much of this work remains of interest, it is naturally based on certain presumptions and perspectives which differ in some significant respects from those held by many people today. Over the past few decades societal changes of unimaginable scope and impact – in the areas of familial relationships, technology, life expectancy and career diversity, and in world-view – have occurred. In addition to coping with personal transitions and challenges, people navigating midlife today are doing so in a global environment in which constant change and uncertainty has become the norm. It is timely for further exploration of the experiences of midlife churchgoers to occur.

Christians throughout the world obviously hold in common many core beliefs and values but the outworking of our faith is inevitably affected by context. This book is about New Zealanders, for New Zealanders. While I do draw upon international research, especially in the opening chapter, which introduces key issues relating to midlife, New Zealanders' experiences lie at the core of this book. All of the people I spoke to came from Auckland, Christchurch and Dunedin. The majority described themselves as "New Zealand European" (or *Pakeha*), although people born in the Pacific Islands, Asia, the United Kingdom and South Africa were also among my interviewees. Demographic details and some explanation of the way that interviewees were selected are provided in the appendix which describes the research methods used. For reasons of anonymity, I am unable to acknowledge interviewees by name, but I am sincerely grateful to every person who was willing to contribute to my research. I felt honoured to learn so much from so many generous people.

I would also like to acknowledge the support of a number of other people. I owe a real debt of gratitude to my doctoral supervisors. My primary supervisor at Otago University, Rev. Dr. Lynne Baab, has written numerous books in the field of spirituality and pastoral care, including books about midlife. While working on my PhD I was extremely grateful for Lynne's constructive feedback, encouragement, energy and expertise. My secondary supervisor, Dr. Kathleen Rushton, is a member of Nga Whaea Atawhai o Aotearoa Sisters of Mercy New Zealand, and teaches Scripture for The Catholic Institute of Aotearoa New Zealand. Kath's erudition and enthusiasm and her ongoing support have motivated me as I have continued to work on this book. Close friends and family members have demonstrated considerable stamina in continuing to express interest in my ideas and writing progress over the past six years. Their unstinting encouragement has helped me to bring this project to completion. I would particularly like to thank Jen Halliday, Kirsten Challies, and Myriam and Michael Cooke for helping me at points when I needed another perspective on my work. I am grateful to Joanna Frampton and Rev Hamish Galloway for reading and commenting on drafts, and my sister Clare Shave for proof-reading early chapters. I would also like to thank Vaughan Park Anglican Retreat and Conference Centre for its generous support. It was wonderful to spend two months as Scholar in Residence there in 2019.

This book is deliberately descriptive rather than prescriptive. Although almost every chapter includes examples of spiritual and pastoral practices that have proven helpful to people in midlife, the range of stories shared and the open-ended questions posed at the end of each chapter are intended to inspire individuals and congregations to explore context-specific responses to the issues that are raised, not to suggest that certain practices should be replicated. I hope that it will offer encouragement to people navigating midlife and to those who would like to support them.

1 — Counting our days

"Teach us to realize the brevity of life,
so that we may grow in wisdom."

Psalm 90:12 (NLT)

Midlife has been described as "perhaps the least studied and most ill-defined of any period in life."[7] According to psychologists Ursula M. Staudinger and Susan Bluck, one reason that midlife has received relatively little attention is that it has not been considered to be a "particularly problem-stricken phase of life." Those in midlife have been considered to be "one of the pillars that maintain societal functioning, rather than appearing to be in need of special support."[8] Middle-aged churchgoers are also often regarded as "pillars" of their faith communities and are relied on to provide support to others. Nonetheless, a lot may be going on for people in this life stage.

"There is a significance about midlife," Bernard (Catholic priest, 52) told me:

> It's not just a continuum. I have noticed that about myself and the people I work with. I think it's a time, typically, of re-examination of one's life. I'm not sure what triggers it. It could just be chronology. You get to a certain age. It's a really fascinating question. I suppose if you are a family person you tend to have finished the education of your children. To some extent, I'm guessing, that's what sparks it off in some of the people who come to see me. I don't have any children but it's still happened. I think certainly for myself, and the people I've spoken to, it's a time of deepening but it's also a time of a new gravity. Certainly, for a while anyway, it tends to have a sort of a sombre feel to it. It's a re-examination. And it's disconcerting because you're not quite sure what's changed.

Jane (Anglican, 55) said:

> I think, for me, midlife has actually been the best part of life so far, to be perfectly honest! *[She laughs.]* It's a time of life when I've felt a lot more comfortable in my own skin – free to be myself. I have a lot less angst and insecurity. There's still an amount of that, but a lot less than there

would have been earlier in life. Although the body doesn't hang together as well and the signs of aging are a little bit more obvious, for myself it's been the best time of life so far, in lots of ways.

These interviewees' comments certainly suggest that midlife deserves closer scrutiny. It is also apparent that people's experiences of midlife can differ markedly. In this chapter we shall look at some different understandings of midlife, identify some key developmental tasks of this life stage, and consider some of the spiritual opportunities that may be associated with them. A number of the topics which are introduced will be addressed more fully in later chapters. In the chapters that follow we shall look more closely at Christian faith at midlife and explore ways that individuals and congregations can support middle-aged members.

Defining midlife

Whenever I speak to anyone about midlife spirituality invariably the first question I am asked is, "What do you mean by midlife?" This invites a reply of greater length than most people are anticipating as there is very little agreement about the age parameters of "middle age." Statistics New Zealand, in the *New Zealand General Social Survey* (NZGSS), identifies four adult life stages with "middle-aged people" being 45 to 64 years of age,[9] and Te Ara Encyclopedia of New Zealand uses the same age parameters.[10] But Waikato University's Population Studies Centre's examination of wellbeing among midlife New Zealanders, *Enhancing Wellbeing in an Ageing Society* (EWAS), suggests that midlife starts at the age of 40 and ends at 65.[11] Research published by The Ministry of Social Development, exploring educational and training issues for those in the workforce, takes the age group 40 to 59 as representative of people in midlife,[12] and a study of leisure time in midlife published by researchers from the Universities of Auckland and Waikato assumes that midlife ends even earlier, as only participants aged 40 to 54 are included.[13] Reporting on the 2014 Neilsen Survey of Wellbeing, conducted on behalf of the Canterbury Earthquake Recovery Authority (CERA), the Christchurch Press described as "middle aged" a group between the ages of 35 and 49 identified as the "new vulnerable" in post-earthquake Christchurch, thus prompting some interesting discussion among readers about the definition of middle age and the pressures facing those in midlife.[14] This is just a snapshot of some New Zealand data. The picture in other parts of the world differs according to culture and life-expectancy.[15]

A leading researcher in the field of midlife psychology, Margie E. Lachman, Professor of Psychology and Director of the Brandeis University Lifespan Initiative on Healthy Aging, suggests that the boundaries of midlife are "fuzzy" as "the nature of midlife varies as a function of such factors as gender, cohort, socioeconomic status, race, ethnicity, culture, region of the country, personality, marital status, parental status, employment status and health status."[16] She writes, "The most common understanding of midlife is that it begins at around the age of 40 and ends at 60 or 65 but it is not uncommon for some to consider middle age to begin at 30 and end at 75."[17] The boundaries are subjective. Unsurprisingly, the older we are the later we believe midlife begins and ends.[18]

Oliver Robinson, Senior Lecturer in the Department of Psychology and Counselling at the University of Greenwich, points out that using age as the basis of categorizing developmental life stages and transitions is problematic because "individuals increasingly live in ways that do not accord with age-graded norms."[19] Medical advancements and increased life-expectancy, changing patterns of participation in education and work, changes in expectations and practices in relationships and family life, and many other factors, mean that it is no longer possible to predict whether people in their 40s may be celebrating the birth of a first child or anticipating the departure of children from home, reaching the peak of their careers or gaining the necessary qualifications to strike out on entirely new ones. As Lachman explains, "Age norms are less stringent for midlife than for periods that occur earlier (e.g., school entry or graduation) and later (e.g. retirement). Many people of the same chronological age are in different life phases with regard to social, family or work events and responsibilities."[22]

Some social scientists distinguish between "early midlife" and "late midlife."[20] Given the complexity and varied nature of midlife experience, and the lengthening duration of middle adulthood as people's life expectancy increases, this distinction can be useful. It recognises that people in their late 30s or early 40s are likely to have quite different responsibilities and preoccupations from those in their late 50s or 60s. Another approach is to think about midlife as the pivotal point between the "first half" and the "second half" of life.[21] This approach draws attention to "the bit in the middle," a period in which some significant changes in outlook often occur. In a helpful short devotional guide, *Facing Midlife*, Tony Horsfall suggests that midlife begins "when we first realise there are probably more days behind us than there are ahead of us."[22] This sort of realisation – and other changes in perspective we shall explore shortly – occurs at different ages for different people.

Assigning age boundaries to midlife is an inexact science but for research purposes it was necessary for me to establish an age range from within which to select interviewees. I chose initially to interview churchgoers aged between 40 and 60, not because I believe midlife to end at 60 but because in New Zealand, where a universal pension is paid to citizens from the age of 65 onwards, many people in their early 60s are beginning a period of transition to retirement. The transition to retirement is very significant but I did not wish that transition to become the dominant focus of my research. Following the completion of my doctorate, I did interview a number of churchgoers who were in their 60s and also a couple in their early 70s who had participated in a programme I was interested in learning more about. The spiritual directors I interviewed were all also in their 60s and 70s.

Midlife crisis?

Paul (Catholic priest, 53) declared, at the very start of his interview, that "certainly there is such a thing" as midlife crisis. Paul had experienced an extensive period of internal struggle, triggered by bereavement and compounded by the Christchurch earthquakes, which led him to seek support and advice from his bishop and also from a psychologist whom he saw three times. Paul admitted that seeking support was a difficult thing for him to do, but he added, "I knew I just needed to bounce it off someone." He told the bishop, "I cannot put my finger on it." To the psychologist, Paul described his experience like this: "I'm happy with what I am doing. I still find fulfilment in what I am doing. But somehow it's like eating the food you like but the taste is not there." Paul said:

> Possibly it's foreign to acknowledge that such thing as midlife [sic]. Because I myself would say, "Ach, it's just a joke thing, you know?" Until you're in it yourself, then you realise, "Hey!" It's good to be able to think about it. It's good to be able to acknowledge that it exists – to know that

there's such a thing as midlife when they're going through a crisis. You actually think the world's falling apart but you don't know why, and is it just you? The reality is, quite a lot of people go through this.

Paul told me that discovering elements of his experience were "reasonably the norm" was reassuring.

At midlife, experiences of disorientation may be "reasonably the norm" but the term "midlife crisis" is somewhat problematic. First, it means a variety of things to different people. As Elaine Wethington, Ronald Kesseler and Joy Pixley note, there is a "disjunction between popular and researcher views of midlife and its 'crisis'. ... Those who are less familiar with the theories justifying the concepts are more inclusive about 'what counts'."[23] The second difficulty is that the scientific validity and prevalence of crisis in midlife is questioned by many psychologists today. For these reasons (and also because this book is concerned with other issues) I shall generally avoid using the term "midlife crisis" other than in the context of quotations from interviewees. But it is certainly worth taking a few moments to look at some contrasting perspectives about this topic.

The term "midlife crisis" was coined by Canadian psychologist Elliot Jaques, who, in an article published in the International Journal of Psychoanalysis in 1965, described a period in which individuals grapple with their place in the world, their remaining years and what's left to accomplish.[24] Others then took up the idea of the midlife crisis and popularized the concept.[25] Much of the literature pertaining to the subject relates to a predictable period of transition occurring at some point in the middle decades of life, which may include a sense of stagnation and alienation, turmoil, and questioning of beliefs, values and self-worth.[26] Paul David Tripp, author of *Lost in the Middle: Midlife and the Grace of God*, for example, identifies "disorientation" ("I thought I knew who I was and what I was supposed to be doing, but now I am not so sure") among a cluster of emotions including discouragement (becoming more cynical than expectant), disappointment (regret at not achieving one's goals or dreams), and disinterest (no longer feeling motivated by things that were once stimulating and attractive) which may be part of midlife experience.[27]

According to specialist neuropsychologist and Anglican priest Joanna Collicutt, in midlife some people may simply experience "a chronic low level of dissatisfaction, expressed in semi-conscious awareness that 'this isn't really me' or 'I am stuck' or 'there's got to be more to my life than this'."[28] While these emotions may sometimes be precipitated by external events – such as relationship breakdowns, serious illness, redundancy, promotion at work beyond one's capabilities or interest, children leaving home, or bereavement – a sense of "uneasiness with one's self and one's world"[29] which cannot be linked to a specific cause is also characteristic of midlife and can prove unsettling.

Recent research conducted by Oliver Robinson and his colleagues from the University of Greenwich, based on interviews with over 900 people, found that nearly one in four people aged 40 to 59 go through an "emotional upheaval" at midlife. Reflecting on these findings during an interview with Kathryn Ryan on RNZ National in 2016, Robinson described midlife as "the peak period of crisis." He added, "It certainly doesn't have an exclusive on crisis, but it is the time when it's most prevalent."[30] Robinson argues, "Although midlife crisis may be an event that only a minority of adults experience, this does not make it any less important."[31]

Those who challenge the scientific validity and prevalence of crisis at midlife, such as psychologists Carolyn M. Aldwin and Michael R. Levenson, claim that although midlife "does normatively involve serious challenges: it is "incorrect to identify midlife as a time of crisis." Rather, they describe midlife as "a psychological turning point" which "may include new insights that can lead to significant changes or redirections in life."[32] Journalist Barbara Bradley Hagerty, author of *Life Reimagined: The Science and Opportunity of Midlife*, agrees. She writes, "There is almost no hard evidence for midlife crisis at all, other than a few pilot studies conducted decades ago." Hagerty suggests, "Midlife is about renewal, not crisis. This is a time when you shift gears – a temporary pause, yes, but not a prolonged stall. In fact, you are moving forward to a new phase of life."[33]

Presbyterian minister and author of two books on midlife, Lynne Baab, perceives the metaphor of "half time"[34] to be helpful as it suggests that pausing at midlife can be both necessary and constructive, allowing a person time to evaluate the past and to prepare for the future. Pausing at midlife, or even feeling "stuck" for a significant period, can motivate us to reflect on our lives and the circumstances, influences and personal choices that have led to the point we have reached. Tony Horsfall considers that the questions that arise for us in this period of life can be regarded as "our friends, not our enemies."[35]

There are further ways of interpreting experiences of disequilibrium in midlife. In *The Happiness Curve: Why Life Gets Better After 50*, Jonathan Rauch reviews a wide range of empirical lifetime studies and big data relating to life satisfaction and age. Rauch concludes that across cultures, and irrespective of gender, age plays a role as a determinant of happiness.[36] One particularly large study collated data from a Gallup survey of 340,000 American adults, on wellbeing, enjoyment, happiness, stress, worry, anger and sadness. Arthur Stone and his colleagues concluded that enjoyment and happiness remain relatively stable across the lifespan but dip at midlife, while sadness shows a slight incline at midlife. More positively, there is a "particularly pronounced decline in stress after the age of 50."[37] The U-shaped happiness curve suggests that while there are a number of aspects of midlife that can be very challenging, it is likely that, given time, things will get better.

Contrasts

Psychologists Carolyn M. Aldwin and Michael R. Levenson comment on the variable and even contradictory nature of people's experiences at midlife:

> For some individuals, midlife is a time of struggle because they are forced to cope with problems such as job loss or failure to achieve critical goals; health problems, both of one's self and also those of parents, spouses and siblings; problems with troubled adolescents or infertility; or divorce, widowhood, and parental bereavement. For others, midlife may be a time of achievement and relative comfort.[38]

Lachman agrees. She notes that while it is common for people in their middle years to be juggling many interlocking obligatory roles and experiencing an increasing number of "overload stressors" (such as those involving children, financial risk and compromised health) midlife can also be a period of "peak functioning in many domains, including some aspects of cognitive functioning and in the ability to deal with multiple roles and stress." She argues, "The portrayal of midlife as both a time of upheaval and a time of mastery is plausible and explicable."[39] The fact that people's experiences at midlife differ markedly is one reason that it can be difficult for congregations to identify how best to support members who are in this age group.

Some contrasts of midlife

❖ Extremely busy

❖ Disorientation – not sure where I am going

❖ Financially a challenging time

❖ Work is stressful or exhausting – I'm not sure I'm in the right job

❖ I go to church mainly for other reasons than worshipping or meeting with God

❖ I feel "stuck" and/or I am "drifting"

❖ I have a lot of responsibility for others – not much time for me

❖ I'm negotiating some big changes in my marriage

❖ I realise I no longer have time to accomplish some of the things I thought I would do one day

❖ Church is one place I go where I hope no-one will ask me to do anything

❖ More flexibility of time

❖ Less angst – more content

❖ More financial freedom

❖ Work is stimulating – I feel I can use my gifts and experience to help others

❖ I find my faith opening up – broadening and deepening

❖ I am enjoying exploring different forms of prayer and/or old forms of prayer are proving sustaining in new ways

❖ Friendships matter to me more than they used to

❖ My spouse and I are enjoying having more time and flexibility to do things together

❖ I now have more confidence to face and deal with difficult things

❖ I feel so much more grateful for really small things

❖ Volunteering and serving at church helps me feel I belong to a community

The above table provides a summary of experiences of midlife most frequently described by the people I interviewed. Something of the complexity and contradictory nature of midlife is captured in their statements. We shall look more closely at many of these experiences in later chapters.

We turn now to some research about midlife development. As Paul's story illustrated, it can be useful to have some theoretical understanding of this topic because awareness of shared aspects of midlife experience can alleviate anxiety for some people. However, we must remember that people's experiences differ. Psychologists Ursula M. Staudinger and Susan Bluck emphasise the importance of taking a "contextualist view" in considering midlife development. They note that individuals enter midlife with different capacities and backgrounds, and "the individual life circumstances of each adult also influence development, resulting in individual trajectories through midlife."[40] Awareness of the diversity of people's situations and experiences is essential if we hope to offer appropriate pastoral care and meaningful spiritual support to people in this life stage.

Tasks of midlife

Social scientists and psychologists suggest that there are a number of "tasks" which engage people's energy during midlife. The tasks they consider to be significant vary, although there are similarities between them. In the mid-20th century, educational theorist and expert on aging, Robert J. Havighurst, identified seven core tasks of midlife:[41]

- ❖ Achieving social and civic responsibilities
- ❖ Establishing and maintaining an economic standard of living
- ❖ Assisting teenage children to become responsible adults
- ❖ Developing leisure time pursuits
- ❖ Relating to one's spouse as a person
- ❖ Accepting the physiological changes of middle age
- ❖ Adjusting to aging parents.

Encompassing career and relationships, biological and psychological change, and the societal demands of midlife, Havighurst's developmental tasks continue to reflect the experience of many (married) midlife individuals today, despite the societal changes that have occurred over the last half century.

Parallels with Havighurst's theories may be found in the fascinating Harvard University longitudinal study of adult development, published in 2002 by George Vaillant. Based on interviews with 824 individuals over five decades, Vaillant concludes that tasks of particular significance in midlife include career consolidation, generativity (finding ways to contribute to society and to benefit future generations),[42] and being a "keeper of the meaning" (which involves a sense of social justice and care for those beyond one's immediate social radius).[43] The "tasks" identified by Havighurst and Vaillant "offer opportunities for the middle-aged individual to learn more about life and about the world while making a contribution to others' well-being."[44]

In *Spiritual Direction and Midlife Development*, Raymond Studzinski describes ten tasks of midlife transition. Studzinski identifies "assessing the limits of achievement," "re-evaluating the life structure" and "balancing polarities" as necessary aspects of development in midlife. "Facing loss, mourning and death," "cultivating care," "gaining wisdom" and "searching for 'the Other'," are also included in his list of "adjustments and adaptations" that must be made at midlife.[45] Studzinski draws explicit links between the tasks of psychic integration and spiritual growth. In her book, *Embracing Midlife: Congregations as Support Systems*, Lynne Baab identifies as "spiritual issues" some further challenges to be grappled with during midlife, including "letting go of the illusion of control," "the call to meaningful service" and "facing old wounds and receiving healing."[46] Baab points out that people who are involved in faith communities are likely to look to their faith for answers when such issues arise.[47]

Dealing with regrets, accepting responsibility for actions and choices which have had an impact on others as well as oneself, and acknowledging the influence that others' actions have had upon one's life can be important aspects of midlife for some people. In *The Psychology of Christian Character Formation*, Joanna Collicutt dedicates a chapter to these issues. Firmly placing human forgiveness within the framework of God's reconciling, healing and transformative work, she acknowledges that dealing with the harm caused to us by others can be very difficult, because of the risks, costs, and sheer complexity of the task. One of the costs of choosing to let go of long-held grievances, which pertains to midlife experience, is that these may have become "part of my story and my identity."[48] The process of dealing with hurts experienced in the first half of life, and opening oneself to the healing grace of God, therefore often requires "the help of friends and advisors inside and outside the church."[49]

Baab points out that people who are involved in faith communities are likely to look to their faith for answers when issues such as these arise.[50] However, when she interviewed members of North American congregations in the late 1990s she discovered that a considerable number of committed churchgoers felt unsupported, or even "abandoned and neglected,"[51] as they sought to address midlife concerns. My own research revealed that New Zealand churchgoers in their 40s and 50s did find support and nurture in being part of faith communities (we shall hear their stories about what was most helpful to them in Chapter 3) but also that some significant opportunities to support people in this age group were being overlooked (a theme we shall explore in Chapters 4, 5 and 6).

Review and reappraisal

According to Harvey L. Sterns and Margaret Hellie Huyck, one of the most common themes in literature relating to midlife is "that midlife spurs the reassessment of one's whole life."[52] Some people, whether due to temperament or circumstances, are more reflective than others, but a sense of the importance of reviewing and reappraising the past, thinking about one's values, talents and the limits of one's achievements, and contemplating the worth and attainability of earlier dreams, appears to be a characteristic of midlife experience, "at least in contemporary Western culture."[53] Review and reappraisal typically occurs over a long period of time, and can be unsettling, as a number of interviewees' comments illustrate.

Karen (Anglican, 52) described a period of "dramatic upheaval" in her mid-30s when she gave up a successful career, embarked on tertiary study, then worked overseas in a completely different role for several years. She felt that time was a significant period of reassessment and revaluation of what she was doing and where she was going. Karen is now in her early 50s. She has noticed:

The same thing's happening again – but not quite – but you know, sort of another questioning and, I don't know how you describe it, time of rethinking things, and changes, and reassessing things. So, I don't know. Maybe I'm having, maybe I've had, two midlife crises or transitions or whatever you call them. And, um, it's not quite in the same way. It's just, maybe, I don't know, taking stock and thinking [*she laughs and adopts the voice of a very elderly person*], "Where have all the years gone? How did I get here?" It's weird. I just find it hard to describe what's actually happening.

Karen described this reassessment as relating to "the whole of life" as she looked at her career and relationships and her faith. She added, "It's confusing at times, yeah." Later in her interview Karen described some changes that she had observed in her faith. She felt that in her 20s she was "certain about things" and had "strong opinions about this, that, and the other – this is right, and that's wrong." Now, she observed, "There are a lot of things that I'm less certain about. And that's OK. ... Probably in terms of faith the important things are still as clear and I'm confident about them. But there's a lot of greyness round the edges."

Michelle (58) is a Catholic sister in a religious order. She described her midlife experience as "quite exciting, really, as well as challenging." In telling me about elements of her inner journey which she considered to be important, she said:

You get to a stage when you think, "Well, what actually gives my life meaning?" You know, I guess prior to that you just lived your life and did all the things you did, but without necessarily reflecting too much on it. I got to a stage where I really thought, "Well, why am I doing what I'm doing?" You know, "Is this actually giving me energy, giving me life? Am I fulfilling the dreams that I had? What is important in my life?"

Michelle told me that she now has more certainty about what she really does believe is important to her. She said, "It's a time when I have stopped and listened more deeply to myself." She added:

Maybe I have previously taken more note of external authority, whereas I think now it's more internal, now my own authority. I'm really trusting that more, not having to rely on feedback from others. I think I'm getting more

OK around who I am and not having to please others too much. I don't always have to be given affirmation, although it's nice to get it.

Frances (spiritual director, 70) has worked with many Christians in midlife, including those taking extended sabbaticals from work and ministry. She said:

> The first half of life is very much geared to the person, you know, becoming their own person, and development of the ego, and their career, and their relationships, and often the focus is from the outside. They're shaped and formed from the outside world, but in the second half of life there's a real shift where we want to become our own persons from the inside. So it's very much an interior journey and re-looking at our lives from that interior place.

Louisa (spiritual director, 66) agreed. She described the first half of life as the period in which people are busy establishing themselves, focusing on external things like getting an education, purchasing a house, establishing relationships and a career, and so on, but "somewhere around midlife the journey goes more inwards." Often, at the midlife point, "people get to know more who they are, not just the persona that they've put out there. There's time to get to know themselves."

By midlife the realisation that the time remaining within which to accomplish goals is decreasing can strike home with new force, although Lachman points out that, when considering the life-span, most people in midlife assume that "there is still a substantial, but not an infinite, amount of time left."[54] By midlife many people have had personal experience of "wake-up calls" such as significant illness, serious accidents, or bereavement, any of which can lead to reassessment of priorities or trigger a new appreciation for life.[55] Whether the awareness that there is diminishing time left to achieve goals comes slowly or suddenly, the realization that, as Jungian psychologist Kathleen Brehony puts it, "if we are ever going to become who we are in the deepest recesses of our being we have got to begin now,"[56] may dawn on us.

Anglican priest, Patricia (58), perceived midlife to be a period during which people often seek to "make sense of who they are and what they're here for." Patricia observed that, for some, "actually looking at their story" can take "great courage." It is not easy to assess how effectively one has lived out one's values or fulfilled the goals one had earlier in life, to reflect on whether earlier aspirations and ideals were realistic, or to let go of hopes and dreams which are now unattainable or no longer seem desirable. Unrequited hope can be "a big deal" in midlife, as sociologist and spiritual director Susan Phillips explained to me:

> When you are younger you are still kind of moving with the hopes; you have this vision of what your life will look like. When you are older it's a matter of acceptance of what your life is and has been. But in that middle period there's that mingling of hope and also dread that hopes won't be realized.[57]

Among those I interviewed, the mixture of hope and anxiety that Susan Phillips identified as being characteristic of midlife experience was most evident when individuals were speaking to me about their work. In midlife, it is not uncommon for people to question the value of their work, to look back at what they have achieved and to reflect upon whether what they have done, or are currently doing, is worthwhile. Whether a person is working full-time or part-time, is paid or unpaid, uncertainty about the worth of one's work, especially if one has been doing it for some time, can be unsettling. Bruce (Presbyterian, 49) who made a significant career shift in his mid-40s, described this experience:

> You think, "Gosh, I should have achieved more by now."... My own experience of midlife has to some extent been around that – looking back over the years of tertiary study, of service in a diverse range of spheres and thinking, "What does it all mean, really? What does it count for? And do I keep doing it?"

Simon (Presbyterian, 48) told me about his role in a large state-owned organisation, where he has worked throughout his adult life. He had recently gained a renewed sense of appreciation about his work and the opportunities his role affords him to serve society and to exercise and develop his own skills and abilities. But this renewed sense of enthusiasm about his work followed a period of uncertainty and restlessness, during which he questioned the value of what he was doing and his willingness to continue in his career, as he explained:

> At times I have thought, what if I were to leave, what would I do? You know, I do have, and have had, reservations about what life holds for me. Is this all that my life's going to be?

Or, ah, is there something else? I had that for a long time. *[Simon pauses to reflect.]* And there's a certain amount of comfort knowing that as long as I choose to stay in my job I'll get paid every fortnight and I'll live a comfortable lifestyle, but yeah, is there something else I want to achieve? Yeah, I have thought like that for a long time, but as time rolls by, I think the older you get, there's also a sense that I'm too old to get into anything new now. *[He laughs.]* You know, I've left my run too late to try something else; I'll just have to resign myself to the fact that this is it.

Simon's reservations and concerns about his work had recently been dispelled by the opportunity for change and growth within the organisation in which he holds a position of seniority:

Just lately I've tried something new in my occupation, gone to a different role, and it's given me a whole new sense of energy, really. And I don't think I need anything else. I think this is actually a really good job. I think I feel quite settled now with the choice that I've made.

Bernard (Catholic priest, 52) told me that men can be "somewhat relieved" to find that this sort of experience is shared by others. He said, "I am able to say to them, 'The last ten men who have come to see me have all said the same thing.' Men tend to be isolated."

Of course, a significant number of people in their 40s and 50s will not be grappling with the dilemmas described by Bruce or Simon. Rather, they will be reaching the peak of their careers and enjoying a period of financial stability and personal fulfilment. Many may be able to use existing skills and talents in new ways, or be able to develop gifts which had formerly been undetected or undervalued by stepping into new roles within or beyond their workplace. Opportunities to exercise leadership and to pass on values and knowledge gained through experience in the workplace can also prove to be extremely energising for people in midlife. At this stage of life, too, it is common for women whose primary work has been in the home to return to paid employment, or increase their hours of work outside the home, as the demands of childcare decrease. For them, the opportunity to mix with colleagues and to engage in new activities, drawing on skills and expertise they have gained in a wide range of situations, can be both stimulating and satisfying. Later we shall hear stories of people who were relishing their work roles and connected the fulfilment they experienced in the workplace with their Christian faith.

Fresh perspective

The process of review and reappraisal at midlife can help people to gain fresh perspective on their experiences, both past and present. According to David Karp, Professor of Sociology at Boston College, once they reach their 50s individuals start to speak of seeing their lives in a "more holistic way."[58] In a study conducted in 1988, Karp's 72 research subjects, professional men and women aged between 50 and 60, felt that they had become much less caught up in the details of everyday life, and were more concerned with the "larger picture." One man said, "I have to put it together in an integrated, synthesized way. And I don't feel that I have to change the world any more. I feel like I have to see what the pieces mean."[59] Others in Karp's study reported being "less irritated by things that would have disturbed them earlier," "more laid back about life," and spending "less time worrying about things."[60] Karp's research was conducted several decades ago, but a number of the people I interviewed described very similar changes in perspective.

Thomas (Catholic priest, 54) spoke to me about shifts in perspective which he attributed to his awareness of the diminishing amount of time he has left to accomplish goals. He said:

> The way that I experience it [midlife] most at the moment is, you know, when you're young you always think, "I'll do that one day. I'll do that one day." And in the last few years I've found that I won't do it. I haven't got time. ... I'm just running out of time.

Both of Thomas's parents died in their early 70s. Thomas is aware that if he lives to the age his mother was at her death, he has only 15 years more left to live. He said, "That's one of the sobering realities of midlife." He continued:

> As an ordained minister, and a person of faith, I cannot imagine the thought that I've only got 15 years left, possibly, without faith. ... I think one of the things that faith does, for me, probably the most important thing, is that it means that ... it's not up to me to do everything within the years I've got walking on earth, because, firstly, as a Christian it's not just about me (there's a whole team of people working

on this), and the second thing is, it's not about achieving. And I think in my early years it was.

Thomas added that he knew the "theory" that "it wasn't about achieving," even when he was studying in his 30s, but he lived as if it was. "And now, I s'pose, looking back, there's enough of what I really put time and energy and anxiety and worry into that's come to absolutely nothing – and a good amount of it I would look back and say has been counter-productive." When I asked Thomas how he felt about that, Thomas described the comfort and hope he draws from "the reality of Jesus present" but admitted, "I feel a bit stupid, I suppose, for not having woken up to it earlier."

Psychologists Carolyn Aldwin and Michael Levenson describe the place of stress, uncertainty, change and loss in the abandonment of unrealistic or even damaging assumptions about the world, and the "fundamental self-reflection" which may arise, as "the basis of the development of wisdom."[61] Psychologists define and measure wisdom in a variety of ways,[62] but a number consider that it has a moral and ethical dimension.

For example, Monika Ardelt, from the University of Florida, suggests that wisdom includes: [63]

- ❖ affective wisdom based on compassion for the plight of others
- ❖ cognitive wisdom, which incorporates the ability to comprehend significance and meaning
- ❖ reflective wisdom, which includes the ability to look at situations from many different perspectives, as well as diminished self-centredness.

Regardless of definition, most people agree that there is a link between wisdom, life-experience and age.

One benefit of life experience can be that, by midlife, knowledge of our own limitations fosters both a more compassionate response to other people and greater reliance on God. Bernard (Catholic priest, 52) told me that losing the "invincible confidence" he had as a young person had brought "spiritual opportunities" including "greater empathy, greater sensitivity to others." By his own assessment, at midlife Bernard has become "less hasty in judging others." Other clergy also spoke about developing greater empathy and sensitivity, something they related both to their stage of life and to their ministry experience. Sandra (Anglican, 58), for example, observed that recently having come through a significant period of upheaval herself had had a positive impact on her pastoral ministry. She felt that her experience had enhanced her ability to relate to parishioners and to "help them through their own stuff." Russell (Anglican, 56) also reflected on his experience in assisting families during times of illness and bereavement. He said, "I think you bring more insights into your ministry as you get into your 50s. I've found that." Don (Presbyterian, 52) provided a specific example of empathy developed through life experience. He told me that he now endeavours to attend the funerals of midlife parishioners' parents. He said, "Through my own father dying, I have made a point, whenever I can, of going to the funeral of a member's parent, which wouldn't have occurred to me when I was 30. I think people have found it helpful that I've been there."

A number of interviewees spoke to me about the complexity of the questions that arise in midlife. Acceptance that there are "no easy answers" was seen by Liz (Anglican priest, 55) as being a characteristic of mature faith developed through life experience. Liz reflected on the way that a couple of her parishioners, who are in early midlife, were coping with some particularly difficult life events. She felt that they are in "a stage in their spirituality" where:

> They're not black and white about things. They've got considerable life experience and spiritual experience as well. It doesn't mean it hasn't been hard. But in some ways I wonder if they've had more resources to cope with that. They're more philosophical, sort of, "We can live without the answers."

When I asked interviewees about the challenges and opportunities of midlife, approximately half of those I spoke to described having greater self-confidence, less anxiety, or a deeper sense of contentment at midlife than they had experienced earlier in life. It was not that half of the interviewees were contented while the other half felt swamped by difficulties: those who described themselves as being happier, less anxious about the future and more grateful for their circumstances also described significant challenges they had faced or were still facing. What contributed to many interviewees' appreciation of their present circumstances was that they had experience of coping well with past challenges and, with God's help, learning from them. They had learned that there were many aspects of life over which they had little control but they were able to "derive meaning from what they had" rather than focusing on "what they lacked or had not achieved."[64]

During his interview, Simon (Presbyterian, 48) reflected on his increased contentment at midlife, saying, "I'm approaching 50 but I think I'm now reasonably happy with my life. It's funny, it's taken me a long time to reach that point in my life." When I asked him how his sense of contentment connected with his faith, Simon said:

> I think too often we forget about the little things in life that we need to be grateful for. Through the earlier part of your life you worry about bringing up your kids and making sure they get a good education, paying the mortgage, paying the bills, planning for your retirement. We're living reasonably comfortably and that's not a focus, not an issue, so it gives you time to reflect on those other things – the enjoyment and pleasures that life can bring you. Yeah, all those other things, which we're really grateful for, that God's created and given us the opportunity to experience. Going for a bike ride, going for a walk up the hill, all of God's creations … I think middle age is quite a happy place for me.

Keith (Catholic, 47) is married and has a son of primary school age. Like Simon, Keith reflected on the blessings of his current situation and the changes he observed in his priorities now that he is in his late 40s. One significant shift Keith commented on was that in the first half of his life he was pretty focused on becoming financially secure but making money now held little interest for him. "Just volunteering time is a bit more of a stimulant to me than, you know, actually earning lots of money. I didn't ever really think I'd be like that," he admitted. Keith referred a number of times to the pleasure and satisfaction he gained from volunteering his time and skills, both in the service of the church and in other parts of the community. When I made the observation that midlife appeared to be a very happy and stable period for him, he replied:

> It's one of those things you can't really explain to someone who's young, but when you sort of get there, you know, you wake up in the morning and you make yourself a cup of coffee and sit on the back deck and, you know, overlook the veggie garden and sort of think, "How lucky am I?"

At the end of his interview, Keith summarised his attitude towards midlife, saying, "I think a lot of people do tend to look on midlife as a big 'ick' but, as I say, I like it."

According to Barbara Bradley Hagerty, those who "thrive" in midlife "shift their energy and attention from seeking happiness to finding meaning, from achieving success to cherishing people and paying attention to moments."[65] Keith's changed priorities, his enthusiasm for serving others, and the great pleasure he experienced as he enjoyed a cup of coffee on the deck at his home, illustrate these shifts. These are significant spiritual movements which are entirely in keeping with Christian faith. We are, after all, repeatedly exhorted in Scripture to seek wisdom and understanding (Prov 3:13), to love others (1 John 4:7) and to pay attention to, and learn from, the least significant of creatures, such as sparrows (Matt 6:25-34) and even ants (Prov 6:6).

Where to from here?

Lachman points out, "The well-being of middle-aged adults affects the many others with whom they interact, give care, advise, or influence. Thus, a better understanding of middle age can have far-reaching consequences."[66] Within the church, consideration of the experiences and needs of middle-aged members is likely not only to benefit individuals in midlife but to have flow-on effects to others, within and beyond their congregations.

The remainder of this book is concerned with faith at midlife. In the next chapter we look at the topic of faith development, through story, metaphor and theory. Chapters 3 and 4 explore midlife churchgoers' experiences of church. We shall look at what people in this age group value about church, and why, and also address some of the challenges facing people in midlife when it comes to church involvement. Chapter 5 focuses on individuals' spirituality and spiritual practices at midlife. Chapters 6 and 7 propose ways that individuals and congregations might acknowledge, celebrate and respond to the spiritual development of parishioners in this life stage.

Questions for reflection or discussion

1. In this chapter, did any of the interviewees' stories or comments particularly resonate with you? Did any surprise you? Why?

2. Reflect on the table headed "Some contrasts of midlife." What stands out for you, if anything? Are there other elements you would you like to add?

3. When you consider your present stage of life, for what are you most grateful? What are the challenges of this life stage for you?

Recommended resources

Hagerty, Barbara Bradley. *Life Reimagined: The Science, Art and Opportunity of Midlife.* New York: Riverhead Books, 2016.

Horsfall, Tony. *Facing Midlife: Bible Readings for Special Times.* Abingdon, Oxford: The Bible Reading Fellowship, 2017.

Lachman, Margie E. "Development in Midlife." *Annual Review of Psychology*, Vol. 55 (February 2004): 305-331.

Vaillant, George E. *Aging Well: Surprising Guideposts to a Happier Life from the Landmark Study of Adult Development.* New York: Little, Brown and Company, 2002.

Van Loon, Michelle. *Becoming Sage: Cultivating Meaning, Purpose, and Spirituality in Midlife.* Chicago: Moody Publishers, 2020.

2 — Faith development and midlife

We thank you for the heritage of thought we have received,
for all that challenged, comforted, was questioned and believed.
We seek for yet more light and truth, in confidence that you
will be, O God, our guide, our goal, in all we seek to do.

New Zealand hymn writer, Colin Gibson[67]

Recently I attended a prayer meeting which was held in a sacristy at the back of a Catholic church. The small room was clearly used as a storage space for a lot of the paraphernalia commonly used by churches during the course of a year and it was consequently somewhat cluttered. Midway through the meeting I found my attention deflected from prayer by the label on the lid of a large plastic tub beside my chair. The label describing the tub's contents said, in very large lettering, "CRIB FIGURES FOR INSIDE CHURCH: BLESSED VIRGIN MARY, ST JOSEPH, 2 X INFANT JESUS (DIFFERENT SIZES)." Once my amusement subsided, it struck me that the description of Jesus coming in more than one size actually provided an apt metaphor for faith development. At some stage in our lives many of us who have had the privilege of following Jesus for some time will discover that the Jesus (or God) we thought we knew is, as the Christian author JB Phillips put it, "too small."[68] What we once believed about God no longer seems sufficient to accommodate all we have come to understand through greater life experience.

Metaphors can be helpful in pointing towards aspects of faith experience that are hard to describe. In an address given to New Zealand spiritual directors in 2011, author and educator Sheila Pritchard employed the image of "concentric circles" as she spoke about her own journey of faith:

> Some years ago, I began to think of my journey as a series of concentric circles. The first was an evangelical Baptist circle. Of course, over the years there were many expansions to that first circle: charismatic experience, a Catholic spiritual director, working in another culture, teaching in an interdenominational mission school, training as a spiritual director in a Jesuit retreat centre, valuing the richness of other faiths ... the circles kept expanding. Over and over again the circle I lived in became too small for the God I was coming to know. Then I came across the phrase,

"Include and transcend," in Ken Wilber's book *Integral Spirituality*.[69] That expressed it perfectly. That's what I had instinctively been doing – including the rich value of each "circle" but transcending its limits to welcome more and more of what was revealed.[70]

The middle-aged people I interviewed obviously did not employ the same imagery as Sheila Pritchard when they spoke to me about their spiritual experience, but in many cases their sentiments were similar. In their 40s and 50s most had come to realise and appreciate that there was a lot that they did not know or understand about God and their Christian faith. While they felt that much about their faith had remained the same, and, indeed, brought stability to their lives, many also said that their desire for a broader faith and deeper relationship with God was increasing.

Rosemary's story

For Rosemary (Catholic, 51), midlife has been a period of considerable change. Rosemary is married and has four children, all of whom are now young adults. When her youngest child started high school, Rosemary had returned to paid employment outside the home, a circumstance which expanded her social network and enabled her to mix with people from different backgrounds. Due to the nature and location of her job Rosemary had been able to participate in some courses in religious studies and pastoral ministries. She also began to attend spiritual direction. As she reflected on her experience she observed, "A lot of those changes instigated other changes, I guess – an opening out into new areas." Rosemary told me that she had always had a desire to be really close to God, but she was aware that there had been changes in her experience of Christian faith at midlife. She said:

> One thing that I guess has changed in midlife is my understanding of God. The desire to be really close hasn't so much changed. ... I would see God as a friend, in my 20s, and I see God as a friend now. But I also see that God is so much more than I could ever have perceived. And so my understanding of him now is that he's unknowable, fully. I probably didn't appreciate that earlier.

Rosemary felt that academic study had contributed to her appreciating so many more aspects of who God is. "There's so much more that I don't yet know about him. I might not have said that in my 20s."

Echoes of Sheila Pritchard's sense of expanding circles of faith experience could be heard in Rosemary's explanation of developments in her experience of church. Rosemary is very actively involved in her local Catholic parish. A significant part of her faith journey has also been many years' involvement in what she called "charismatic circles." Rosemary told me that while she is now "enjoying the more contemplative side" of Christian spirituality she still finds it "deeply ministering to be in that charismatic worship space." She said, "I find it very easy to be with God in that space, and encounter him there very deeply. It's very moving for me." Rosemary spoke further about her sense that God meets with her in both contemplative and charismatic contexts. She summed up her thoughts by saying, "I like the fact that God is not limited to one area of spirituality and he will use whatever is helpful for any individual."

As she thought about changes in her faith, Rosemary employed the image of the church as an aviary within which she had felt secure throughout her life. She described coming to the realisation that this aviary has an open top through which she can fly. The open-topped aviary enables her not to escape the institutional church but to explore beyond limits she had taken for granted. At midlife, Rosemary retained the security, familiarity and comfort of her own tradition but she also felt blessed to be able to broaden her experience and understanding by exposure to others' insights. Gratitude for all she was learning and experiencing appeared to be an integral part of Rosemary's midlife journey, in life and faith alike. Rosemary said, "For me, my experience of midlife is one of freedom. I guess it feels expansive – it's still expanding. There are opportunities I can take hold of." She felt, for example, that her broadening experience of faith enabled her to contribute in new ways to her church.

Jane's story

Like Rosemary, Jane (Anglican, 55) considered midlife to be a period of opportunity as well as challenge. She described some significant events that had been part of her midlife experience, including the death of a parent, change of vocation, and returning to New Zealand after living overseas for many years. She also commented on some of the physical changes and other challenges of midlife. Nonetheless, Jane expressed a greater sense of ease within herself which she linked to her faith. "I feel a lot less angst before God, I suppose, if that's a way of putting it. Just more conscious of being loved and less needing to toe the line – that's the general trajectory, I think." She continued:

> I feel like for a lot of my Christian life there's been this little bit of a tension – like a balancing act – between kind of wanting to stay within the right boundaries and do the right thing and yet recognising that God is also bigger than all that, you know? I've always been conscious of that tension.

Jane explained that, in the past, part of her didn't want to "keep within the fences" but she knew that she needed to. At midlife she has felt greater freedom not to do so. She said, "Midlife, I feel like the emphasis is much more on the outside of the fence, if you like. Feeling less constrained by the boundaries and the structures and more aware that actually God's a whole lot bigger than all of that – even though that's still kind of important."

Jane identified tensions regarding the blessing of same-sex couples who have been married as "the presenting issue" which was of current concern in her local church and within her denomination. She said:

> I find myself a lot less bothered about it than I would have once. Not that it doesn't matter. It's not that doctrine doesn't matter or boundaries don't matter, but I can just see the other side of it. I'm still figuring this out ... the idea that it can be both/and. I'm more comfortable than I used to be with actually there are aspects of my faith experience that are at odds with each other, that are kind of contradictory or paradoxical. But that's sort of OK. Yeah.

Jane felt that shifts in her faith were difficult to explain, especially while they were occurring – an experience with which many Christians might be able to identify. She elaborated:

> Things that 10 or 15 or 20 years ago I would have thought quite black and whitely, "This is right and this is wrong, and God says so, and I need to abide by that," now I think, "Yes, but ..." and I seem to be able to more comfortably live with the "yes" and the "but" in way that I once couldn't. But I'm still figuring out how that all happens.

Rosemary and Jane's expanding perceptions of God, and their sense of being less constrained by boundaries which they had hitherto willingly accepted, illustrate some patterns in faith development which, over the past few decades, theologians have observed and endeavoured to describe within various theoretical frameworks.

Images of spiritual development

Many people turn to metaphors and images to express truths about spiritual growth. These can be helpful as they may be interpreted and understood in different ways throughout our lives.

A journey

The metaphor of the spiritual life being a "journey" is used so frequently today that many people barely think of it as being metaphorical at all. It is, of course, a Biblical image. Biblical stories of individuals and groups of people who move with deepening faith from the security of what is known, into the unknown, are illustrative of the myriad possible directions that life may take and the place of faith in responding to periods of transition and uncertainty. Among many Old Testament examples, we might think of Moses and Aaron leading God's people out of Egypt (the Exodus), or Abraham and Sarah's faith as they obeyed God's call to them (Gen 11:27-12:9, Heb 11:8-12). Such stories hold multiple layers of meaning, and in a number of faith traditions they are recalled and recounted regularly. Within the Old Testament, the people of God are repeatedly encouraged to remember how God has led them in the past so that they may have confidence that God is with them in the present and will be in the future. The New Testament is also full of journeys, both literal and figurative. Jesus' own journey towards Jerusalem and ultimately to the cross is of huge significance to believers who seek to follow "the way" of Christ.

New Zealand theologian Kevin Ward's work in the field of Sociology of Religion suggests that the metaphor of "journey" may have particular resonance today as "a spirituality of seeking" or "quest" (as opposed to affiliation to the institutional church) has assumed increasing dominance since the 1960s, in New Zealand as in other parts of the world.[71] It is an image which may also resonate with people who have already travelled some distance in life and in faith and find themselves looking both backwards and forwards over their lives.

Some interviewees spoke to me about their experience of literal journeys which had spiritual significance for them. Pilgrimages, which have held a significant place in Christian history, are experiencing a resurgence in interest and engagement both among people of faith and those who claim to have no religious belief at all.[72] Many of those who are embarking on these journeys are in midlife, as the statistics recorded by the Pilgrims' Office of the *Camino de Santiago* (The Way of St James) demonstrate. From the almost 350,000 pilgrims that arrived in Santiago de Compostela in 2019, 189,505 (54%) were between 30 and 60 years old. 65,103 pilgrims (18.73%) were over 60. Among my interviewees, three had walked or cycled this famous pilgrimage route. Hugh (Baptist, 52) described his experience:

> What I found really, really helpful was to slow down my life for five weeks to the pace of life, to the speed of walking. Disengaging from the media, from what was going on at home, interacting with others on the pilgrimage, the pace of life dropping back to the next café or the next town. It was a great opportunity to reflect and think.

Hugh was very conscious of the history of the pilgrimage he made. He said, "They've got a saying on the Camino that the Camino calls you, day by day, and there's a truth to that. People have been walking it for 1,200 to 1,300 years. There's a sense that you are joining something much, much deeper than yourself."

Pope Francis writes, "Walking is one of my favourite words when I think about being a Christian and about the Church. ... I think this is truly the most wonderful experience we can have; to belong to a people walking, journeying through history together with our Lord, who walks among us."[73] Alongside fellow believers, "we walk with the Lord, in the light of his way."[74] Many Christians draw consolation and courage from this beautiful image of the life of faith.

A slinky, spiral or labyrinth

Biblical scholar Walter Brueggemann has described a sequence of orientation-disorientation-reorientation within the book of Psalms, reflective of the contours of human experience. Brueggemann suggests that the psalms both mirror and provide opportunities to respond to the rhythms of human experience: times of stability, in which "there is no great movement, no tension to resolve"; times of dislocation and loss of equilibrium; and times of reorientation into which enters recognition of "a genuine newness which is wrought by gift."[75] Brueggemann's paradigm of life's rhythms provides a coherent yet flexible structure within which some elements of midlife experience may be explored in the light of faith.

Frederic M. Hudson, author of numerous books and articles on adult learning, development, and life planning, portrays human development as a "cycle of continuity and change" rather than something that occurs in "progressive, straight lines." As in Brueggemann's model, "people experience stability for a period of time, followed by a period of transition and re-evaluation, followed by more stability."[76] Hudson employs a memorable simile when he depicts adult life as being "something like a large slinky, with cycles that go on and on. Each new life period is different from yet similar to the last one."[77] In *The Psychology of Christian Character Formation*, Joanna Collicutt employs a similar image when writing about spiritual development:

> The trajectory of the life of faith has something of the spiral about it. Images of straight roads and ladders do not do it justice. A spiral staircase might be nearer the mark, but it would have to be highly convoluted. Perhaps the image of a three-dimensional labyrinth is the nearest we can get.[78]

Labyrinths take different forms but each has a single circuitous path that winds backwards and forwards until it reaches the centre. It is not a maze; there is no possibility of getting lost and there are no dead ends. To walk a labyrinth as an act of meditation and prayer can be a profound experience. Interest in physical labyrinths has been growing in recent years. Every experience of labyrinth prayer is unique but people from a range of faith traditions attest to its value.[79]

When we find ourselves revisiting issues we thought we had resolved, or returning to lessons we thought we had learned, it can be helpful to recall that growth is recursive. Reflecting on images such as the spiral, slinky and the labyrinth can help us gain a fresh perspective, particularly if we feel that we are "going round in circles."

Seasons

Another image that many people find helpful when considering psychosocial development and spiritual growth is that of "seasons" (Eccl 3:1-8). There are obvious parallels between stages of life and seasons of the year.

Daniel Levinson, author of *The Seasons of a Man's Life*, a seminal study of midlife development, observes that each season has its necessary place and contributes its special character. Each is equally important, and, although the pattern of the seasons is stable, change occurs within the seasons and between them.[80] Levinson's decade-long study of the lives of 40 men draws upon the developmental frameworks of Carl Jung and Erik Erikson. Jung argues that the first half of life is oriented primarily to development of the ego and conformity to the outer world, and suggests that interiority and integration of incongruent parts of the self are central to a person's development in the second half of life. Erikson identifies a critical antithesis in middle adulthood between "generativity" and "self-absorption and stagnation."[81] A theme that receives additional emphasis in Levinson's work is the significance of transitions. Levinson's depiction of the life cycle incorporates predictable periods of transition between four eras (or seasons) of human development. These transitions may be times of "profound inner conflict" as they mark the end of familiar and perhaps cherished aspects of life, as well as presaging new, possibly daunting, experiences ahead. Levinson observes, that it is rarely easy "to accept the losses the termination entails; to review and evaluate the past; to decide which aspects of the past to keep and which to reject; and to consider one's wishes and possibilities for the future."[82]

Author and educator Parker J. Palmer also considers seasons "a wise metaphor for the movement of life." He writes, "The notion that our lives are like the eternal cycle of the seasons does not deny the struggle or the joy, the loss or the gain, the darkness or the light, but encourages us to embrace it all – and to find in all of it opportunities for growth."[83] In fact, it is in times of transition, when reliance on self is so often shaken, that many of us may be most open to God. As Jacques Philippe, a Catholic priest in the Community of the Beatitudes, points out, "The situations that make us grow are precisely those we do not control."[84]

Organic models of growth and fruitfulness

The Bible suggests that spiritual growth is organic and fruitfulness is a natural outcome of rootedness in God. The Old Testament depicts those who are faithful to God as being like "trees planted by streams of water, which yield their fruit in season" (Ps 1:3) or "willows by flowing streams" (Isa 44:4). Within the New Testament

Jesus describes himself as "the true vine," the Father as "the vine-grower," and his followers as "branches" (John 15:1-8). He prays that his disciples will "bear fruit, fruit that will last" (John 15:15). Paul writes of the "fruit" – love, joy, peace, patience, kindness, generosity, faithfulness, gentleness, and self-control (Gal 5:22-23) which develop as we keep "in step with the Spirit" (Gal 5:25).

Sociologist and spiritual director Susan Phillips helpfully points out that in the spiritual life the concept of fruition, which "has to do with receiving grace and allowing it to work in oneself and through oneself,"[85] provides a necessary counter-balance to cultural attitudes which frequently "equate striving with thriving."[86] Images of rootedness and fruitfulness illustrate the connection between personal development and co-operation with the work of God. These images reinforce the truth that it is God who works in us, enabling us both "to will and to work for his good pleasure" (Phil 2:13).

Holy mixed metaphors

In *The Psychology of Christian Character Formation*, Joanna Collicutt notes that although "the fruit-bearing tree is a very helpful picture of the spiritual life," it is, "like all metaphors ... not complete in itself."[87] She suggests that multiple images are necessary for a fuller understanding of development in the Christian life. Alongside "the flourishing plant" she draws on another Biblical metaphor, that of "the fit body,"[88] to explore truths about the psychological and spiritual growth. The dynamic image of a person running a race, straining forward towards a goal (Phil 3:13-14) balances the evocative but static picture of the fruit-bearing tree.

Phillips also draws on "holy mixed metaphors,"[89] when she writes of "rootedness" alongside "journeying."[90] Phillips believes "the melding of the imaginative domains of garden and journey allows for some of the wisdom we see in modern developmental theory, which portrays human psychosocial development as involving growth in autonomy (like the forward movement on the road) coupled with maturing in interdependency (like the ecology of the garden)."[91] Certainly more than one image is needed to illustrate the complexity of faith development throughout life.

Faith Development Theory

American theologian James Fowler was, for much of his career, Professor of Theology and Human Development at Emory University. His most well-known book, *Stages of Faith: The Psychology of Human Development and the Quest for Meaning*,[92] was first published in 1981. The key concepts of Fowler's research continue to be taught in theology programmes at tertiary level and have been included in the training and formation of many clergy and spiritual directors currently serving in New Zealand. Drawing on in-depth interviews conducted between 1975 and 1979, the psychosocial and psychological frameworks of Erik Erikson, Jean Piaget and Lawrence Kohlberg, and the theology of H. Richard Niebuhr, James Fowler concluded that six stages in faith development can be recognised across a range of faith traditions. Over the decades since the publication of his initial research Fowler's work has been utilised and adapted by many other writers and researchers in this field.

Before describing Fowler's theory, I would like to acknowledge that the notion of "stages" can be problematic when it comes to talking about faith. We know from observation and experience that linear models of spiritual growth do not do justice to the uniqueness of individual faith journeys, and (quite justly) we may feel uncomfortable about putting people into spiritual boxes. Nevertheless, while acknowledging it can be helpful to have some understanding of Fowler's stage theory for two reasons. First, it can be heartening to learn that aspects of our personal spiritual experience are shared by others. For example, Fowler's research revealed that faith development "is a process of alternations between times of provisional balance and coming unbalanced, then finding recovered balance in a new place."[93] The realisation that this process is "normal" can come as a great relief to people who, at points of disorientation, may feel that they are in danger of losing their faith altogether. Second, having a theoretical framework provides terminology for us to draw upon when we are speaking of experiences we may otherwise find difficult to describe. Shared language can help us to understand and to support one another even if our expressions of spirituality may differ.

Although Fowler uses somewhat complicated descriptors for the six stages of faith he identified – titles that others have frequently sought to adapt and simplify[94] – his work is so widely referenced it is useful to have some familiarity with the terms Fowler himself employed. The first two stages of faith described by Fowler – "Intuitive-Projective faith" and "Mythic-Literal faith" – are closely connected to features of childhood development. Trust in parents and authority figures, development of a sense of right and wrong, understanding of cause and effect, and engagement in stories at a literal level, are all important characteristics of these first stages of faith development. Fowler acknowledges that some people remain in the literalist stage beyond childhood, but most adults in midlife are more likely to be operating within one or more of the three stages that follow.

At Stage 3 of Fowler's model, "Synthetic-Conventional faith," people find security in belonging within, and conforming to, a group which adheres to a defined set of beliefs and behaviours. At this stage, faith is relatively unreflective. Alan Jamieson explains, "Adults at this stage tend to know what they know, but they are generally unable to tell you how they know something is true without referring you to an external authority … such as the Bible or the Pastor."[95] Fowler notes that, regardless of age, many individuals can and do find equilibrium at this stage of faith.[96] He also suggests that religious institutions often thrive when the majority of their members are operating at this stage.

Fowler calls Stage 4 "Individuative-Reflective faith." As the title suggests, at this point of faith development individuals become less reliant on external sources of authority and they may begin to question what they have learned and believed. The transition from conformity to more independent faith, which may (or may not) be precipitated by external challenges, can be a rocky journey for some people. But for many people this transition can be a very rich period of exploration and discovery in their faith.

Fowler suggests that Stage 5, "Conjunctive faith," is rarely reached before midlife. It is at this stage of faith that people become more conscious of the limits of reason and are willing to embrace the fact that there is much that they cannot know. As Fowler puts it, conjunctive faith "accepts as axiomatic that truth is more multidimensional and organically interdependent than most theories or accounts of truth can grasp."[97] It is "alive to paradox and contradictions"[98] and inclusive of other faith traditions. People at this stage of faith may gain a new appreciation of mystery, of religious rituals and symbols, and of aspects of their faith tradition that they may have formerly rejected. Although faith at this stage may have broad and porous boundaries, it is "owned and firmly rooted."[99]

According to Fowler, only a very few people make the transition to the sixth stage, which he calls "Universalizing faith." As the name suggests, at this stage of faith people find freedom to live in oneness with all people, willingly sacrificing themselves for the sake of universal justice and love. Mother Teresa and Mahatma Ghandi are two figures Fowler associates with the sixth stage of faith. Catholic columnist Ron Rolheiser's description of "mature discipleship" as "becoming ever-wider in our embrace" illustrates Fowler's sixth stage.[100]

Fowler's model of faith development has helped many people to understand and traverse some complexities in their faith journey but, like any model, it has its limitations. Since the publication of *Stages of Faith* other writers have proposed metaphors of faith development which are more flexible.[101] No matter how different patterns or phases in faith are described – whether one thinks of "rooms, terrains, stages, styles, dimensions, zones, spaces or places of faith"[102] – all theories of faith development reinforce the understanding that faith development is a life-long process. Moreover, faith-development theories are not prescriptive but descriptive. Faith is a response to God's invitation, and faith journeys are always unique. If faith becomes a matter a comparison (or competition) with others we are stepping into unhelpful territory. Fowler emphasizes that no part of the faith journey can be considered "better" than any other. He insists that "each stage has the potential for wholeness, grace and integrity and for strengths sufficient for either life's blows or blessings."[103] We might do well to remember the parable of the Pharisee and the tax collector, which Jesus told to some who "trusted in themselves that they were righteous and regarded others with contempt" (Luke 18:9- 14).

Tony's story

Tony (spiritual director, 56) referred to Fowler's framework as he spoke to me about changes in his faith and his church involvement at midlife. Tony considered that the period from his mid-40s onward had been a "time of transition in terms of faith experience." Tony had been an active member of a Baptist congregation for many years but despite his sense of loyalty to his church he began to feel a sense of "dislocation" between his faith and church life. Around this time he encountered Fowler's research on stages of faith and Alan Jamieson's work on churchless faith,[104] and found both helpful. "It was nice to see my experience explained that way. Affirmed, if you like." Tony laughed as he added, "That's what's going on! Nobody told me about that." Tony felt that at that time his church was "sort of doing Stage 3 things" while he was doing "the hypercritical Stage 4 thing" and being independent, but also "entering Stage 5 where you can kind of re-engage with everything in the past, but in a new way." During this period, he continued to attend the Baptist church "off and on" but also found avenues outside his parish which helped him explore contemplative forms of spirituality and expanded his experience and expression of faith. He felt that his faith had "bloomed and blossomed."

It was not until his early 50s that Tony decided to move to a different church. At the time of his interview he had been worshipping for several years in a church he described as "high Anglican." Tony admitted that he found some of it "a bit weird" – "vestments and the incense and so on" – but there were also many aspects of the services that he valued. He told me that he appreciated being able to re-engage with ritual. He also felt that the services provided a "sense of connection with the past." He liked "the focus on the church year (the calendar and so on), and the creeds, and the careful attention to words that carry meaning, and the sort of multi-sensory experience of Mass." He described his experience of the services:

> It's very incarnational. It involves the whole of you. And there's movement around. I mean even the simple things like when the gospel is read, the gospel is brought down into the middle of the congregation, everybody turns to face it. You sort of think, "Oh, that's amazing." You're not just reading a book, you know? We actually do something physically in relation to what's being read, so yeah, I've found that quite attractive.

Despite changes in the expression and practice of his faith at midlife, Tony felt that his theology had not actually changed very much. He still believes much the same as he did before "but it's just much more expansive now." He considers his theological understanding to be "fairly conservative" though his expression of it is broad. Tony told me he could identify with a Canadian theologian he had once heard who described himself as having "a clear centre but fuzzy edges." Tony summed up his spiritual experience at midlife by saying, "So the last ten years really has been about exploring different ways of expressing my faith."

Faith transitions

Many of the spiritual directors I interviewed spoke of transitions between faith stages as being periods of disorientation and dislocation. Louisa (66) told me that she had attended a course for spiritual directors which focused on "the stuck place" that Christians can find themselves in at various points in life, including midlife. The course presenter suggested that when people find themselves in a stuck place, "there's something for rejoicing in that. It might not feel like a great place to be, but it's a prelude to a newer, fuller, richer season." But the "stuck place" Louisa described can often feel like a huge obstacle to be overcome. Another spiritual director, Matthew (61), spoke about a book which he felt addressed this experience helpfully. He explained that Janet O. Hagberg and Robert A. Guelich's *The Critical Journey: Stages in the Life of Faith*[105] has similarities with Fowler's *Stages of Faith*, but in Hagberg and Guelich's model, between the journey outwards and the journey inwards, there is "the wall." This is when people strike a set of issues that make it feel as if it is going to be very difficult to go to the next stage. Matthew said, "I kind of recognise a lot of that as the sort of stuff that people have at midlife."

Matthew also observed that in some cases he has worked with directees who, when coming up to the wall, have chosen to retreat to more familiar ground. In an article comparing faith stage transitions with cross-cultural transitions, Adrienne Thompson, who is a spiritual director, supervisor, and occasional writer for a range of New Zealand publications, observes, "It is important to remember that in moving from one stage to another something is lost and left behind."[106] This can be extremely unsettling. Some people may begin a "panicky search for substitute churches, leaders, books" to replace old "spiritual props."[107] Some may also feel guilty, if they attribute disorientation or spiritual malaise to personal failure.[108]

Developmental expectation

It can be difficult for churches to support individuals who are working through questions of identity and questions of faith. Lynne Baab writes, "Certainly, in our communities of faith, we embrace the concept of enabling our members to 'turn toward greater life or wholeness.' But we often don't understand what is happening in the midlife years, so we lose an opportunity to come alongside members in this life stage."[109]

Both the clergy and spiritual directors I interviewed discussed this issue. They noted, first, that Christians in midlife who are questioning aspects of their faith, or who feel that certain church practices are no longer meaningful to them, are likely to find it very hard to talk about these things at church. It can be difficult for churchgoers – particularly middle-aged churchgoers upon whom congregations commonly rely – to find a safe place to share their doubts or spiritual dilemmas without unduly distressing people who do not share the same concerns. Second, many churches do not cultivate what James Fowler calls a "climate of developmental expectation."[110] Ensuring that mature Christians have some awareness and understanding of faith transitions (whatever labels one puts on faith stages) can reduce distress and enable individuals to take greater responsibility for their own spiritual development. Several spiritual directors observed that some parishes, and some members of the clergy, do this better than others.

Matthew (spiritual director, 61) accepted that it can be difficult for parishes to accommodate the needs of people who are struggling with questions that may arise in the second half of life as well as catering for those "that do need the *Alpha*[111] and the straightforward message of the gospel." He said, "They've got so many other things they're trying to do, which are more geared to people in the first journey than the second journey, I think. So if we could have *Beta* to go with *Alpha* ..." He laughed, leaving his sentence unfinished. He added, "Without rocking the theological boat too much, we could do more. Churches could help to normalise these experiences and give people some pointers about where they can find help." Matthew said:

> I think what people really value is if they can find support ... if they can find a framework that's got some long-tested wisdom to it, and it's not going to ask them to go back in

some box that they feel they can't go back into theologically or personally.

Tony (spiritual director, 56) described the discouragement experienced by some Christians when, in midlife, former ways of praying no longer prove sustaining. He questioned where Christians can go if "former ways of thinking or believing ... don't work any more." Alluding to Alan Jamieson's work on church-leavers in New Zealand,[112] Tony said:

> What happens if they're in crisis? Do they hide their own crisis and doubt, to help the younger ones? ... I mean that's where the bulk of the running of the churches lies. So how can they be doubtful when they're the ones the whole structure sits on? That's quite a problem. Expressing doubt at church is actually really hard, because (as Alan's research shows) then you're either considered to be backsliding or giving up on God, or just not being loyal any more. So where can you say those things, and be held as you explore them, without being lectured?

Tony suggested that spiritual direction can provide "a safety net" for people facing crises or faith dilemmas. "What they are experiencing is hard, but not abnormal," Tony observed. If people feel they need to leave their churches – "a huge loss for the churches and for the individuals who have hung in there as long as they can" – then spiritual direction provides an opportunity for those people to be cared for.

Clergy and congregation members that are able to accompany those who are engaged in what Jamieson calls the "work" of deconstructing parts of their faith that are "no longer relevant, meaningful or viable,"[113] and the ensuing work of faith reconstruction, can also be immensely supportive during these points of transition. In an article entitled "Fowler, Faith and Fallout," Andrew Pritchard, who worked for many years in spiritual direction, ministry supervision, and the training of spiritual directors through Spiritual Growth Ministries (SGM), observes:

> It is appropriate for churches, especially those who value evangelism highly, to base their programmes and practices towards the needs of those at earlier stages of faith. However, if the needs of those who move to later stages are ignored, or worse, seen to be a distraction from the purpose and mission of the church, many of those won in

evangelism will be lost in the passage of time, not because they have grown cold but because they have grown![114]

Churches that cultivate a culture of developmental expectation are most likely to retain their midlife members and to attract others who have become disenchanted with church because changes in their faith have not been understood. Pritchard describes a number of constructive ways that churches might respond to the needs of people who are questioning their beliefs or possibly finding former ways of praying inadequate. He also points out possible pitfalls that churchgoers might avoid and suggests positive approaches that individuals might adopt when they find themselves facing dilemmas in their faith. Pritchard's article is available on-line and, although published some time ago, remains a valuable resource for clergy and congregations seeking to help parishioners navigate transitions in faith.[115]

Don (Presbyterian minister, 52) observed that it can sometimes be difficult for people to find a safe and accepting place to explore some of the paradoxes and hard questions of faith within their own churches, not because the churches lack resources or personnel but because individuals may be concerned about the impact of their questions on other people. Recalling a parishioner who no longer comes to church regularly, but certainly had not lost his faith, Don said, "One of his issues is how can he ask the questions of the Scriptures that he wants to ask without feeling like he's being naughty. He wants to be able to sit down and talk about things without upsetting someone else's faith."[116] While there is already a well-resourced network of small groups within Don's parish where significant questions of faith may be discussed openly, his church is considering establishing another group that could meet on a monthly basis in a different setting (such as a café), to delve deeper into particular topics.

While most of the spiritual directors and some of the clergy I interviewed were concerned about these issues, the majority of the churchgoers who spoke to me were not concerned about them at all. Like Rosemary and Jane, whose stories we heard at the start of this chapter, most regarded any shifts that had occurred in their faith as positive. Others felt that their faith had remained "much the same" in midlife. Andrew (Anglican, 44) considered that his faith had remained "rock-steady," supported by the stability of the institutional church. Andrew has had a strong faith since his mid-20s, and he said:

> That has kept me on firm solid ground. So while, I guess, the issues of day-to-day life come and go, and overwhelm me from time to time, falling back on what I know to be true and rock-steady has always been good. Nothing has come along to actually shake that faith and confidence I have, so far. *[He laughs.]* So that's been good. So, no, I wouldn't say my faith is any shallower or any deeper. It's just been fairly solid, I think.

Andrew did acknowledge that at midlife "there are certain issues and crises that start coming up." He mentioned that these might be related to finances, work or family, and observed, "It's the stage where people do start worrying about issues and things." Andrew added, "The church is a very slow-moving engine. *[He laughs.]* And so, while we may have our ups and downs, you can always know that, yeah, the church services, and the faith, and the principles, and everything it entails, it's going to be solid. It's a solid foundation."

Malcolm (52) had a Catholic upbringing but had little to do with the church after his teens. He now attends an Anglican church. When asked about shifts in his beliefs and values, Malcolm did not feel that he had changed dramatically, but he described significant gradual shifts that have occurred in his adult life. He said:

> I'm just carrying values that I have always had that were instilled in me when I was young. ... I think maybe you are just aware of those things in a different way as you, you know, go through your life. And perhaps there are different levels of importance that you attach to them at different stages of your life.

Malcolm still considered himself a Christian when he was away from the church for 30 years. He felt he may have been expressing Christian values in a secular way but they were still important to him. When asked if he could explain a little more about the way some of his values and priorities have changed, Malcolm said:

> I think, you know, when you're younger, maybe in your 20s, 30s and perhaps even 40s, you're just busy living your life – well, that's my experience. I guess in my 40s and now my 50s, I am more conscious of the spiritual aspect of life and what that might mean for me and my work and, you know, in other environments, rather than just me personally. *[He*

pauses.] But it's just an awareness. It's not necessarily an activity, if that makes sense.

When it comes to supporting individuals' faith development, and helping people to ponder deeper questions in life, it is wise to acknowledge that there are limitations on what churches can do. We need to consider carefully what it is sensible to attempt. It is also important that individuals who are in midlife seek for themselves resources and opportunities that will nurture their spiritual formation both within and beyond their places of worship. The willingness of clergy and church leaders to assist parishioners in exploring avenues for spiritual growth which lie beyond their own churches may be a significant factor in nurturing faith development. Whatever terrain people are traversing in their faith journey, we all need to encourage and build up others' faith, (1 Thess 5:11), to pray for others (Eph 6:18), and to take particular care of those who are struggling as their faith develops (Roms14:1-15:2). These are issues to which we shall return in the next two chapters as we look first at what midlife churchgoers frequently find helpful about their church involvement and then explore some of the challenges that can affect people's engagement in church in the middle decades of life.

Questions for reflection or discussion

1. In this chapter, did any of the interviewees' stories or comments particularly resonate with you? Did any surprise you? Why?

2. When you look back at your own journey of faith, perhaps over the last five to ten years, are you aware of changes in your beliefs, or in your understanding of God, or in the ways you pray? Or have things been pretty stable for you over this period?

3. Consider the images of faith development described in this chapter. What images do you find helpful? Which do you do not find so helpful? Why?

4. At the moment, where do you find support for your spiritual development?

5. What might you like to pray about, or act upon?

Recommended resources

Baab, Lynne. *A Renewed Spirituality: Finding Fresh Paths at Midlife*. Downers Grove, Illinois: Inter-Varsity Press, 2002.

Hagberg, Janet O. and Robert A. Guelich. *The Critical Journey: Stages in the Life of Faith*, 2nd ed. Salem, Wisconsin: Sheffield Publishing, 2005.

Jamieson, Alan. *Called Again: In and Beyond the Deserts of Faith*. Wellington: Philip Garside Publishing, 2004.

Pritchard, Andrew. "Fowler, Faith and Fallout." *Reality Magazine*, Issue 33. <http://www.reality.org.nz/articles/33/33-pritchard.html> (8 May 2020).

3 — Part of the Family

Come in, come in and sit down, you are a part of the family.
We are lost and we are found, and we are a part of the family.
Children and elders, middlers and teens, singles and doubles and in-
betweens, strong eighty-fivers and street-wise sixteens,
for we are a part of the family.

Hymn writer, James K. Manley[117]

In 2018 the Anglican Diocese of Auckland published a "Healthy Church Model" designed to support self-review within churches.[118] This model, which was based on a range of church review resources from New Zealand and overseas and developed after wide consultation over two years, identified four key dimensions considered to be vital for a "healthy church." These were:

1. *Knowing God* – acknowledging that relationship with God through Christ is the heart of Christian faith and is both communal and individual in its expression.

2. *Growing in Christ* – requiring individual commitment and a supportive environment in which to continue to learn and develop as disciples.

3. *Shaping Community* – nurturing our relationships and caring for one another within the "household of God" (1 Tim 3:15).

4. *Living Beyond Ourselves* – remembering that we exist for a purpose beyond ourselves: we are called to bear witness to our faith and serve others as we seek God's reign of justice and peace on earth.

These four elements of church life (and some further details about them) were displayed in quadrants surrounding a circle within which were the words, "Glorifying God, the Holy Trinity." Other denominations have similar aspirations for their members and some have developed comparable frameworks within which similar values are expressed. For example, South-West Baptist Church, a large suburban church in Christchurch, developed a logo placing *God, Self, Each Other and The World* at four equidistant points around a central cross.

Such models, perhaps especially when presented graphically, emphasise the interrelatedness of various dimensions of the

Christian life. In loving others within the church, and being loved and supported by them, our appreciation and understanding of God's love for us and for others, and our courage and will to serve God wherever we find ourselves, are strengthened. In working out our faith in various capacities in the world, our beliefs and assumptions about ourselves, others, and God are challenged, and we grow in dependence upon God.

If churches are "healthy" members of all ages will be nurtured in their faith and equipped to live as disciples of Christ. However, half of the ministers and priests that I interviewed stated that, in their experience, the needs of people in midlife are not given a great deal of consideration within the church:

1. There's nothing targeted for them. And yet I think … that in fact it's quite a critical area because people are confronting, often quite unexpectedly, these issues. Have we got anything targeted for them? No. Sorry to say that. (Bernard, Catholic, 52)

2. How is the church addressing midlife? Um, I don't think it's doing it very well. Especially with the fact that I'm not really thinking about it! (Yvonne, Presbyterian, 58)

3. To be honest, when it comes to negotiating the middle years, in specific terms, or trying to be helpful, we don't really do anything like that. (Russell, Anglican, 56)

4. We don't have something specific for people in midlife … but if we know there's a need we address it. (Paul, Catholic, 53)

5. Sorry, I'm drawing a blank. It probably means we haven't been intentional enough. (Greg, Presbyterian, 62)

These comments, taken out of context and grouped as they are, indicate that there may be room for some consciousness-raising among clergy and congregations when it comes to reflecting on the needs of parishioners in midlife. Having said this, all of the clergy who made these remarks went on to qualify or modify the statements they had made. These five church leaders and the other priests and ministers who were interviewed were able to provide numerous and diverse examples of ways that their churches were in fact offering spiritual or pastoral support for people in this life stage.

People in midlife who choose to attend church do frequently find it "hugely meaningful," said one Anglican priest, Patricia (58), whether or not what happens there is targeted specifically at people in their own age group. Patricia noted that by this stage of life people "will probably have made a decision whether they are living out the faith in a traditional church-based organisation or not." It was Patricia's belief that many middle-aged people who go to church do "find community, and acceptance, belonging, encouragement and nurture in that space."

I asked churchgoers in their 40s and 50s to tell me what they valued most about their church involvement. Unsurprisingly, given that most of the people I interviewed attended church fairly regularly, the vast majority had no trouble identifying some positive elements of their church experience. Many said that they valued significant connections they had formed with clergy, church leaders and other members of the congregation, thoughtful sermons or homilies, liturgy and church music. One Presbyterian interviewee, Grant (55), summed up many people's comments about church when he told me that "at the heart" of what people appreciate about their churches is "good teaching, good worship and good fellowship amongst the people." In addition, interviewees whose churches had a strong sacramental tradition told me that receiving communion was central to their church experience. Another notable feature of interviewees' comments was that people from a range of church types were very grateful for opportunities the church provided for quiet reflection and prayer during services or at other times.

In this chapter and the next we shall explore midlife churchgoers' experiences of church. This chapter focuses mainly on aspects of church life which middle-aged interviewees spoke about with gratitude and appreciation – things about their church experience that they valued and were important to them. In Chapter 4 we shall direct our attention to some of the challenges facing people in midlife when it comes to church engagement and the corresponding challenges that clergy and congregations can have in endeavouring to care for midlife members. The division between these two chapters is somewhat artificial. It is difficult to draw a distinction between aspects of church life that are helpful and those that are not so helpful to members, not only because what is appreciated by one person may not seem at all important to another but because individual parishes differ so greatly that what one church does well (for example, in offering support to married couples) may not be going so well (or be completely overlooked) in another parish. In addition, some things that might seem to be "working well" for middle-aged churchgoers might be able to be improved upon if carried out a little bit more intentionally.

The following table summarises aspects of church involvement which were most frequently identified by interviewees as of importance to them.

What do people in midlife value about church?

❖ Shared values and beliefs

❖ Having a sense of community, and of communion, with congregation members and with members of the wider church throughout the world or throughout history

❖ Several aspects of services of worship, including music and liturgy (of a range of types), teaching, and participation in the Eucharist/communion

❖ Relationships with trusted clergy

❖ Care of children and families

❖ Intergenerational relationships, providing opportunities both to give and to receive

❖ Small groups, whether structured or unstructured, meeting regularly or occasionally, with a social or more explicitly spiritual focus

❖ Opportunities to learn and grow through participation in programmes such as marriage and parenting courses, DVD series, and theological education

❖ Being able to contribute to parish life, using gifts and talents and drawing on life experiences

❖ Feeling supported when choosing to take on fewer or different responsibilities within the church

❖ Practical and spiritual support at times of difficulty, received from people in leadership and from fellow parishioners

❖ Quiet, prayerful space – churches being open, contemplative services, silence, retreats, time for reflection

❖ The availability of counselling, mentoring, or spiritual direction

Naturally many of these things are appreciated by people in other age groups as well as those in midlife, but in this chapter we shall think about why churchgoers in midlife, specifically, might value some of these particular aspects of church.

Community

A study carried out by Auckland's University of Technology (AUT) in 2015, found that, compared to 29 European countries that were involved in the same study, "New Zealand fared the worst when it came to social connections and community."[119] Of the 10,000 New Zealanders surveyed, almost 40% met with others socially once a month or less, and only 4% said they felt close to people in their local area. Overseas research suggests that people in midlife may be some of the loneliest members of society. Drawing on a range of studies, Oliver Robinson of Greenwich University observes, "Midlife is the peak era of occupational and civic responsibilities for most people, and friendship network size decreases by over a third compared with young adults."[120] Increasingly many middle-aged people live alone, are geographically disconnected from their families, and, due to developments in technology, frequently work in isolation.[121] As a result of the Covid pandemic, since this research was undertaken the numbers of people working in isolation has increased.

Karen (52) is a member of an Anglican parish. She talked to me about why she attends church:

> It's for the teaching and also for, you know, mixing and mingling with people, and the companionship. Well, particularly living alone. I mean I'm with people during the week at work, but I live alone. Even though I'm an introvert I do like to be around people on a Sunday morning and feeling we're in the same place with the same aim. And it's good to be encouraged and part of a community. It's for that sense of community. That's why I do it.

After her interview had concluded, Karen elaborated on this theme. As Karen's comments applied to the many people in New Zealand who live alone – and almost a quarter of New Zealanders live in one-person households[122] – I asked if we could re-start the recording so that she could repeat what she had said. She added:

> In daily life there's not always a huge sense of community. For example, here I am living alone, and I don't always see a lot of my neighbours. Yes, you're out and about with other people but you're not interacting with them. So church, and the sense of community that provides, is a really important part of my life. Shared vision, shared goals, shared values, and a shared sense of identity.

In his interview, Richard (Catholic, 48) also suggested that the church is a place where middle-aged people who might otherwise feel isolated may find genuine support. Like Karen, Richard lives alone. In his experience the church provides a context within which "unity and connectivity" may be found. He said:

> As the world is becoming a lot more individual the church is offering that sense of unity and connectivity which is really important. All of the things that supposedly connect us more now are really isolating us more. They're actually making people much more lonely. So the church is still real, as people do turn up bodily there. And while you can be thinking very individual thoughts while you are there, you still are very aware that other people there are primarily doing what you're doing.

I asked Richard if he was describing not just a sense of participation but of community. He replied, "It's community and also communion. Community is immediate, and the communion thing is the whole connecting down the ages and to heaven – so it's all there. It's very rich in that way."

Some of the ministers I interviewed were very conscious of these issues. Sung-ho (Presbyterian minister, 53), who had, at the time of his interview, lived in New Zealand for 15 years, expressed concern about the social isolation experienced by many people in this country. When I asked him what he considered to be the most significant needs of people in midlife he paused for quite some time before saying simply, "I think they need more friends." Sung-ho's parishioners have told him, "We are living in a lonely society." He added, "Overcoming, coping with, loneliness is true actually in the church as well." Another Presbyterian minister, Don (52), also identified "that loneliness thing" as a significant issue for people in middle age, particularly for those who are single, but also for couples who are childless or whose children have left home. As the nest empties, parents can find that networks of support that had revolved around the common interests and needs of their children are lost, and it can be hard to maintain friendships or to establish new ones. And as retirement looms, people who have invested a lot of time and energy into paid work may find themselves anticipating with some anxiety the loss of workplace relationships.

Paul (Catholic priest, 53) ministers in a large parish and is very aware of the need to offer opportunities for social connection for churchgoers who are in midlife. Paul observed that it is in midlife that people are most likely to shift house and move to a new parish but because people can go to Mass at any church it's easy to assume, in a big church, that a new person is just visiting on one day. He acknowledged, "So we don't reach out to that person. And you can be doing that the whole year, and no-one said hello to you." Paul noted, "Church can be a lonely place if you are a shy person and don't reach out to others, you go to a parish and no-one reaches out to you." Paul endeavours to make his regular parishioners aware of this. He has introduced biannual wine and cheese "welcome evenings" for newcomers, and morning tea is served after Mass each Sunday.

Many churches invite church attendees to meet together before or after services for a cup of tea or coffee, or sometimes a light meal. These informal gatherings are clearly considered by clergy and congregations to contribute to a sense of fellowship among churchgoers of all ages. Those of us who have opportunities to connect regularly with others in contexts such as these can easily take for granted the value and potential impact of simple hospitality when so many individuals in our communities are "suffering from disconnect."[123]

The building of close bonds between members of the church is not incidental to Christian discipleship but integral to it. After all, Jesus identified "love for one another" as the quality by which others would identify his followers (John 13:34-35). In his apostolic exhortation, *Evangelii Gaudium: The Joy of the Gospel*, Pope Francis writes:

> The individualism of our postmodern and globalized era favours a lifestyle which weakens the development and stability of personal relationships and distorts family bonds. Pastoral activity needs to bring out more clearly the fact that our relationship with the Father demands and encourages a communion which heals, promotes and reinforces interpersonal bonds.[124]

Small groups

In order to promote and reinforce interpersonal bonds many churches encourage members to join small groups. Small groups can be contexts within which people are able to share with others their struggles, joys, questions and discoveries. They also afford opportunities both to receive support and to offer it to others. Judith (Catholic, 60) has participated in a lot of small groups within both Protestant and Catholic parishes throughout her life. She described small groups as "critical to the Christian life," not only because of the material that may be covered within them, but "more so for fellowship and praying with other people and walking through life together." Judith identified one of the groups she had been part of as "quite a midlife group" (although it wasn't called that). The members who met had children in "that older age group" so they "were all walking together at that same stage of life." She said, "We didn't always particularly look at midlife issues or anything but we were quite aware of the stage of life, so that was supportive."

As Judith had been in a number of different small groups and had mentioned the advantages of meeting with others who were in the same stage of life, I asked her what she perceived to be the advantages and disadvantages of groups which catered for people of a similar age and groups which are less homogenous. Judith felt that own-age groups were particularly important for youth. She then acknowledged that groups that are similar are probably "easier." But Judith also marvelled at the fact that absolutely diverse people are drawn together by God – people that we just wouldn't mix with or have contact with otherwise – which "deepens your understanding of people and helps you see things from different perspectives." Diversity within small groups and within congregations was mentioned repeatedly by middle-aged interviewees as one of the most positive aspects of their church involvement.

Over 100 Catholic parishes in New Zealand are part of an established network of small groups called "Passionist Family Groups." These are intergenerational groups in which the emphasis is on building relationships. Each group is encouraged to get together once a month for a "low cost or no cost" activity, to extend acceptance and support and "simply and joyfully experience Christian life with others."[125] Several of the Catholic interviewees I spoke to mentioned Passionist Family Groups. They pointed out that, as with many other initiatives, the success of these groups is dependent on the level of commitment to them demonstrated by parish priests and congregational leaders, but where they are operating well connections between parishioners can be forged and enriched.

Sally (49) is a foundation member of a Passionist Family Group that was established 20 years ago. She explained to me how the groups in her church were formed. Parish coordinators allocate families to groups so that each group includes all ages from young children through to grandparents. Sally said that the thing she particularly liked about the Passionist Family Groups "is that you do get to know the range of ages."

Sally felt that the support her small group provided was "fantastic." She gave two examples of ways in which having established relationships with people of different ages had been helpful to her and to members of her family. When her children were young, she could easily find babysitters because there were teenagers within their Passionist Family Group that her family knew well. Now that her own children are teenagers, the active interest and support of an older couple in the group has meant that her 17-year-old son has gained "real employment" in a part-time role. She said, "That certainly would never have happened if we hadn't had that contact through knowing them." A Catholic priest from a different parish, Paul (53), observed, "The Passionist Family Group gives the children another set of, or more sets of, the next generation as well. I think we need that. I think young needs the old, the old needs the young."

Opportunities to mix with people from a range of age groups may be taken for granted by many people who attend church regularly but for some New Zealanders who have no church involvement it can be difficult to establish or maintain intergenerational relationships, even within families. It is common, for example, for grandparents to live in different cities from their adult children and young grandchildren, and (despite the sense of connectedness that communication technology can offer) the inability to meet with family members in person can be a source of real sadness for many.

A number of middle-aged interviewees described close relationships they had formed with older parishioners at church – stories we shall hear in Chapter 6 – and clergy also identified ways that people in midlife and older folk both benefited from connecting with one another. Sandra (Anglican priest, 58), for example, told me about a day programme for the elderly in her community, offered through Presbyterian Support, which some of her parishioners attend as volunteers. Sandra described the positive effect this had on a fairly shy middle-aged woman who had lost both her parents. This parishioner enjoys being a volunteer and has established lovely relationships with the elderly folk. She continues to visit one of the elderly men who has left the programme and gone into a home. The middle-aged parishioner now has somebody to whom she can offer some care, but she, too, is blessed by the relationship. Sandra said, "That's been really nice just to watch across the generations." Relationships between people in different stages of life provide rich opportunities for middle-aged Christians to give and to receive, and to grow in faith.

Friendships

The church can also play a positive role in helping people who are in the same stage of life to connect with one another. For men in midlife this is particularly important. A five-decade longitudinal study of adult development from Harvard University revealed that in later midlife, as they approach retirement and their focus on achievement declines, men's need for community and affiliation increases.[126] Friendships become a higher priority. As Janet Ruffing, Professor Emerita of the Practice of Spirituality and Ministerial Leadership at Yale Divinity School observes, "Older adults as compared to emerging adults place more emphasis on relationship and communion while younger adults are more concerned about their ability to act in the world."[127]

These shifts were illustrated very clearly in Don's interview. One of the things Don (Presbyterian minister, 52) considered significant about his midlife experience was that he had found himself becoming "much more intentional about connecting up with people." He told me that he now makes it a priority to meet with a male friend for coffee quite regularly, for example. Don said he was not quite sure how this shift came about. He paused to think about it, then said:

> I think that in some respects I think maybe it's having less to prove, but I don't feel quite as driven as I used to be, I don't think. ... I work pretty hard, really, but I am going home at 5 o'clock much more than I used to. It's kind of related to thinking, "Well what's really important in all of this?" And one of the things is this friendships thing, I'd say.

Don went on to provide an example of a case where he and his wife had rescheduled plans in order to prioritize time with friends who wished to catch up with them on a Friday night when they had intended to go away for a few days:

> My reaction a few years ago would have been to say, "Thanks for asking, but we can't go because we are heading away." But *[my wife]* and I had a quick chat and decided we'd delay leaving until Saturday morning so that we could go to the movies with our friends. That probably doesn't sound like a big deal but it's different to what would have happened ten years ago, I'd say.

Middle-aged men commonly have fewer social networks outside work than women but church can be a place where they are able to build strong relationships with one another. This was certainly something that both clergy and male churchgoers wanted to talk to me about. Priests and ministers spoke about the pressures facing men in midlife and the need for the church to encourage men to make time to spend together. Men in midlife described a variety of ways that they had connected with other men in their congregations.

Greg (Presbyterian minister, 62) believes that women are well catered for in the church, with mid-week groups where they have coffees and lunches, "Music and Movement" for pre-schoolers, and so on. "But the guys – we have breakfast together on a Friday morning, and we meet for prayer after we've set up here on Sunday, and we talk about all sorts of stuff. No agendas." The men also have film nights fairly regularly. They don't have a study but just meet as "guys without an agenda." Greg told me that the men "seem to be hungry for the fellowship." He then added, "When I think about the age of these guys, they're all in the age group that you're talking about." When I observed that the men who were making time to attend were clearly enjoying spending time together, Greg agreed:

> It is wholesome. How do you describe wholesome? It's not dull and boring. We'll sit and have a beer over a game of pool. But I know I'm not going to get awful language. And I've never heard anything even negative in a tone of voice, about their ladies, or their kids. There's never going to be a little backhander about anything. Now it's very rare to find where you can actually just be a guy in that situation where it's wholesome but it's still fun. Not geeky.

Greg added that he would like to invest more time in addressing the men's needs as he thinks that there are times when it's good for the men and women to be separate.

Andrew (44) attends a fairly large Anglican church and is part of a study group which meets fortnightly. He told me that he would be "more than happy" if the group met weekly. Andrew feels that it is important to be part of a small group "to get the relational side of things and personal encouragement in the faith journey." He said:

> It's not something you're going to be able to get from attending the kind of service we go to on a Sunday; there's too many people, and, with children around, it's too busy. You can connect at a social level at that sort of a service but the deeper stuff has to happen in homes.

Andrew's group is for men only, which he feels allows them to discuss things that they "probably wouldn't want to discuss as a mixed group, particularly when it comes to men's feelings, things they're struggling with, problems that they're having." The group has also been able to use some materials which have particular applicability to men, including an Australian resource entitled "The Men's Series."[128] This DVD series focuses on eleven issues of importance to Christian men, and includes episodes on work, midlife, parenting, health, sex and pornography, money and generosity, depression and anxiety, and mates. The scope of topics the group discussed and the trusting relationships that he had formed with other members were both appreciated by Andrew.

Grant (Presbyterian, 55) reflected on some of the challenges of men's ministries for those in midlife. He said, "When you look at the topic of men's ministries, it's quite a thorny issue, in that we can be sort of very difficult to get together in a group. From my perspective it's more achievable when there's something else to do." Although his church holds a men's breakfast about once a month, and men of all ages are welcome, it is held at a time when Grant is on his way to work. Occasionally his parish holds a men's movie night, and other activities are sometimes organised for men, but Grant still felt that involving men in midlife is "sort of difficult" because men in this age group are "doing stuff."

Grant then shared with me some significant changes that occurred in his life over the past decade. I asked him if he felt that the church had been able to support him while these changes were occurring.

In response to this question, Grant said that it had been, due to the close relationships he had formed with a group of men in the "set-up team" who put out furniture each week before church:

> Working in the set-up team I've got to know a bunch of men very well. We always joke about it. It's like a men's support group and the church gets set up as a side-effect of it. You know, quite often we have a good 20 minutes or so once we've finished set-up, before the next sort of major activity group of people come into the church, when we can just sit round and have a yarn and have a cup of coffee and chill out.

Sandra (Anglican priest, 58) spoke about the stress many of the middle-aged men in her congregation were experiencing. While they may not want to meet up for a Bible study, "because some of them would just not be into that," she felt that they might enjoy going out for a motorbike ride, or a bit of four-wheel driving, or a barbecue, and things like that:

> That kind of relational stuff, for some of those guys is actually really important, because I know that a lot of them are really stressed. And whilst I can go and have a bit of a chinwag with them, you know, as a female minister it's possibly not connecting sometimes. ... Women are good at organising groups and coffee mornings, and they like doing that. And the old retired guys love it *[meeting regularly for a coffee]* because they've all got plenty of stories to tell. But you know, for working men, often they don't necessarily have that connection. They don't necessarily have that talk-time with their colleagues at work because they're so busy. They might talk a little bit about it when they go home, but they might not. So, a place for them to kinda unwind and sound off if they need to, or encourage each other, I think's important.

Sandra went on to give an example of an event organised by a man in her congregation, for the men, which was a barbecue with boutique beer tastings. She said, "It was such a brilliant event. And they all got talking. I would have loved to have been there."

Of course, women also appreciate the support of friends and can value opportunities to spend time with others from their congregations. Sandra mentioned that for several years a group of about half a dozen female parishioners, who were a little under the age of 40, went away on "a girls' weekend" and they always invited her to join them, which she appreciated. She sees the value of sometimes "retreating out of normal life" but it's not always easy to work out how to do that, especially with middle-aged women who may be working and busy. "Dragging them off for a weekend and just doing something fun, and being refreshed, I think would be a really nice thing to do. But it takes a lot of organising." She felt that the same thing could be really good for the guys that are working. She thought it would be beneficial to them if they could "just go off and have a guys' weekend out in the country, or do something." Sandra contrasted that sort of relaxing weekend, which provides a "change of pace and space," with "trying to get things like vestry retreat days and things like that. They just don't want to do it. They don't want to waste a Saturday doing that stuff." Sandra sounded perfectly accepting of this perspective. "I think it's often in that change of pace and place, that's when a lot of the true relating kind of goes on."

Whether social, pastoral or spiritual concerns are the primary focus of any event or gathering, whenever churches support opportunities for people to build relationships with one another multiple needs are addressed. Bonds between parishioners, established and sustained within and beyond the organized activities offered by the church, are essential to people's sense of connection with the church and, ultimately, to their sense of being cared for by God. These friendships can become a significant source of stability and hope during times of challenge or crisis and can also provide encouragement and accountability in the Christian life.

Children and families

How churches respond to children matters enormously to their parents. Among the middle-aged churchgoers I interviewed, there were several who spoke with great enthusiasm about ways that the church catered for their children's needs. Churches did this in very different ways. The common denominator was that parents were happy when they felt that their children were made to feel welcome and valued members of the congregations to which they belonged.

Keith (Catholic, 47) described ways in which his seven-year-old son is included and involved at church. At his church there is a "children's liturgy" on Sundays. The children can go out for half an hour and do their own programme, and when they come back into the church the priest interacts with the children in the service. He "gets down amongst them" as they share their pictures and other activities. Keith described it as "precious" to see the children with smiles on their faces, loving that time. Keith and his wife are involved in serving in a number of ways during church services and also during the week. His pride was evident as he told me about the way that his son helps him with activities such as taking up the offering, cleaning the church, putting out things for morning tea, and so on. Keith observed that there can't be too many people in the church who don't know his son. He concluded, "It's a very warm, friendly church."

Murray (Anglican, 44) has teenaged children. In his church, too, children are encouraged to participate in the services and older children have opportunities to be involved in the formal structures of the church and in the organisation of events. This is not mere tokenism. His son is currently serving on vestry, and Murray is pleased and proud that his son's academic skills are being used and developed in that context. His son has also been involved in running social events, not just for youth, but for the whole parish. Murray also loves the fact that in their church, "Kids are free range – in other words, they have the run of the place, if they want to have the run of the place." He added, "The worst mistake people make in parishes is telling the kids off for being noisy and stuff like that." Murray's own sense of being part of a welcoming church family is linked to the congregation's acceptance and inclusion of children.

The connections parents in midlife can make with other Christians who have children of a similar age, and who may be grappling with similar issues, can also enhance their sense of belonging to their church community. Andrew (44) and his wife attend a large Anglican church which holds multiple services on Sundays, one of which offers a very good children's programme. He told me that they had chosen to attend that particular service "because of the children." Then Andrew made some observations about the congregation at the service he attends. He said, "It puts us with other people in the same stage of life who've also brought their own children along. From that aspect it's beneficial to us because afterwards, around tea and coffee, we can discuss the issues we're having." Later, however, Andrew noted that the different services tend to split up the age groups of people and therefore the diversity of the whole parish is not reflected in each congregation. Each congregation tends to be rather homogenous in terms of age. As Andrew put it, "It's more or less people at exactly the stage of life that we're at." Andrew felt that in some ways this was a pity.

Some churches hold special services or events which have an intergenerational focus, such as "Messy Church."[129] These occasions can be extremely effective in engaging middle-aged adults with young children, including those who are not familiar or comfortable with traditional ways of doing church. Ordinary Sunday church services often also include elements which engage parishioners of all ages. This can benefit everyone. Sandra (Anglican priest, 58) noted that while big churches may have the privilege of being able to offer a variety of services and programmes this isn't necessarily always a positive thing for parishioners with families:

> I don't know if it actually does any good. If you take kids out of church until they're twelve, then why do they think they're suddenly gonna want to start coming to church? They've never been before; they've always gone off to their programme. Church seems boring compared to that, so, "Why should I go?" *[She laughs.]* And then they opt out. Whereas if they've been a part of things, and they've been putting the candles out, or collecting the money, or doing a reading, or whatever, from when they are little, church is just familiar to them.

As we have seen, a conviction that their children are welcome and happy to be involved at church can be a significant factor in contributing to middle-aged churchgoers' attachment to their parishes. It can also contribute to their perception that their own needs are being met. However, support for children may not (by itself) be sufficient to sustain the faith of midlife members. This problem is not easy to address. It is a topic to which we shall return in Chapter 4.

Attending a Sunday service can be difficult for individuals in midlife who are juggling family commitments especially if they are the only members of their households who consider church attendance a priority. Therefore, flexibility around how and when people can be involved at church is important to people in their 40s and 50s. Grant (Presbyterian, 55) told me that he liked attending a service that started with breakfast on a Sunday and was finished by 9:45am. Although he no longer had children at home himself, he believed that the early start and finish suited families. He said, "It's family-friendly, but it's also sort of older-people friendly as well. You can get up, get going, and then if want to you can go and join friends for lunch, or whatever, and have a relaxed morning, or come home and work in the garden." Karen (Anglican, 52) described the pattern of worship in her own parish which includes a "Prayer Book" service at 8am, which is mostly attended by older people, and a 9:30am service for "all ages." She observed that although the later service offers a separate children's programme some younger families choose to attend the 8am service (where materials for children are available) because they prefer the time of day. Malcolm (Anglican, 52) appreciated being able to attend a Tuesday evening celebration of the Eucharist after work not only because he found the style of the service spiritually nurturing but because his wife and other family members were not churchgoers. Attending the Tuesday evening service allowed him more time with his family at the weekend. Liz, the priest at Malcolm's church, told me that the midweek evening service was attended by several midlife parishioners who came directly after work. She was also aware that one of those who attended the midweek service had a young family, including a three-year-old.

The Covid pandemic catapulted many churches around New Zealand and around the world into using technology more creatively so that people who were unable to attend church could still connect with other Christians as they worshipped God. Some churches found ways not only to enable parishioners to join in services of worship but also to participate in new or existing programmes that had formerly not been accessible to them. An organizer of an early evening *Alpha* course offered on Zoom described the motivation behind offering the course online, and the impact it had in enabling the participation of some people with children at home. Rosemary (Catholic, 52) said:

> We decided to do it because *[during lockdown]* we noticed so many families connecting on our Facebook page who weren't regular churchgoers. Some took us up on the invitation to join us on-line for *Alpha* and those who did attend were very grateful and they said that their faith was enriched by being able to attend the course. The parents said that if it hadn't been on Zoom they wouldn't have attended, but because it was a lot easier for them to attend, they tried it.

Churches are continually finding new ways to serve and connect with their communities. People in midlife, who can sometimes find it difficult to participate in church events and activities, obviously benefit when churches respond creatively to this issue.

Opportunities for service and for reflection

An integral part of authentic Christian discipleship is "remembering that we exist for a purpose beyond ourselves: we are called to bear witness to our faith and serve others as we seek God's reign of justice and peace on earth," as the Anglican diocese of Auckland's description of a healthy church puts it. Or, to draw on a higher authority, to remember that "faith by itself, if it has no works, is dead" (James 2:16). However, while people in midlife may have great capacity and desire to serve others, many also find that they are increasingly drawn to the "inner work" of review and reappraisal, as we noted in Chapter 1. Opportunities to serve and opportunities for reflection are both needed and valued by people in midlife.

Service

I have asked many Christians in midlife about areas of service they are involved in, both within and beyond the church. It has been a joy to hear them speak with such enthusiasm about ways they feel they are able to contribute to their communities. In addition to their paid employment – an aspect of midlife experience we shall look at in Chapter 4 – a significant proportion of the people I interviewed were serving on parish councils, carrying out practical maintenance projects for their church, were involved in formal mentoring or educational programmes, sharing leadership of children's ministries or were leading small groups of a variety of types. Beyond the church, they were assisting with fundraising for other organisations, serving on school boards of trustees, cooking meals for people in need, and actively supporting food banks and charitable second-hand shops. Two interviewees spoke of their commitment to the "prophetic role" of the church; one described his involvement in "low level politics" in the community, and the other was actively involved in working with the church to speak out about certain issues such as euthanasia. Other interviewees described mowing lawns and doing odd jobs for neighbours, providing transport for acquaintances who needed assistance to attend appointments, cooking and serving food at neighbourhood events, supporting children's music groups, and completing maintenance projects in schools. It was quite evident from their comments they were finding fulfilment in responding to the needs of people outside the church by exercising their gifts and "playing to their strengths." One midlife interviewee, Keith (Catholic, 47), described volunteering his time as "a stimulant."

Phil (Catholic, 53) expressed the view that the church is "just so huge" that everyone can find a place to be involved and included. Some of the ministries he identified as being areas Christians in midlife might wish to be engaged in were offering hospitality, working with refugees, supporting those who are "down and out" by working for St Vincent de Paul, singing in choirs, and serving on parish councils or school boards. Phil also identified ministries and activities that he felt were particularly helpful in supporting people in midlife, including groups for men,[130] marriage encounter groups to support people in their marriages, parish picnics and midwinter meals. "There are even Catholic sports' clubs," he added. Phil concluded, "Whatever your thing is – you're kinda involved in." Phil himself gained enormous pleasure from serving as a mentor in a pre-marriage course offered in his diocese (a role we shall hear more about later).

Clergy acknowledged the significant contributions that many middle-aged Christians make in a range of voluntary roles within their parishes. A number of priests and ministers perceived that parishioners' voluntary service was not only of benefit to the church but also a way in which midlife parishioners' own needs were being met. When Russell (Anglican, 56) was asked how effectively he thought the church supporting people in midlife, he identified "opportunities to contribute," particularly to the governance of the parish, as being important to people in this life stage:

> If you looked at our vestry, generally, the majority would be in that 40 to 60 age group. Definitely. And I think that they really find it very empowering to bring some of their skills and offer those skills to help the parish. You know, legal skills, accounting skills, general management-type skills, health and safety type skills. So that's a big thing.

Patricia (Anglican, 58) noted, similarly, that midlife churchgoers who are involved in volunteering and helping "find a sense of community and support in doing that, because it's often when they're doing something like that that they will be sharing their own challenges and dreams, and so that becomes a good place."

Patricia told me that she enjoys tapping into and releasing parishioners' gifts and desires in areas of service as particular needs and gaps arise within the church. She likes to see ministries develop in an "organic" way within the church. She said, "I'm very much one to, personally, to try and look at what God's doing, and join in." I asked Patricia if she had any thoughts about how to ensure that the ideas of all parishioners could be heard and incorporated, as shy members of a congregation who are conscious of a gap or need within the church, or who would like to serve in a new role, may not always have the confidence to approach the vicar or vestry. Patricia said that in more than one parish she has held an "Exploring Our Gifts" Sunday, fitting with the Bible reading of the day, at which, after a brief homily, she has issued a questionnaire and given people time to fill that in. The questionnaire covered all the things in parish life that people might be on rosters for:

> They had the opportunity to indicate what they were involved in, what they might like to be involved in, what they might like to also give up they could note, and then "other" – so anything else that they wanted to write down. And out of that a number of additional people are now involved in all sorts of areas. ... For me, it's enabling people to be open to the Spirit of God working, you know, in their lives, and giving that permission to, yeah, try something new!

As it happened, I had interviewed one of Patricia's parishioners, Murray (44), who, without prompting, had mentioned this questionnaire. He was enthusiastic about it because it had provided him with the opportunity to take on two new roles. First, he had offered to serve as a cantor within the church. He admitted, "I'm quite shy. I've always been able to sing." Murray told me that he now really enjoys being able to get together on a Sunday with four or five other very musical people from the congregation. Murray also offered to cook at the City Mission with a friend, a role he is enjoying as well.

A number of the churchgoers I interviewed spoke of the joy and fulfilment they were experiencing in discovering talents they did not know they had, or had not formerly had the opportunity to employ. With the support of clergy, several of them had taken the initiative in establishing and assuming leadership of new programmes, having perceived that needs existed which were not yet being met. These "gaps" prompted them to step up and contribute to parish life in ways that were meaningful for them and which had the potential to make a significant difference to others. They experienced what Presbyterian theologian and writer Frederick Buechner describes as "deep gladness,"[131] in being able to serve God in these ways.

Alison's personal experience led her to do something about addressing a need she found existed in her congregation. Alison (Presbyterian, 59) was widowed in early midlife. She received a lot of support from Christian friends both at the time of her husband's death and since, but she said, "I've really struggled. It's very hard being a widow at 41. We don't fit a demographic. The churches don't know what to do with you." Alison gave several examples of ways that widows and single people were inadvertently neglected within her church. These things led to her decision to start a group for the older single women in the parish. She invited a counsellor to attend and to help them identify what was difficult about their situation, and what was good, and the people who attended found that very helpful. Various members of the group that Alison established have continued to meet every Sunday after church for lunch at a café, although Alison herself now participates only occasionally as she has assumed other responsibilities. She is now part of her church's leadership team and she continues to speak up when she feels the needs of people who are not part of family groups are being overlooked. Exploring ways that churches can better support single Christians is beyond the scope of this book, but I would point people with an interest in this topic in the direction of the British website Single Friendly Church (www.singlefriendlychurch.com), which is packed with stories of single Christians' experiences and practical suggestions for congregations to consider.

Like Alison, Ian (Presbyterian, 41) had taken the initiative in introducing some new programmes and activities to his church. He identified this as a shift which was related to his stage of life. He said:

> I guess the big thing is when you're younger you make use of what is suggested to you, or maybe activities or opportunities that the church provides. I think as I've got a bit older it's become more about getting to know myself

and if there's an urge there to see if I can fulfil that, or actually start something which fulfils that.

Ian provided two examples. There wasn't a home group at his church, and he valued home groups, so he started one. He also established occasional Saturday night worship sessions after chatting with others at his church who, like him, felt that their Sunday morning services were rather lacking in the scope and style of worship they found most enriching. In reflecting on these things, Ian said, "I see more now that I am a part of a community." He is glad to contribute to his church community by sharing his gifts to meet shared needs.

By midlife many people have a fairly well-developed understanding of their gifts and strengths and this knowledge influences their choices of ministries both within and beyond the church. Approximately a quarter of the middle-aged churchgoers I interviewed explained that they had learned to be selective about the ways in which they chose to serve in the church so that they could effectively spend their time and energy in areas of service for which they felt well equipped, outside the church as well as within it. They were happy to contribute but they did not feel compelled to say yes to every request made of them, having learned (sometimes from painful experience) not to capitulate when undue pressure was placed on them. A significant number of the people who spoke to me felt that they needed to relinquish some of their responsibilities at church for a time. We shall hear more about some of their reasons for doing so in Chapter 4.

Members of the clergy were aware of the potential for middle-aged church volunteers to become over-burdened. Greg (Presybterian, 62) ministers in a "family-friendly" church which holds non-traditional services in a school hall. He believes that some people in the midlife age range who come to his church have been hurt through "burnout" in other churches. These are people who have been "unappreciated" after serving the church in a range of capacities. Greg said, "The only way they could get off the roster was to leave. They had to leave the church to have a break." In Greg's parish everyone is "stood down" at the end of a year of service. They get personalised letters of acknowledgement from Greg and the opportunity to reapply to serve again if they would like to do so. Greg also ensures that volunteers get a lot of acknowledgement and appreciation regularly throughout the year as well as at the end of the year. He expressed the belief that some people who have been hurt by church "have been hurt by being used, actually." He noted, though, that clergy do need to rely on the laity, and trust them, if clergy are not to be "run ragged."

It can be difficult for ministers and priests to discern how much time or energy members of their congregations can manage to contribute to activities within the church. Individuals in midlife can themselves find it difficult to gauge how they may best contribute to their communities of faith while coping with transitions and adjusting to multiplying or diminishing responsibilities in other spheres. A particular challenge for individuals in midlife is that although fulfilment is often found in serving others at work, at home, at church and in the community, in this stage of life people need time to reflect on the meaning and significance of these activities and to take stock of where they have been and where they are going.

Reflection

Churches can play an active role in supporting parishioners in midlife by providing opportunities for them to reflect on their roles, not only at church, but in their workplaces and in the community.

Liz (Anglican priest, 55) told me how her church was trying to help people to reflect on their roles within the community. She described a series of public talks that her church had been hosting in cafés, and the worthwhile nature of these, both for the listeners and for the presenters themselves. At these evening events presenters from within and beyond the parish had the opportunity to talk about the intersection between their work and faith. At the time of her interview two parishioners in midlife had recently spoken to the congregation at one of these events, and Liz said how interesting it was for her and for other members of the congregation to hear them describe their sense of God's call to serve as doctors in an impoverished community over 20 years ago. Liz considered it "one of the joys" of the evening to hear them telling their story to fellow parishioners. She would love to give parishioners more opportunities to share their stories, "even within the church service pattern." But she admitted, "It challenges me, too, because the danger is we sort of polarize or just get so church-focused."

Some people are delighted and honoured to talk about their work or areas of community involvement, whether during a church service or at another event, whereas other people would run a mile if asked to speak in public. Fortunately there is scope within the church for a wide range of opportunities for reflection to be offered. One Catholic churchgoer, Richard (48) told me how much he appreciates the fact that the church is a "reflective place." By this he meant two things. First, Richard considered that church is "thoughtful." In the midst of the world's complexities, the wisdom that is offered by the church is bigger than the individuals' wisdom or insights within it. The church "offers a bigger framework of understanding." Second, Richard described the church as "reflective" in the sense that it provides "thinking space" for individuals. Richard perceived that the space that is created during Masses, when other interruptions and demands are removed, to be very valuable, particularly as people have so little thinking time in their lives now. He noted that outside Mass times, too, Catholic churches are almost always open during the day so that people can come in and have some quiet reflective space which can be hard for them to find in other parts of their lives. "So there's lots of ways that the church can really help, and does, but are not always understood," Richard said.

Richard observed that time for reflection can be particularly valuable for people engaged in some of the tasks of midlife – and it can be hard to come by. It takes time to reflect on our work, relationships, values and beliefs as we seek "a more congruent living out" of our "inner and outer lives," as one spiritual director, Julie, put it. Bernard (Catholic priest, 52) described midlife as a period of "re-examination" during which individuals feel drawn to explore questions such as, "What's my life about? The activity: Is it worthwhile? Is it true? Does it have a meaning and purpose beyond this world?" Bernard is currently involved in establishing a new residential retreat centre which he is sure will provide many opportunities for people in midlife. He said, "People are longing to get away to try to attend to these unresolved things that have sprung up in their life."

It is perhaps not until people have a little bit of life experience that they come to realise – whether they are able to articulate this or not – that being able to connect effectively with the world requires a "godly balance" between "contemplation and action; between detachment and engagement; between hard slog and flow,"[132] as Joanna Collicutt explains. The church is one context in which deeper questions about life can be pondered. People in midlife benefit greatly when time and space for this to occur is provided.

Silence

Given that midlife is not only very busy for many people but is also a period during which the desire to pause, review and recalibrate naturally increases, it is not surprising that many middle-aged people find silence helpful. Nearly half of the middle-aged churchgoers I interviewed said that they had recently participated in contemplative services, vigils, or retreats – a number for the first time – and, without exception, they had found these experiences worthwhile. In addition, a similar proportion of interviewees stated that they valued the fact that the church provides a peaceful, reflective context within which they can experience some stillness in the midst of their busy lives. But it was not simply desire for personal space being expressed by interviewees when they commented on the value of silence in helping them to reflect on their lives and faith. Even though most struggled to find words to describe their experience the clear implication of their comments was that that in silence they encountered God.

I asked Keith (Catholic, 47) how the church is able to assist middle-aged people who may be struggling with regrets, or with things that have happened to them earlier in life. His response was immediate: "You can sit in the church, and it's, you know, it's quiet." Keith explained that because of the voluntary roles he holds at his church, including responsibility for church maintenance, he and his wife have a church key and can enter at any time. He continued:

> You can go in and sit down, and, you know, just let it all wash over you. And after a while you sort of feel good about life in general. And then you see there's a light bulb out and think, "I must fix that on the way out." *[We both laugh.]*

Keith's church remains open until about seven o'clock at night so that individuals can pop in. He told me that many people make use of the church building in this way. Keeping church doors open so that people can enter and spend time with God is perhaps a form of outreach or ministry which deserves greater recognition.

In some denominations services which allow an extended period of time for people to sit quietly in God's presence may occur at particular points in the church year. Spending time in sustained silence with others can help people to become attentive to God in a special way. Murray (Anglican, 44) told me that not long before his interview with me he had attended an Easter vigil for the first time. In the evening there was a short service at their church and the church had remained open until midnight. Murray stayed for a couple of hours "praying and thinking." He said:

> Good time to de-stress, actually. Put your life in perspective again. Because you're thinking about the loss and what was contributed to you by him placing himself on the cross, and the sacrifice he made. It was a good time to reflect. I couldn't have done it all night, though!

In the Catholic church opportunities for people to attend Eucharistic Adoration may be offered. Thomas (Catholic priest, 54) explained a little bit about this practice:

> It's interesting that in the Catholic Church in the Western world one of the biggest growth things in parish life in the last ten years has been Adoration of the Blessed Sacrament. Which is nothing. Silence. Nothing. The presence, the reality of Christ present, but no-one's doing anything. The people are coming and going in their own time. People come to church, come in in silence, don't talk to anyone, stay there for 15 minutes or an hour, and then leave again, in silence. We say, "This is the heart."

Another Catholic priest, Bernard (52), told me that Adoration is "full of people in midlife. At midlife, I think you become a bit more attentive to spiritual things."

In some Catholic dioceses people choose to make a commitment to attend Eucharistic Adoration weekly at a specific time. I spoke to one man whose wife – being "pretty proactive" – had signed both of them up to be on this roster. Peter (73) told me how he spends his hour at Eucharistic Adoration. He sometimes begins his time of silent prayer by reading two or three pages from a devotional book.[133] "I sometimes use that as a focus for it. That would take no more than 10 or 15 minutes but provides some thought to reflect on." Peter then sits and asks, "What are you trying to tell me, Lord?" Peter admitted that initially he found it difficult because he "quite likes to talk, whereas in Adoration it's a little bit more about listening." He added, "But the Lord persevered with me." Although Peter feels that sometimes the time drags (and he has to be careful not to nod off) at other times he is able to enter deeply into prayer.

Peter had attended Adoration on the morning of his interview and he told me about this experience:

> I was just thinking this morning that God started it all, he's keeping it going, he knows what the end purpose is. What is my role? You know, I'm supposed to be a helper here. What is it that I'm supposed to be doing now to help you fulfil your vision? That's the sort of thing that comes through. ... One of the things I asked for this morning, I wanted to be more than just a sort of fair-weather friend. ... I opened my eyes and I thought, "Cripes, the hour's gone!"

Although Peter "quite likes to talk," and still finds a great deal of spiritual nourishment in communal contexts, silence is playing an increasingly important part in nurturing his relationship with God.

Anglican Bishop Jeremy Taylor (1613-1667) wrote, "There should be in the soul halls of space, avenues of leisure, and high porticos of silence, where God walks."[134] If we believe that spending time in silence is likely to help people to listen to God – whether that is in a structured environment or in other contexts – then we will work to ensure that silence can be found within churches of every denomination and every type. We might be further motivated to prioritise silence in our churches, including making space for silence during services of worship, if we are conscious that it will not only be members in midlife who will benefit. In caring for one cohort within our congregations we will also be supporting people in other age groups who can feel bombarded by words in church, such as those with dementia. Joanna Collicutt writes:

> Too many words can mean that we can't hear ourselves think and, more importantly, we can't be attentive to the still small divine voice. Too many words are not only pointless, not only idolatrous, not only a mark of anxiety, but they are also counterproductive. They can build a barrier between human beings and the life of the Spirit. ... When we pray, we are participating in a love relationship, and you don't need many words for that.[135]

Experiences of worship

Before we conclude this exploration of the elements of church most valued by middle-aged churchgoers, let us attend to what they said about church services themselves. In speaking with churchgoers and clergy it quickly became apparent to me that there is no correlation between age and attraction to a particular style of church service. Some middle-aged churchgoers appreciate informal services of praise and worship which enable them to express their emotions freely, while others find freedom within formal liturgy. Some like contemporary music, whereas others prefer traditional hymns or choral music. For many Christians the celebration of the Eucharist (or receiving communion) is regarded as the focal point of a service of worship. And thoughtful sermons or homilies that help people in midlife to reflect on their faith and life are universally valued. As we have already noted, churches that have a strong focus upon children and offer forms of worship that are engaging for families can be very attractive to churchgoers with children living at home. Middle-aged Christians who are juggling multiple responsibilities and busyness can also be drawn to contemplative services. For some, midlife can be a period of openness to exploring unfamiliar styles of worship.

Music

Half of the churchgoers I interviewed spoke about the importance of music in their experience of worship. There was a broad spectrum of tastes in music among them.

Judith (Catholic, 60) and Richard (Catholic, 48) both sing in church choirs. For Judith, singing in a choir is primarily "something little I can do to make this offering to God, to make other people's spirits soar, and to also reflect the beauty of God in the music" but in recent years it has also become "the fellowshippy bit" of her church experience. Judith loves "that sense of doing something together." Richard described the way he experiences God through sacred music. He said, "I have a good sense of the transcendent God through the Church's music. I have that sense of God's bigness, my smallness, not in a dismissive way, but in a really good way, to know that I'm not the centre of my own universe." Like Judith, Richard felt that involvement in choral music contributed to a sense of belonging. He said, "There's a whole lot of things that you would probably seek in other groups if you didn't have music. The people that are drawn into the music, that's a family within the church."

Some of the people I interviewed attended more than one church because they had particular musical preferences. Gail (41), who belongs to a large Anglican parish and attends a Sunday morning service at that church, sometimes goes with her family to an evening service at a Pentecostal church. Gail's preferred style of worship is not offered at the Anglican parish – Gail laughed as she expressed the view that at times the music "sort of feels like a bit of a funeral march" – but she and her husband are committed to the parish because they believe that the church offers a strong children's programme which is "good for the kids." The Pentecostal church they sometimes visit holds an early-evening service on a Sunday, which lasts one hour. There, a children's programme is offered concurrently, so Gail and her husband can attend the service and really enter into the style of worship that they most enjoy. Gail admitted that they leave immediately after the service without making personal connections, "which for us is unusual," but "we get the worship side that we felt we were missing."

Ian (Presbyterian, 41) belongs to what he called "a community church." He described the Sunday services in their parish as fairly liturgical in structure, with some songs at the start and hymns later in the service, including "a little bit for everybody." Some parishioners, including Ian, enjoy a more contemporary style of worship. The Saturday night praise sessions which Ian had organised were intended to supplement, rather than replace, the Sunday services. They are held only once every few months as some of those who wish to be involved are quite busy with young families. Ian was clearly glad to have been able to facilitate these gatherings and enjoys participating in them. A number of other interviewees exercised flexibility about their involvement in services incorporating a range of worship styles. This flexibility and openness to a variety of styles of worship and forms of prayer was commented on by clergy as characteristic of churchgoers in this life stage.

Patricia (Anglican priest, 58) described her own journey of spiritual exploration at midlife as an "adventure." She told me that for many years she had been part of a church where she was very involved in children's ministry and music ministry. "I was pretty busy on a Sunday morning," Patricia said. "I would tend to look for somewhere for nourishment in the evening, if I could." Patricia moved from her original denomination to the Anglican church by "quite an involved route that God was very much part of." Along the way she drew nourishment from "quite a mixture" of different forms of worship, including Celtic, Taizé, more traditional sacramental services, and more modern services. She "dipped into Pentecostal and charismatic areas as well" and felt that these contributed to her spiritual formation. "I was really very open," Patricia said. She added that she also took children along to a range of churches as part of their faith development in their Sunday programme. The Sunday school leaders spent a term taking the young people to the Chinese Church, the Salvation Army, the Samoan Church, and so on, to help them to understand that they were part of something that was much bigger and also diverse. Patricia is aware that her diversity of faith experience has helped her, in ministry, to understand people and to meet people "where they're at" spiritually. She added, "And it's OK to change along the way."

A number of the middle-aged churchgoers I interviewed shared Patricia's attraction to unfamiliar expressions of spirituality. They spoke of encountering God as they attended church services of different types and also as they were exposed to a range of resources and faith experiences beyond the church services they continued to attend. Several had changed denominations at midlife.[136] As individuals' faith develops and their circumstances change some may seek forms of worship and prayer which help them to respond to God in new ways – a topic to which we shall return in Chapter 5. Church services that accommodate and foster the willingness to explore in liturgy, theology and in spirituality can therefore be beneficial to Christians in midlife.

Sermons and homilies

Almost half of the midlife churchgoers I interviewed stated that sermons or homilies provided encouragement to them. They spoke with great respect of preachers whose faith, integrity and wisdom were evident in their words and in their lives. Interestingly, three of the Catholic interviewees who placed a lot of value on homilies commented on the fact that the priests whose sermons they most appreciated were elderly.

Michelle (Catholic, 58) has the opportunity to attend services in a number of parishes because she travels widely as part of her current role within the church. When she is not away, Michelle worships in two quite different contexts. One is a cathedral, which has a very inclusive multicultural congregation. She also attends services held in a chapel in her workplace. Michelle spoke with warmth and appreciation about an elderly priest who officiated at services held there. She told me, "He really just preached the gospel and helped us to take hold of something so that when we left that Mass we would have something to really reflect on during the day.

He'd really speak about his own life experience and I could relate to that."

Sally (Catholic, 49) also described, with warm affection, a previous parish priest. He was an elderly man with whom Sally enjoyed having "reasoned conversations" about topical issues. He delivered very thoughtful sermons. Sally told me that she used to email those sermons to her father in another part of New Zealand, and he loved them too. She reflected that that particular priest – whom she felt, being elderly, was aware of most stages of life – would be able to give guidance to someone in any stage of life. Phil (Catholic, 53) had a very similar perspective of the homilies and of a previous parish priest. He said, "The homily means a lot more to me now. ... I guess it came from having a priest that was so good at unpicking the liturgy with his homily where he related it to the real world. And this was a 70-year-old man who had such life experience."

Nina (43) attends an evangelical Anglican church. When I asked her how the church has helped her to cope with midlife issues she said, "Probably as an individual – not really." But she immediately added, "Sermons provide a lot of support." At Nina's church the sermons are recorded and made available on-line. Nina really appreciates being able to listen to the sermons at home, as well.

Patricia (Anglican priest, 58) told me that she considers it an "enormous privilege" to be able help people connect with God, "to offer that 'holy ground,' the 'I–thou' relationship," as parishioners struggle with a range of life experiences. In her homilies she endeavours to relate to the Scriptures to what is going on in people's lives, acknowledging that there are challenges that all of us share.

Holy ground

"Church is not what we do; it is what God does, although we participate in it,"[137] writes Eugene Peterson, author of *The Message* paraphrase of the Bible. Rowan Williams, the former Archbishop of Canterbury, expresses a similar sentiment in words which I find immensely helpful to recall on occasions when I have the privilege of preparing and leading church services myself:

> When we think about liturgy and shared worship, what we have most to think about is whether the actions and the words performed convey any sense that something is happening that nobody there is doing. ... Liturgy comes

alive when that's the sense people have, whatever form the liturgy is taking.[138]

This sense of sacred mystery – that something is happening during worship "that nobody there is doing" – was described by a number of interviewees. This was most marked in their descriptions of receiving communion.

Phil (53) has only recently become a member of the Catholic Church, although he has attended Catholic services with his wife and children for much of his adult life. Phil described the connection he feels with God and with others when he goes to communion. Similar experiences were mentioned by other midlife interviewees from both Catholic and Anglican churches. Phil said:

> For me, as I get older, I find great comfort in going to Mass. You know, Mass is a time of reflection. You're just sort of very much "in the zone". It's meditative, you know? … There are times when I go and I am so tired and it doesn't make any sense … but then you go to communion and that's the point in the Mass where you say, "Well, it don't really matter what I've taken in and what I haven't taken in, I'm with the team here." And you feel that connection.

Phil described his experience of receiving communion as "very fulfilling." He said, "This is the comfort I need in my life. And you know, it's amazing." The fact that liturgical practices and lectionary readings are stable and predictable also bolsters Phil's sense of connection with Christians throughout the world:

> The beauty of the Catholic Church, or any church system, is you go to a church service or you go to Mass anywhere in the world on any particular day and it's the same reading. You know, there's this unity to it all that appeals massively, isn't there, really?

Malcolm (52) had a Christian upbringing. He was christened in the Catholic Church and he attended a Catholic primary school. But he "shied away from church and religion for the next 30 years." Malcolm now regularly attends a mid-week Eucharistic service held at an Anglican church not far from where he works. He told me about his attraction to this service and the small community of believers amongst whom he has found himself:

> I could just sort of sneak in on a Tuesday evening and I didn't have to front up with a congregation. It was always

a smaller gathering. You know, half a dozen to a dozen people. And um, I don't know, it was just easier that way, rather than turning up for a Sunday Mass. And that sort of suited me. I found that was enough, really.

Malcolm appreciates the contemplative style of worship offered at this service. "There's more silence and the liturgy's fairly formal. And I just like the space that that gives you." The service does not include a homily or sermon, but Malcolm does not miss that, as he attends for the "ritual of the Eucharist." The service takes half an hour. "It's just easy to slot into your week," said Malcolm, but he emphasised that this was not the only (or primary) reason he chose to go at that time:

It's a different thing to a Sunday service. I mean I always felt that I could just come in, be there for it, and go. There's no need for conversation. You're in your own space. It's not a communal thing. I mean, people are coming together, but it's a bit more individual. I went to it for a long time and I didn't even know people's names. I saw them week after week, but I didn't know their names.

Later in his interview Malcolm reflected further on this church experience. His comments reveal that, although he appreciates not being required to engage in conversation, he does have a sense of deep connection with others who attend the midweek service he attends, and he draws strength from their prayerful presence. Describing himself as a fairly "passive participant," Malcolm said, "I guess I go for spiritual nourishment and I feel I get that." He elaborated:

When I go there and sit amongst that congregation, um, compared to my work, and all the people I deal with during the week, I just get the sense that there's real spiritual power there, in these frail people. Real or perceived, I don't know. But it's like – they're very gentle people. And just that whole thing, it just seems like there's power in it. You get a sense of that, which is almost an oxymoron.

Malcolm's consciousness of "spiritual power" among the people was replicated in Judith and Jane's accounts of receiving communion.

Judith (Catholic, 60) described as "surprising" the support for her faith that she feels she receives from the church "through sensing the devotion to Christ of other people." At communion she experiences "the foot of the cross being really level," as she explained:

> When you go to Mass you just see other people filing up reverently, taking communion, all expressing their need for Christ. Rich and poor, together and not-so-together, and young and old, and I just find other people's devotion to Christ – because it's not in a showy way at all, it's just this humility – I find that really supportive. I find that inspires devotion in me, too.

Jane (Anglican, 55) described going to communion as a "leveling" experience:

> I remember thinking once, years ago, watching people go up to communion, it's almost like a pictorial thing of the gospels, really. Everybody, all these different people, no matter what stage of faith they're at, or what level of education they have, or whatever, they can all go up the same way, and we all get the same food, and we all need it just as much – I quite like that. I like the visual demonstration of it, week after week.

Jane felt that her appreciation of the place of communion in worship was deepening as she aged. She thought that this "might be a kind of midlife change." She explained that when she had attended a Baptist church for some time, earlier in her life, the sermon was "the high point" of the service, but in the Anglican Church the Eucharist is "the grounding thing, the focal point" in the service. "A good sermon's a bonus!" Jane said, with a laugh. But there's an "objectivity" about communion which she appreciates:

> It brings you back, week after week, regardless of what state you're in. It brings me back to the heart of my faith and it's tangible – that's a key part. It's not a matter of what state I'm in this week; it's just the elements are offered to me again, and I receive them again. The sermon is still important to me in terms of encouragement and reminders, or whatever I need, but the Eucharist is the focal thing for me.

These churchgoers in midlife encountered God both through the tangible elements of bread and wine and through the experience of a faith community within which "words like Jewish and non-Jewish, religious and irreligious, insider and outsider, uncivilized and uncouth, slave and free, mean nothing" (Col 3:11, *The Message*).

As we have seen, many churchgoers in midlife find a huge amount to value in being part of a supportive faith community.

Nonetheless, in the middle decades of life it is not uncommon for people to attend church services less regularly and to be less engaged in congregational activities. These changes can occur even if individuals' previous experiences of church have been very positive and they still consider their faith to be important to them. In the next chapter we shall look at some of the factors contributing to these shifts and consider ways that churches might respond to them.

Questions for reflection or discussion

1. In this chapter, did any of the interviewees' stories or comments particularly resonate with you? Did any surprise you? Why?

2. What aspects of your church involvement have you valued in the past? What do you value at the moment? Give thanks to God as you remember and reflect on these things.

3. If the church you attend was to be reviewed using the "Healthy Church Model" designed by the Anglican Diocese of Auckland, where might it be doing well? Where might there be points for development?

4. Think about the fulfilment you experience when you are able to use your gifts and life experience both within and beyond the church. What forms of service attract and energize you? What roles or responsibilities might you need to relinquish at this time? Who might support you as you explore these questions?

5. What might you, or your church community, like to pray about or act upon?

Recommended resources

Baab, Lynne. *Embracing Midlife: Congregations as Support Systems.* Bethesda, MD: Alban Institute, 1999.

Pope Francis. *Evangelii Gaudium: The Joy of the Gospel.* London: The Incorporated Catholic Truth Society, 2013.

Johnstone, Carlton. "Understanding the Practice of Church Two-Timing." *International Journal For The Study Of The Christian Church* 9:1 (2009): 17-31. <http://www.tandfonline.com/doi/abs/10.1080/14742250802577382> (3 November 2016).

Van Loon, Michelle. "Why Friends Disappear When You Reach Midlife." <http://theperennialgen.com/why-friends-disappear-when-you-reach-midlife/> (30 April 2020).

4 — Challenges

"May there be balanced rhythms in our lives, O Lord.
Work and rest; company and solitude;
Sound and silence; activity and stillness;
Doing and waiting; giving and receiving."

8th Anglican Bishop of Auckland, Bruce Gilberd[139]

By one measure of New Zealanders' "subjective perception of the importance of religion to their life and identity," Christians in midlife identify less closely with their religion than those in other age groups.[140] Geoffrey Troughton, Joseph Bulbulia and Chris G. Sibley have explored responses to the question, "How important is your religion to how you see yourself?" posed in the New Zealand Attitudes and Values Study in 2012.[141] Participants ranked their answers from 1 (not important) to 7 (very important). Analysing the responses of the 3,505 New Zealand participants who identified as Catholic, Anglican, Presbyterian, or simply Christian with no further definition (NFD), the authors found that in Catholic, Anglican and Presbyterian churches there is "greater strength of religious identification among younger respondents than among each successive age group into middle age."[142] Beyond middle age, strength of religious affiliation increases. According to this measure, then, a significant number of New Zealanders in midlife who are affiliated to mainline churches do not perceive their religion to be as important to them as those who are younger or older than themselves.

In many congregations throughout New Zealand people in midlife are conspicuous by their absence. Although the focus of this book is not on church leavers – I would commend to readers who would like to think more deeply about that topic Alan Jamieson's work examining the experiences of Christians who have left evangelical, Pentecostal and charismatic churches in New Zealand[143] – there are obviously some factors, both within and beyond the church, that affect both leavers and "remainers." Despite all the aspects of church involvement which are valued by those who do attend, churchgoing may seem less attractive, or simply become more difficult, for people in midlife.

There is a range of reasons for this, including (but certainly not limited to):

❖ *Family* – responsibility for children and/or parents, lack of time, other commitments and priorities, exhaustion.

❖ *Work* – pressures related to work and/or insufficient opportunities to connect what happens at church with what happens during the rest of the week .

❖ *Major life events* – when significant challenges arise church may be a place of nurture or a difficult place to be.

❖ *Spiritual development* – the potential for midlife to be a period of discovery and deepening faith can be underestimated within churches.

These were themes that arose frequently in the interviews I conducted. In addition to these issues, there are undoubtedly also periods in the lives of particular parishes (and denominations) when congregations are forced to grapple with other problems that can have a significant impact on the involvement of middle-aged members. The list above is not an exhaustive summary of factors affecting the church participation of Christians in midlife but reflects the dominant concerns of the interviewees with whom I spoke.

Family responsibilities

Margie Lachman and others involved in psychological and sociological studies of midlife suggest that the "central issues" of midlife centre around "generativity, caring and concern for others in the work and family spheres."[144] However, at the same time as dealing with these responsibilities, people in midlife are also addressing "their own needs for meaningful work (paid or unpaid), health, and well-being. The need to balance multiple roles and manage the conflicts that arise is a reality that is characteristic of middle age, regardless of one's specific lifestyle or circumstances."[145]

"Midlife adults are at the height of assuming responsibility for others and midlife is typically the time of greatest influence and most frequent intergenerational contact," Lachman observes.[146] Many people in midlife bear some responsibility for children (of a wide range of ages) and/or elderly parents, and some also take an active part in supporting grandchildren. These responsibilities can have a significant impact on people's relationship with the church, both in terms of what they hope to receive from congregational involvement and in how much energy they have to expend on church activities. For some middle-aged people a primary means of maintaining a developing faith is to hunker down and try to maintain some sort of devotional life while learning how to love those closest to them.

When it came to responsibility for family members the most common themes raised by interviewees were:

❖ Busyness – "I was enabling everyone else to do everything – and that is what I thought a good mother did, anyway – and then there was nothing left for me."

❖ Complexity of parenting (particularly teenagers) – "Just there's no manual for it. I wonder whether I have done enough, whether I am doing enough, whether I should be doing more, whether I'm doing it right."

❖ Transition to an "empty nest" – "Potentially I'm going to feel a little bit lost."

❖ Care for parents – "Before the losing of them is the caring for them, and the whole role reversal and journey that takes you on."

❖ Bereavement – "I realised that that line between life and death is such a tiny thin one."

It can be difficult for churches to support members who are dealing with significant familial responsibilities. Interviewees' comments about pastoral care are peppered throughout this chapter and we shall look more directly at this topic towards the end of it.

Care for children

Gail (Anglican, 41) has a young family and she works part-time. Her story is worth recounting in some detail as it illustrates a number of issues that can affect churchgoers who have children living at home. Gail told me that for some years she and her husband attended a large Pentecostal church. When their children were very young Gail spent most church services out in the crèche with her children – not an uncommon experience for parents with young children – and she experienced a significant sense of loss in being unable to participate in worship. Gail also felt somewhat isolated at this time because she was a "stay-at-home mum" in a city where she had no family support. When Gail spoke of her struggles to a friend, her friend lent her a worship CD. This simple act of kindness had been very important to Gail and in her interview she recollected it with some emotion. Gail told me that being able to play the CD at home had been "just amazing."

On moving to another city Gail and her husband looked for a church that offered a strong children's programme and they ended up attending their local Anglican church. Gail said that she and her husband both felt "mature enough" in their faith that, even if they themselves got little out of their church attendance, "We are not going to fall away; we'll just sort of endure it." Later in her interview, however, Gail described some significant transitions and challenges she had been dealing with. Not only had she and her husband moved cities, which had meant she had need to make new friends, but she had returned to paid employment and was finding it difficult to juggle commitments at home and work. Gail was also adjusting to some serious health issues that had recently emerged within her immediate family. Despite the evident complexity of her personal circumstances, Gail appeared a little disconcerted when I posed the question, "What further support or opportunities would you like to see the church offer to help you in your faith journey in midlife?" She said:

> I don't know. You kind of think about it in terms of how it's going to help our kids. You kind of put your own – *[dawning realisation]* – maybe something for us, rather than for our kids would be quite nice wouldn't it? *[Gail laughs, then pauses for quite some time as she processes the question, before continuing.]* You always think "What's going to be good for the kids?" but you put yourself on the backburner, so I am not quite sure how to answer that question – something I suppose that's for the middle-aged people rather than those that depend on them?

A number of the people I interviewed suggested that if children were well catered for within a parish then parents would generally consider that they, too, were receiving support. For example, when I asked Raewyn (Presybterian, 47) to identify ways in which the church was providing support to her, her initial response was, "There are a lot of opportunities for the family to be involved in the church and to be nurtured by the church, I suppose." It is natural for parents to place a high priority on the nurture and care of their children, and support for families is very important. However, unless their own spiritual development is also fostered – unless there are elements of what occurs at church that are meaningful to them personally – there will certainly be some midlife churchgoers that are "coming each week who are leaving internally," as Alan Jamieson observes. These people are present, "but inside the lights are out. Other things keep them coming – their children, friendships, playing in the band etc. Yet they are not engaging in the way they would have previously."[147]

If what is happening at church does not seem meaningful to people in midlife, people in this age group are likely either to disengage or seek sources of nourishment elsewhere (or perhaps both). As Gail's use of a worship CD at home and her attendance at another church illustrate, Gail had found food for her soul outside Sunday morning services. She was also a reader. When I visited her home I noticed a book by Philip Yancey entitled *What Good is God?*[148] lying open on the coffee table. Gail told me she had been finding the book helpful as it addressed a raft of concerns that had emerged for her just a few years earlier as multiple stressful events had caused her to question some aspects of her faith. Although she had little time for reading – as she said, "Sometimes sitting down and reading can feel like a bit of a luxury" – Gail appreciated the fact that resources were available through her church's library and she availed herself of them when she could. Other middle-aged interviewees were also finding different forms of support for their faith outside church. This is a topic we shall look at more closely in Chapter 5.

Gail also told me that she and others at a similar age and stage to herself were "pulling back for a little bit" from commitments at church because they found it difficult to juggle all their responsibilities. Gail had withdrawn from a hospitality roster. She was relieved that no-one at church had made her feel under any pressure to continue, especially as she and her husband had felt under a great deal of pressure to commit a lot of time to roles within their former church (where simply being on the welcoming roster had demanded attendance at a lot of meetings). Gail said that, at that time, her husband's work had suffered because he was so involved in serving within the church. She and her husband are now aware that burnout and getting priorities out of balance can be an issue. Gail said, "No-one's going to say to you, "Stop. You are doing too much. Your life is out of balance. You need to look after your family, or all that kind of stuff." She described her current congregation and its leaders as being very good in terms of not pressuring people, and added, "If we did feel pressure, we could feel uncomfortable there and could be thinking, 'Well, hang on – are the people here really in touch with what life is like?' I sometimes felt that at the big Pentecostal church."

Many of the people I interviewed – clergy, spiritual directors and churchgoers alike – expressed concern about the pressure that churches can inadvertently place on middle-aged members. This is an issue that people often raise at spiritual direction. Louisa (spiritual director, 66) noted that it is not uncommon for people who have been very active and committed to the church in their younger years to "pull right back, or even pull out in midlife." While she attributed some of that withdrawal from church involvement to family and work demands, Louisa also wondered if it could be "a kind of exhaustion." She said, "You know, they give so much in those early years." Louisa acknowledged that in her own denomination being very active and involved is seen as good.[149] "It can be all-consuming in terms of service and ministry and busyness, where busyness is really held up as a goal to be attained." She added:

> I wonder if people draw back – I wonder what that means for their faith. And if they pull back at midlife, and the stages of faith, or the midlife crisis, or "the stuck place" happens, do they toss it all overboard? I don't know. I have got no answers to that. But those are questions I am interested in.

These are significant questions, to which there are many possible answers. We shall explore some of these in Chapters 6 and 7.

The "empty nest"

A number of interviewees reflected on the transition to having an "empty nest." Sally (Catholic, 49), has four children, the youngest of whom is fourteen years old. She told me about the busyness and financial pressures that her family had experienced over the previous few years, before commenting on recent changes in family dynamics. Sally said that, despite the fact that three of the children still live with them, there are more and more times that only she and her husband are at home. Although that is "kind of weird – and did take a bit of getting used to" she considers it also to be "quite nice." Sally said, "It's a change I've welcomed. I am quite looking forward to getting my own time back." Sally now feels less worried about her children and is pleased to see them growing in independence. She added, "You're not so in their world any more. They're off doing other things that you don't know about. You've just got to think hopefully you've done enough and they'll be fine."

Sally then noted that this stage of life allows more opportunities for personal reflection:

> I guess with middle age you do end up with more time to yourself, and you are exploring, like, "What is it that I want?" Whether it's learning to claw yourself back from being a mother, or a wife, or a daughter, or whatever, as far as spiritual growth goes. ... When the kids are younger you are so busy and life is so frantic you don't have that time, or you don't make the time, and now (even though I'm working in a full-time job) I probably do have more time to be thinking about that.

Whether Sally's growing interest and willingness to think about some significant questions was acknowledged by anyone within her church was not something she mentioned.

Debbie (Catholic, 51) observed that for people who have had children it "can be a big adjustment" when children leave home. She told me that she included herself as well as others she had talked to when saying that this event can raise feelings for women such as, "What is my purpose? I've been a mum for how many years, and all of a sudden nobody wants me. I'm not needed." Awareness of the potential challenges of this transition was a motivating factor behind Debbie's choice to seek employment as her youngest son approached the end of his schooling. But Debbie also described having a sense of freedom now that her children have reached adulthood. She explained that when she and her second husband married they already had three children, so they were parents right from the start. They are now getting to spend time together alone more often than they have done before. She said, "There's an enjoyment there, because we haven't had that. Not much. So I'm really enjoying this stage of the journey."

Others also described their experience of children leaving home "and all that that brings" as being largely positive. Patricia (Anglican priest, 58) used the word "celebration" as she described the process of watching her children move into adult life and making adult choices. She felt that this was "generally a very positive time." Russell (Anglican priest, 56) spoke about seeing his children now "launched into life." He said, "In some ways that feels quite satisfying." All of these interviewees were aware that they had been considering their own choices and values during this period of transition. They expressed openness to change in their lives and in their faith. There are opportunities here that parishes could certainly explore.

Care for parents

Due to the increased longevity of men and women in Western societies it is common for people entering midlife to have at least one remaining parent. The needs of elderly individuals and the capacity of family members to support them differ.[150] Sociologists Norella M. Putney and Vern L. Bengtson point out, "At midlife, the need to care for an elderly parent may coincide with the launching of one's own children, or caring for children still in the nest, or continuing responsibility for adult children who have returned to the nest, an increasingly common occurrence."[151]

There is some debate about "the extent of caregiver burden experienced by the sandwich generation, and indeed over the validity of the phenomenon itself,"[152] but care of parents, children and grandchildren, even when not occurring simultaneously, remains a significant aspect of midlife experience for many New Zealanders.[153] Only one of the people I interviewed explicitly identified the pressure of caring for parents and children simultaneously as being a major challenge in midlife, though two others mentioned having this experience. Six others described their experience of providing practical long-term support for parents without speaking about the impact of this on other relationships within their families.

Linda (Anglican, 58) acknowledged how difficult she found it to balance the responsibilities of her paid employment with the needs of her elderly mother, her two adult children at home, her commitment to look after a grandchild one day each week, and keeping in touch with friends and with those within the church for whom she has pastoral responsibility. At the time of the most destructive of Christchurch's earthquakes, in February 2011, the multiple pressures of Linda's familial and work responsibilities were compounded by the need to respond to traumatic events experienced by members of her extended family and by the numerous losses affecting people within her church and throughout the city. Her adult children, who could no longer live in their own accommodation, returned to live at home. Linda described trying to juggle caregiving roles for so many people at the time of the earthquakes as "a very intense experience." Describing the experience several years later, she became tearful when telling me that at that time she had had to say to others, "I can't care for an elderly person, and my family and my job." Although that period of crisis has passed, Linda perceived that the Christchurch earthquakes have had far-reaching effects for families and for individuals, which the church should continue to be mindful of in catering for adults in midlife:

> You've lost your income, or you've lost the retirement you thought you were going to have. You've lost the culture and all those beautiful things, the heritage. ... Your family dynamics have now changed. How do my adult children get into the property market, or rental, or what are the wisest choices for them? What are the new issues that have come, or are part of midlife?

Even if one discounts the impacts of the Christchurch earthquakes, "new issues" are arising with increasing frequency for many people in middle age. Psychologists Putney and Bengston note that intergenerational relationships, and living arrangements, have changed. In the past, "it was the needs of elderly parents that prompted a co-residential arrangement with midlife children," but now the elderly are more likely to choose to live independently and "young adult children are the ones in need of support by midlife parents. More than ever, midlife parents are a safety net for their children, and their grandchildren."[154] Nonetheless, several of the middle-aged churchgoers I interviewed had assumed responsibility for providing practical and emotional support to one or more of their parents as their health declined.

Debbie (Catholic, 51) has lost both her parents and her father-in-law as well. She told me, "Before the losing of them is the caring of them and the whole role reversal and the journey that that takes you on. That was very rewarding but really challenging." After her mother's death Debbie's father's health deteriorated so he moved in with Debbie and her family, living with them for 18 months before entering full-time care for the eight months before he died. "So we had him living with us, and then having him in care. So just that feeling of, you know, needing to still care, whether they are with you or not, that sort of thing. So that was a big change." I asked Debbie if her church community had been supportive. She said, "People were loving with food, and support and practical stuff – that was wonderful," then added:

> I don't know. Not a lot could be done. You know, when Dad was sick and he was in and out of hospital and it was doing my head in – I was just worried – words were the only comfort. There was nothing that could be done. It was just a journey that we all had to go through. ...The whole parent illness and death thing, it was pretty hard. Hard, hard, hard. Yeah. It's just how it is, I guess.

Murray's father was diagnosed with a terminal illness and as his health declined he needed a lot of support. In caring for his father Murray (Anglican, 44) "actually took on too much." He said, "It overwhelmed me at the end." After his father's death Murray was diagnosed with chronic fatigue and had to have several months off work. He also relinquished all responsibilities at church. Murray said, "When I got ill I stepped down off everything. I stopped doing everything." Several years down the track, Murray is once again fully involved in parish activities but he admits that he still appreciates being able to take a break from his responsibilities on occasions. He loves going to services at a nearby Presbyterian church with his wife sometimes. "We toddle off there some Sundays," he said. "We don't go to [name of Anglican church] every time. And it's quite nice to sit down and not have to be involved or pushed into doing something."

A number of the priests and ministers I spoke with expressed concern about the needs of people caring for elderly parents. Sandra (Anglican, 58) spoke of friends who have been in this situation. These friends have met once a month for coffee over the last 15 years, and as their parents have required more help they have appreciated being able to talk about the challenges they have been dealing with. Sandra said, "Meeting on a social basis, being able to talk about that, has actually been a really important support, you know." Sandra suggested that congregations can play a role in helping caregivers in a number of ways, primarily by listening to people talk about their situation and concerns but also by providing opportunities for caregivers to have a little time to leave the house and do something recuperative.

Sandra went on to tell me how hard it can be for people in midlife to deal with the death of parents, especially if a relationship with a parent has been difficult. Mixed emotions can arise and there may be unresolved issues to face. She said, "You need to be a good listening ear, I think, at, you know, for that stage of life." When I asked Sandra about the place of bereavement courses or counselling, Sandra agreed that it was good to be able to get people "hooked into something that's going to be long-term for them." She said, "I can't sustain that listening-ear stuff with people that are going through all that sort of thing, so if I can do the initial listening and then suggest that they do go to a counsellor, or whatever ... there have been cases where that's been really helpful." Sandra felt that, as a vicar, she had well-established networks she could tap into and refer parishioners to. She identified a particular counselling service with a wide variety of counsellors as being "not too expensive." She reiterated that she considered it important to be able to link people in to "regular counsel."

Another Anglican priest, Patricia (58) also spoke of the importance of being able to connect churchgoers who are caring for family members to resources and services within and beyond the parish. She said, "The church is well-placed to be supportive, and it's important to be aware of the network possibilities, and to guide people to what is available, as well." Patricia described a leaflet that had been put out by Anglican Care[155] regarding the support of people with dementia in the congregational setting. The publication includes suggestions around support of carers. She had also shared books about these issues with carers within her own parish, as well as resources about grief and trauma. I asked Patricia if she considered it worthwhile to invite someone to come to the church to speak about issues such as bereavement, or whether it is more helpful to send an individual to a course or to a counsellor to speak with someone one-to-one about their experiences. She said, "It depends a lot on the groups that you have in your church." There are some groups within Patricia's parish, such as the women's group, that are pretty good at organising their programmes for the year and choosing the speakers they want to have. They have autonomy and can make their own choices about what they think would be worthwhile. Patricia valued and appreciated the work of these groups but acknowledged that some – particularly men – could fall through the cracks. She described a resource about grief, written specifically for men, which she has been able to share with male parishioners, then added, "I think we can have a role in enabling church members to connect with what is useful to them."[156]

Bereavement

A predictable aspect of midlife experience is the loss of one or both parents. It is "perhaps the most normative stressful life event of midlife,"[157] according to Carolyn Aldwin and Michael Levenson. Aldwin and Levenson note that the death of the first parent may lead to middle-aged offspring having to assume greater responsibility "not only for their own lives, but for the remaining parent," but the loss of the second parent is an even more significant event: "While relatively little hard data exist, it is likely that losing the buffer of the parent generation leads to a shift in identity and perhaps in values and behaviors."[158] As one middle-aged interviewee, Alison (Presbyterian, 59) expressed it, part of the significance of losing both parents is that "then you realise, 'we're it'."

Several interviewees spoke to me about their experiences of bereavement at midlife. As well as describing the loss of parents, two mentioned the death of a sibling and one spoke about the loss of a spouse. A number described the place of their Christian faith in responding to these events. Judith (Catholic, 60) shared two experiences of bereavement. When Judith was 40, her eldest sister died suddenly, in an accident. Judith told me that this shook her sense of identity as she felt that her sister was an intrinsic part of who she was, and an integral part of her childhood and past. The fact that there was no chance to say goodbye was also something Judith found very hard. Her sister's death, unlike the death of older relatives before, made Judith realise that "we are all vulnerable." It happened out of the blue. Judith said, "That was a big thing for me to deal with."

At the age of 53, Judith joined the Catholic Church after many years of active involvement in another denomination. She said that she has observed a different attitude towards death among Catholic people:

> Suddenly death was part of life, I realised. A widow would come to Mass two days after her husband had died. *[She sounds surprised.]* To me it had been this unexpected event that shouldn't be there, and almost to be feared –death is out of the ordinary. That's how it had been. And now it was part of life.

Judith said that she had always found consolation from her faith in times of bereavement, but Catholics even pray for the dead (something which Judith added took a bit of getting her head around) "and I realised that that line between life and death is such a tiny thin one." Having a sense of the communion of saints gave her an understanding of death that was "pretty helpful" when her mother died. "It doesn't take away any of the grief, but I think that for me death is in a healthier perspective," Judith said.

During his interview, Phil (Catholic, 53) also talked about the place of his faith in God in coping with loss. Phil came from a big family with 13 aunties and uncles. He told me, "When you're in a big family you are always going to funerals. So it does make you think about your own life and your own spirituality, really." Phil's father died quite suddenly at the age of 54, from a brain haemorrhage, when Phil was 23. Phil's sister died of cancer when she was 47. Phil said:

> I've had quite a lot of early death in my family and that's always made me think about, you know, the afterlife, and what Christianity says about that, and what I needed to sort out for myself in terms of where we're all headed and how we, you know, connect in death, and things like that.

Phil went on to explain how cumulative losses in his life (including the death of a much-loved priest whom Phil considered a "grandfatherly figure") were influential in his decision, at the age of 50, to make a commitment to the Catholic Church. He said, "If there's one thing you want to be, it's buried in the Catholic Church. 'Cause there's this sense of comfort in death that Catholic churches seem to have. There's this sort of normalcy about death that I like. 'Cause it's going to happen to us all." The awareness that death is something that is "going to happen to us all" intensifies in midlife. In fact, this awareness is often considered to differentiate the midlife transition from other life stages.[159]

Sometimes the comfort and care of God can be most acutely felt at times of vulnerability; bereavement may create a "thin place" or "thin time" during which God may seem especially close. As Judith and Phil experienced, suffering may spark deeper awareness and appreciation of the interdependence of all people. At times of loss many churchgoers find solace in their faith and in the support of others who share in the hope of resurrection. But it is also true that when difficult or tragic events occur faith can seem precarious. A sense of being abandoned by God and out-of-step with fellow believers can be a very real part of the spiritual journey at such times. Some Christians may carry additional burdens of guilt or shame if they feel that they could or should be doing better because they are believers. They will not necessarily feel comfortable talking about these experiences with others. Nor may they wish to attend services of worship.

In a book borne out of the experience of the death of her adult daughter, *Celebration in Times of Grief and Sorrow*, Helen Bent, Anglican priest and then Head of Ministerial Training for the Royal School of Church Music in England, describes the sense of disorientation which can cause people to stay away from church at times of grief or trauma. Her book explores ways in which church leaders may minister more sensitively to those who are hurting "especially at those times when everyone else seems to be having a good time."[160] She reflects on the particular value of the Psalms – often prayers of raw honesty – which have proven to be profoundly helpful to people of faith over the centuries. As the compilers of *A New Zealand Prayer Book: He Karakia Mihinare o Aotearoa* explain, the Psalms "give words to some of our deepest feelings in the face of life's experiences. Whether for joy, worship and exaltation, or degradation and rejection, or hope, faith, love, anger, or despair, the psalms contain verses that reflect such moods."[161] Helen Bent observes that the church calendar, too, holds within it "times of darkness and waiting intermingled with times of celebration." She writes, "The tensions of real life are already there in this familiar annual cycle if we are prepared to tease them out. And rituals and symbolic actions that go beyond words alone may open us up to new treasures in the darkness."[162] Bent's book, which is part of the Grove series about pastoral and theological topics, is a rich resource for anyone who wishes to support Christians at times of grief by exploring the place of lament as well as joy in services of worship.[163]

Work

Work can affect people's ability and willingness to make church involvement a priority. It is not simply that work (whether paid or unpaid) takes up a very significant proportion of most people's time, although that is, in itself, something that is worth addressing from a Christian perspective. An even more significant problem can be that, too often, middle-aged churchgoers can find it hard to make connections between what they expend their time and energy on during the week – and which contributes significantly to their sense of identity – and what happens at church on Sunday.

Harvey L. Sterns and Margaret Hellie Huyck, researchers in the field of Life-Span Developmental Psychology, believe that "one of the most intriguing issues in adult development and aging is the importance of work in people's lives."[164] It was certainly a topic that was frequently and fervently spoken about by my interviewees. Each of the following work-related experiences was mentioned by one or more of the people I interviewed:

- ❖ Juggling work and family responsibilities – "Making sure that work doesn't rule you."
- ❖ Peak of career – experiencing fulfilment and/or financial reward – "I've always believed that you pick up bits and pieces through different jobs, and through different scenarios you find yourself in, and they'll always come in useful later on down the track. And I kind of feel that in this job I'm in now I'm getting to use everything, really."
- ❖ Returning to paid employment after a significant period of time out of the workforce and discovering or rediscovering gifts and skills – "It's a big change, but it's one that I'm really ready for and excited about."
- ❖ Questioning the value of one's work – "Is this all there is?"
- ❖ Finding work physically or emotionally more challenging than in the past – "You get physically tired."
- ❖ Concern about the future – "As I get older I think I need to find something different because my body's going to wear out."
- ❖ Redundancy – Going through "the good, the bad and the ugly."
- ❖ Approaching retirement – "What I'm doing now I can never do again. So these are precious years. And you want to invest them as positively as you can, because it won't last forever."

According to Sterns and Huyck, in midlife "one of the common refrains is the desire to balance work and other commitments more successfully."[165] Unsurprisingly, the desire for better work/life balance was expressed by a lot of people I encountered during the writing of this book.

Gail (Anglican, 41) spoke to me about the competing demands of work and parenting. Her two children are now both at primary school. Their schooling has allowed Gail to return to work on a casual basis, which she has felt some responsibility to do in order to contribute financially to the home. While she is glad to be working again, Gail does not want her identity to become too caught up with her work, as she felt it may have been prior to becoming a stay-at-home mum. She explained:

> I'm not like career driven. I don't want to get to the top of the ladder, because I think there is a cost associated with that and the cost can be my health, or my family, or my marriage or … And I think that's the change from when you first start in the workforce. There's a myth out there that as a woman you can do anything, you can have it all, and I don't think that's true, that you can have it all at the same time. You can have one thing, and then you can have another thing, but that whole image of everyone juggling everything – I don't think it's healthy. And I think something gets dropped. You only need a tiny change and everything's blown out of the water. So it's the challenge of doing what I need to do, to earn what I need to earn, still being available to be here for the kids when they need it, and being engaged with them because you want to be – you get fulfilment with that.

Phil (Catholic, 53), who is a full-time secondary school teacher, also described the demands of work with respect to health and family life. He felt that his children had sometimes been affected negatively by the commitment he had made to his work. He also spoke frankly about some of the personal challenges he has experienced in his chosen career. He told me that he struggled to be as productive and committed as he had been when he was younger, and said, "I wouldn't be surprised if I make a career change in the next couple of years, actually." He explained, "Working in a stressful working environment is not conducive to one's mental health. I have found it mentally more tough than I have physically more tough." Alluding to my own background as a high school teacher, Phil said:

> Partly, also, Anne, you just get resentful of working long hours, don't you, as a teacher. And you get physically tired. It's a very very physically demanding occupation. Physically and mentally. You're on the go, you're just constantly managing people. And, you know, there are other jobs that seem so much more appealing at this age, aren't there? [He laughs.]

Like Phil, Murray (Anglican, 44) acknowledged some concern about his future work prospects due to the physical demands of his occupation. Although he found many aspects of his work rewarding, and believed that what he did was appreciated and valued by others, Murray felt that aging was likely to affect his ability to continue to do it:

> As I get older I think I need to find something different, because my body's going to wear out, you know. And you are looking at that. I know that as I get older, my hands, if your hands don't work you can't do electrical work.

Sustainability of work, including the ability to tolerate and cope with the physical and emotional demands of particular roles, can be a significant concern for some people in middle age. But many people I interviewed also described finding their work stimulating and satisfying, and, at midlife, were glad to have opportunities to use their gifts and life experiences in the context of their paid employment.

After a change of career direction in his 30s, Malcolm (Anglican, 52) worked for a large corporation for 13 years before starting his own business in central Christchurch, at the age of 46. For Malcolm, the decision to start his own business "came back to self-determination – having a bit more control of your destiny." Due to the nature and location of Malcolm's business the major earthquakes in Canterbury, which occurred in 2010 and 2011, created a lot of work for his company and extended his sphere of influence within the city. He told me that he felt as though he was in "the right place" and, due to his education and experience, "well prepared" for the position in which he found himself. Although Malcolm spoke rather hesitantly as he endeavoured to describe the relationship between his work and his Christian faith, the connection was clearly important to him:

> I'm doing things that I feel I should be doing, even at work. So I think there's a – I haven't sort of vocalised this before – but I think there's a spiritual aspect to work as well, which might sound a bit strange, but there is. Work affects people and affects how people interact and relate to each other, and downstream of that's their welfare. ... It's not divorced from a sense of some higher purpose as well, rather than just doing your work for your work, and earning money. I

do have a sense that there's something bigger at play, and I'm just part of that, however that works out.

With respect to his work, Malcolm felt that he looked at things through the "prism" of Christianity, but he said that he found this difficult to explain. When I submitted that quite a few people do talk about the fulfilment they find in using their gifts at work and feeling that they are doing things that are connected with their spirituality, Malcolm agreed. "It's part of who I am. I'm not just a spiritual person when I go to church," he said.

Nina (Anglican, 43) was very interested in the connection between work and Christian spirituality and she addressed this theme in some detail during her interview. Nina holds a responsible position in the health sector. Her professional role is demanding and at one point the pressure of work had been exacerbated when restructuring occurred in her workplace. Nina told me how grateful she was for the sustained support she had received from an elderly friend within her congregation who was interested in Nina's work and had been glad to pray with Nina about it. Nina had also appreciated being able to attend a theology course entitled "God at Work,"[166] which was about Christians in the workplace. Nina told me that she was interested in a key idea raised in the course, which was how the church can affirm the value of people's work. She talked about a range of ways that this might occur, such as the minster affirming different groups of people, from "up the front" – praying for teachers at the start of the year, for example – or by having small groups within a church praying for a particular group of workers, week by week. The lecturer had also suggested that people from similar work backgrounds could arrange to meet and talk about the issues of faith and work that relate to their own field. Nina thought that this would be helpful "because it's affirming of all of us, it's supportive of all of us, once we go back out into the workplace, and it also raises the value of this group of people." Nina felt that it was very important to connect what happens on Sundays with what happens on Mondays, whether people are in paid employment, voluntary work, or at home. Nina was also sufficiently interested in the connection between faith and work to have read books on the subject, and, among other works, identified Timothy Keller's *Every Good Endeavour: Connecting Your Work to God's Plan for the World* (London: Hodder and Stoughton, 2014) and Alistair Mackenzie and Wayne Kirkland's *Where's God on Monday? Integrating Faith and*

Work Every Day of the Week (Colorado Springs: NavPress, 2003) as useful texts.

It is not unusual for Christians to understand their work – including voluntary and unpaid work – in terms of vocation. It is really important, therefore, for churches to value and honour the work that people do during the week. Most churches could make more explicit acknowledgment of the importance of parishioners' weekday employment and be much more proactive in helping them to reflect on the connection between their work and Christian faith. Historically, the "theology of work" has been the subject of close scrutiny within the church, in both Roman Catholic and Protestant traditions, and there is a wealth of resources available on the topic that congregations might find it fruitful to explore. For example, Catholic teaching relating to "Human Work" as explained in the *Pontifical Council for Justice and Peace's Compendium of the Social Doctrine of the Church*[167] raises many interesting and important issues which could be discussed within small groups of any denomination. For people seeking materials for personal reflection or for group discussion the "Theology of Work" website[168] provides numerous articles exploring topics related to work as well as studies about topics such as workplace conflict, ambition and ethics at work. Devotionals for individual use about other work-related topics, some based on Scripture, are also available on the same website. *Professions of Faith: Living and Working as a Catholic*, edited by James Martin and Jeremy Langford,[169] is a collection of reflections on work and faith written by people working in a range of environments, including in the home. People struggling to find work-life balance at midlife might find it particularly helpful to explore resources relating to Sabbath observance. Lynne Baab's *Sabbath Keeping: Finding Freedom in the Rhythms of Rest*[170] is an accessible book on this theme.

Liz (Anglican priest, 55) admitted that she sometimes needs to remind herself to honour parishioners' work within the community during the week rather than focusing too narrowly on their ministries within the church. She said, "A good number of those in midlife that I see at the moment do see what they are doing in the week as their ministry." As we noted in Chapter 3, Liz's congregation celebrated the contribution members were making to the community through their employment by holding occasional evening events at which individuals spoke about their work. Liz felt that these occasions had been inspiring for those who attended and also helped the presenters themselves to reflect on the connection between their work and their faith. Each person's unique call to follow Christ was affirmed by their faith community. An interviewee from another church, in a different city, Tony (spiritual director, 56), told me how grateful he was that his professional role had been acknowledged in a church service; he felt blessed to know that there were congregation members upholding his work in prayer. This had not been the case in his previous parish. The lack of connection he experienced between his work and worship on Sundays had been a factor in his decision to move to a different denomination.

I am aware that workshops relating to work are occasionally held in some churches. In my own church an evening event was held where an outside facilitator encouraged us to talk with one another about the particular joys and challenges of our jobs. Those who attended – all of whom were in midlife – found this helpful. It not only enabled each of us to look at our circumstances through the "prism" of Christianity but helped us to get to know one another much better. Members of many congregations may in fact know very little about what other parishioners do during the week. One interviewee, Murray (Anglican, 44), an electrician who was extremely enthusiastic about using his skills to support others on a voluntary basis, felt that there were a lot of other people within his parish with a range of professional backgrounds and work skills but "most people don't cotton on to what other people do and what they can contribute." He considered that this was a missed opportunity, both for the workers themselves and for those they had the potential to assist.

All of the priests and ministers I interviewed were sensitive to work-related issues affecting their midlife parishioners. Most of the clergy commented on the fact that the demands of work for people in this stage of life mean that the time and energy that they are able to commit to activities within their parishes is limited. Don (Presbyterian, 52), for example, observed that his team of elders, most of whom are in midlife, "are able people, so they have a lot of other calls on their time." He gave examples of some demanding leadership roles these elders held in various workplaces, then said, "There's a limit to what they can commit to beyond the regular meetings that we have." Liz (Anglican, 55) said that she found it a challenge to find a balance between providing a place for laypeople (a number of whom worked in "helping professions") where they can "sit and stop" while also being a place where they can contribute. Yvonne (Presbyterian, 58) observed that people who are in "high-powered jobs" just want "something stable and regular, you know, not too challenging. They want to be chaplained, actually." With a laugh she added, "I think, well, it's probably reasonable. They just want to be looked after and not have too many things required." Sandra (Anglican, 58) expressed a similar opinion. She observed that a lot of those who are working full time are experiencing a great deal of stress at work. These people "just want to come on a Sunday, be part of it, but don't want to do too much."

Sandra was clearly very aware of the need of "gentle, very grace-focused ministry" for people under stress. She spoke of the multiple pressures many people within the midlife age range, in her congregation, were experiencing:

> They're tired, and so you kind of learn to just give them permission to take some time out, or back off a bit, or um, yeah, not put a lot of stuff on people. 'Cause there's often many people that are going through that whole, you know, needing to change jobs, needing to slow their own jobs down, somehow; there seem to be a lot of people that are frustrated up to here *[she gesticulates]* with the pressures of work, so church needs to be a place where they don't feel pressured but they've got something to contribute. And I also think that many people of that age, if they've got their own families, their kids are growing up and moving off to become independent, so that changes life for them again. Some of them have got real struggles with their families and just need a lot of listening time and encouragement.

Sandra later went on to describe her parish as one with "a culture of really caring for each other" which, although she did not say so, her own sensitivity and style of leadership clearly fostered. For example, Sandra told me that she considered "cultivating a culture of prayer" to be part of her priestly role. In addition to providing services which include prayer for healing, in some ordinary Sunday services she encourages parishioners to pray in small groups about particular issues, even if silently. She said, "It's quite permission-giving – you know, do what you need to do. I figure if we can't pray for each other, what are we doing here? I have seen that really supportive of people particularly that are struggling with stuff."

Pastoral care

The churchgoers I interviewed had differing experiences of pastoral care within their communities. Their experiences reflected the priorities and skills of church leaders and the effectiveness of pastoral care structures within parishes, as well as individuals' willingness and ability to seek support when desired. Only five of the first 20 midlife churchgoers I interviewed for my doctoral research described specific occasions when clergy or pastoral workers offered them pastoral support. Five others said that in their parishes the needs of those in midlife are rarely acknowledged. One Anglican interviewee, Karen (52), believed there was little awareness of the needs of midlife churchgoers in her parish: "Like there's not much going on *[in midlife]*. So you just leave people to their own devices." A number of other interviewees felt that the pastoral care offered to people around their own age was limited. Raewyn (47), who worships in a Presbyterian parish said, "People of my age are more sort of doing things to help others, or to be involved. I don't think we expect support." Whether or not pastoral support is expected, it was evident from the experiences that interviewees described that were times when greater awareness of individuals' circumstances would have been appreciated. Let us attend to midlife churchgoers' experiences and comments before reflecting on clergy responses to the challenge of providing pastoral care for people in this life stage.

As a child, Phil (Catholic, 53) had been taken to Sunday school in Presbyterian and Methodist parishes, but he had for many years attended a Catholic church with his wife and children. Phil was eloquent about the place of his faith and the support of his church at a time of significant ill health. At the age of 45 Phil discovered he needed major heart surgery. His medical diagnosis was quite unexpected and Phil found himself "panicking" when given only one week's notice of his operation. He and his wife attended Mass at their church one night during that week. The priest, who had had a similar operation, spoke personally to Phil and offered him reassurance:

> Being there and just sort of feeling that sort of shared experience – on so many levels – on a spiritual level, on practical level, of a guy who had been through everything I was about to go through, you know, it just made me deal with things a whole lot better.

After the operation Phil received a lot of on-going support from the priest and from lay people within his parish. Church members came up to Phil after Mass and asked how he was getting on and said it was great to see him. "Tons and tons of people were friendly and helpful," he said. Reflecting further on this experience, Phil made the following observation:

> In parishes you get a cross-section of people, who've all been through stuff, so you know about the stories of the older and the younger and you see it happening all around you. And you know that you're going to have support. And I always felt that. You can't not, really, when people know that you're in strife. They always rally round you. And it's gorgeous that they can do that. But they do. They really do.

The fact that so many of his fellow parishioners were willing to make the time to ask Phil how he was, and to talk to him about their own experiences, was clearly something that he found moving and very helpful, yet it seems probable that most of the individuals who spoke to him would have been unaware that their words and actions meant so much to him, and few would have considered their comments to constitute "pastoral care." In supporting people in midlife, however, it is lending a listening ear or speaking a few words of encouragement that can be exactly what is most needed. The most effective care for people in midlife may often be provided by church members interacting in ways that seem quite commonplace, as Phil's story illustrates.

Karen (Anglican, 52) lived with her widowed mother for six years prior to her mother's death. Karen was unable to identify specific ways in which the church had supported her around the time of her mother's final illness but she acknowledged that a factor that contributed to the church's lack of attentiveness to her situation was that their parish had been seeking a new vicar at the time, and the new vicar was unaware of her circumstances and history. Karen knew that had she asked for a pastoral visit someone from the church would have come to see her, but she had been reluctant to request it. Karen then reflected on the composition of her congregation, which includes younger families and elderly people, as well as some middle-aged couples with older children who are in the process of leaving home. Apart from herself, Karen could not think of any single people of her own age in her church. Having mulled this over, she added:

There's actually probably quite a lot of people coping with different changes. You know, looking after elderly parents or kids leaving home and that kind of thing. But it's not really an area that's acknowledged or dealt with at all. It's really very much focused on the younger age group. And everything is sort of targeted around that.

Karen was philosophical about this situation:

I guess partly it's there's only so many resources and you can't hit everything and so you target it in certain areas. And ours is very much directed to the kids and the youth and the young families' support. Which is fine, because you need people coming in, otherwise the church just gets older and older and dies.

I asked Karen what form pastoral support for people in midlife might take. What would be practical and helpful? She paused before replying:

I guess it's hard to know. I guess even just finding out what people are dealing with. 'Cause I am sure there is a lot going on. ... Finding an opportunity to meet and just talking with people about what they're dealing with, what challenges they're facing. Or maybe they're expecting people to put their hand up. A lot of people wouldn't. They just get on with things. Well, I wouldn't! I wouldn't make an appointment to see *[the vicar]* and go in and say, "I'm dealing with all this stuff." ... I'm sure if I went to somebody and said, you know, "I'd appreciate a visit," somebody would come, but you don't always want to be requesting it. You want somebody to notice or, you know, have an arrangement where you go around certain people so that everybody gets something once a year. They make contact and say, "Let's catch up for something-or-other."

The difficulty in finding an appropriate balance between offering pastoral support to parishioners and waiting for people to ask for it was a recurring theme in interviews.

Nina (43) attends an evangelical Anglican church. Nina felt that her church does quite well in supporting people in crisis – she gave an example of a needy family in her parish that received wonderful wrap-around care from the whole church community – but she expressed concern about the lack of support for people who are dealing with less obvious issues:

> There are also the others that are out there that don't
> have huge significant issues like the death of a spouse or
> someone who's got a really serious illness – but it could be
> that someone's son is going through a troubled time, and
> they don't know what to do. They don't get much support.
> They are in midlife and they've got a young person who's
> struggling. Where do they get support unless there are
> friendships that they've built? It's more that group that I
> kind of … *[She trails off, but her silence implies real concern
> for the people who may be overlooked.]*

When I suggested, "These might be significant needs, but not
necessarily acknowledged needs?" Nina agreed, and suggested that
perhaps clergy need to think about "how we cover those people, in
some way."

Nina had given this issue careful consideration. During her
interview she itemised what she considered to be some of the most
significant pastoral needs of people in midlife. She observed that
many people in midlife are coping with a lot of change, and she
also identified multiple responsibilities that may be held by people
in this life stage. Nina noted that people in middle age are often
looking after teenagers and elderly folk at the same time, and, she
pointed out, these people are often in senior roles at work as well:

> So there's quite a lot of pressure that they're having to
> juggle. And I suspect that a lot of our families are probably
> struggling in some areas. The quieter families may not
> get as much support as they might not say, "We need
> some help." But someone saying, "How's it going?" or just
> popping over to have a visit, blah, blah, blah, that would
> come out.

Nina felt that establishing a formal pastoral care structure at her
church would help these pastoral conversations to occur. She
said, "It just seems to be pushed aside all the time. And it's been
an issue for many years. And I just don't understand that. And I
don't think the informal – just through the kumara wireless[171] – is
really always effective." Nina then remarked on what she called
"the yo-yoing between individual responsibility and corporate
response." She acknowledged that "there's stuff that individuals
can do" to find their own support from someone else, including
from people outside the church, but she felt that there was a need
for a "coordinated approach" within the church so that laypeople

have an idea about what to do when they hear of issues coming up, and can tap other people on the shoulder to help, too.

Nina described some additional challenges faced by multicultural congregations, such as her own, as different cultural groups have different practices and different ways of viewing the Christian life. For example, some cultures focus more on the immediate family whereas others have a more extended-family approach to events. Nina thought that perhaps a diverse pastoral care team of some sort could help with those differences, or "just an awareness, actually, that some people do things differently" could be helpful. She went on to explain that in some cultures the family would expect the minister, not an assistant minister or a pastoral worker, to pray with the sick, for example. "There are some things like that, that are just different, and we need to be mindful of."

All of the ministers and priests I interviewed expressed the hope that, at times of struggle or distress, individuals would find support and experience grace through their involvement in congregational life. But clergy admitted that the pastoral needs of midlife parishioners can be difficult to address. There are obstacles of a practical nature in reaching out to people of middle age that do not exist for people in older or younger age groups. Moreover, the complexity and variety of issues that people in this stage of life are dealing with demand a multiplicity of sensitive, empathetic and creative responses from those in church leadership and from congregation members, sometimes over a long period.

It is obviously difficult for clergy and congregations to address the needs of parishioners who, for various reasons, do not readily share their problems or concerns. In large parishes, especially, churchgoers who feel unable to let others know about their difficulties, or do not wish others to be aware that they are struggling, can easily miss out on receiving tangible support. In the context of speaking about the needs of parishioners who are caregivers, Paul (Catholic priest, 53) said:

> Often it boils down to whether you reach out or not – whether you make yourself known, that you need care or not. There might be people out there who say I've neglected my duty. My simple answer is, "I don't know that you're sick. ... No-one told me." And it's the same for the carer. Unless they are active and they're involved in things and people pick it up and tell me, then they could fall

through the cracks, too. Secondly, some people are very, very personal. These things are decided within the family and they don't want it out there.

Nor does the "routine pastoral call" always work so well for people in midlife, as Liz (Anglican priest, 55) explained:

> I'm just very aware with a number of my midlifers that the only way we manage to catch up is to have a coffee during the work day, if it works for them to do that, or after school, or early evening, or something like that. And I suppose I've got the flexibility to do that. Which is a very different model from the "norm" of going to the home. And so that's interesting. It's a different model, and perhaps a bit more needs-driven.

Liz explained that sometimes middle-aged members of her congregation might ask if they could meet for a coffee if they want to talk about something, rather than inviting her to their home, whereas older folk invite her for morning tea or lunch for a longer engagement and tell her all about their family, and so on. For those in midlife:

> It seems to be more, "Um, yeah, it would be good to catch up some time, but I'm busy. How about we just fit in a coffee?" And that's fine. And you do what you do. Or otherwise a sort of a needs-based thing, like, "I'd just like to touch base with you about something." But again it seems more purpose-driven or intentional, perhaps because of the juggle of so many things.

Having acknowledged the advantages of meeting midlife parishioners in neutral venues for coffee, Liz paused, and then noted that there are benefits in continuing to visit parishioners' homes, such as being able to meet parishioners' non-churchgoing partners. But such visits need to be organized in advance. Liz added, though, that she would probably still "pop in" on older people.

Another interviewee, an ordained Presbyterian minister now working in a role outside a parish, shared Liz's perspective about the challenges of meeting with middle-aged churchgoers. He regarded cafés as being ideal settings within which to meet with parishioners in this age group, for a number of reasons. He said:

> There's a generational thing involved there. One of our younger elders said that to our largely elderly session. "If

you want to connect with me," she said, "don't try to visit me at home because I'm never there. If you roll up and I'm off to hockey, or whatever, I'm not going to have time to talk with you. If you want to connect with me, flick me a text, make an appointment, and we'll meet at a café." So that is a significant generational shift.[172]

Cafés do have several drawbacks as contexts for pastoral interactions. Some are acoustically-challenging environments. It can be more difficult to pray with another person in a café (if that seems appropriate). And, of course, somebody has to pay for the coffee.

I am able to share two examples from my own experience about the appropriateness of different contexts for different sorts of pastoral conversations. About six months after my mother's death a priest from the Anglican church I attend on Sunday evenings contacted me to see how I was getting on. His suggestion that we meet for a chat at a quiet central-city café was not only convenient for us both but meant that our conversation occurred in an environment in which I felt comfortable. I remember this occasion, and the priest's kindness and understanding at that time, with gratitude. On another occasion, when I had received some difficult news regarding my health, a minister from the Presbyterian church I attend on Sunday mornings visited me in my home. Home felt like the right place for that particular conversation. As with so many other aspects of care for people, flexibility and sensitivity are essential.

I spoke to Sandra (Anglican priest, 58) about the contrasting needs and expectations of midlife churchgoers and the elderly with respect to pastoral care. I asked her, "What works, what are the challenges, and what are some of the opportunities or solutions?" She paused for some time to consider this, and eventually said:

> It's got to be relational, obviously. We're not a parish that does heaps of social stuff but I think a culture of trying to connect people through meals or coffees, or things like that, is a good way to do it. It's not easy to do it, in the sense that that's demanding as well, to try and have meals with people, or invite people for meals.

Sandra noted that in her parish, over the years, it's been better at some times than in others. "As people have got tired or busy or whatever, they kinda don't go down that track," she said. She went on to tell me that some of the middle-aged members of her congregation meet informally. Some parishioners want to do motorbike stuff together, and others meet up on Friday nights for tea, for example. Sandra thinks these things are great. However, the danger of those informal arrangements is that "there are people missing out on that kind of connection, because they're newer or they're not necessarily outgoing, and so you've got to kind of formally do it."

At another point in her interview Sandra described how some of the middle-aged members of her congregation were supported by older parishioners:

> I think often people in that stage, say something happens, say in their family or work, that's really overwhelming, they think, "Nobody else would have these problems here, and if they knew my child was going through this, or whatever, they just wouldn't understand." And then they'll start talking to somebody who says, "That happened to me. And I'm right with you." ... Some of those families that I see that, you know, their adult children or young adult children are going through crises, or whatever, there's been people in the parish that have had that happen to them 20 years ago, and they have actually just got alongside and quietly prayed with them, encouraged them.

When it comes to pastoral care, there is a lot of food for thought in the comments made by interviewees. During difficult times people in midlife are often able to harness many personal resources and to draw on wisdom and strengths gained through life experience. But regardless of their ability to cope with challenges, middle-aged people still appreciate the support of clergy and fellow parishioners. The most crucial component in extending pastoral care to churchgoers in this life stage (and, by extension, to people of other ages) is to make time to ask other people how they are and what they need, and then to listen attentively to their answers. "*Titiro, whakarongo, korero*"[173] – Look, listen, then speak. This sounds simple, but can be difficult to put into practice.

Others issues and possible responses

In addition to the challenges of midlife already described in this chapter, priests and ministers commented on other issues that they felt were closely connected to the welfare of parishioners in their 40s and 50s. Greg (Presbyterian, 62), Patricia (Anglican, 58) and Liz

(Anglican, 55) shared some examples of relational issues affecting people in midlife within their parishes. Don (Presbyterian, 52) and Sung-ho (Presbyterian, 53) talked specifically about marriage at midlife. Yvonne (Presbyterian, 58) was the only interviewee to speak about ways that the church might provide support to women who are approaching or going through menopause.

Some members of Greg's church are divorcees who are dating and are thinking about whether to live together or not. Then there are some who have been widowed young. Some have left other churches because they have felt guilty, or have been made to feel guilty, because they are divorced. "What do we provide there? I can't answer that," says Greg, except for "as much TLC as we can." Patricia identified a number of relationship issues that can typically arise at midlife, including people re-evaluating their marriages, the empty nest syndrome, sexual issues and intimate relationships breaking down. When I asked her how well the church is doing in supporting people who are having relationship difficulties, Patricia said she would not like to make a blanket statement on it. "We could spend another afternoon talking about that," she said. Patricia admitted that while she hoped that the church would be "a place of grace where people can really talk about that," she thought there was plenty of room for improvement. "And probably it will vary hugely from place to place," she added.

Liz pointed out that, in supporting couples in midlife, an additional challenge for churches can be that some people in this stage of life come to church on their own, but have a partner who is not involved. Liz wondered if there is, now, "perhaps more acceptance that people can be in quite different places within a partnership spiritually and there is no sort of felt obligation that they have to come along to keep up appearances." Liz said that in responding to this situation her church is considering "how we still have events, you know, social or community events, where people can feel comfortable for their partners to come if they'd like to."

Don observed that marriages can be in difficulty at about this stage of life. Don's own parents separated when his father was about 50 or a little younger, something which he attributed to "classic midlife crisis type stuff." Don said, "I'm not sure if that's talked about a lot." In Don's church the subject of marriage is addressed in sermons, and the *Alpha Marriage Course*[174] is also offered, once a year or so. This seven-part programme presents practical tools designed to help couples communicate more effectively, resolve conflicts, develop greater sexual intimacy, improve relationships with extended family, and addresses a number of other important topics. It is well received by people in midlife. Don and his wife have also found it helpful personally, even though they have participated in it several times (as they are part of leading it). "The Marriage Course has, I think, been more helpful for the people who have been married some time, than the younger newly-marrieds," said Don. "It's the fence at the top of the cliff."

Sung-ho also believed that programmes addressing issues relating to marriage, and marriage counselling, can be of value to middle-aged Christians. He noted that in midlife many couples become free of ties to children's education and have more time for each other. There can be time "to redevelop or enhance their relationship." Sung-ho said, "They are not newly-wed but I think that would be helpful, to rediscover." Yvonne had a similar opinion. She shared something of her own experience of marriage as she and her husband are both approaching retirement. Yvonne felt that the departure of their children from home has meant that she and her husband "have to re-think who we are as a couple, and how we will live."

Yvonne raised the subject of menopause, a topic which is frequently mentioned in literature relating to midlife but was mentioned by very few interviewees. As Yvonne observed, "In terms of women in midlife, you know, the menopause thing is certainly out there, and not often talked about." Yvonne invited a counsellor to come and speak to women in her church about this topic. There was a lot of interest – about 30 people attended – and although the evening didn't go quite as Yvonne had anticipated, she still thought it was worthwhile:

> I think it's something you could easily do every year – just a one-off every year, just to help people talk about it. Because they would say to me, "No-one talks about these things." When I mentioned it at church there was quite a lot of interest from the younger women as well. I was trying to get a range of people coming so the younger ones can think about it and the older ones can help. But in the end the younger ones didn't come.

Although, on this occasion, there were fewer interactions between group members than Yvonne had hoped, she said, "The idea is good.

I think that's definitely a way the church can help – by bringing up some of these subjects."

Almost all of the clergy I interviewed suggested that it could be helpful for Christians in midlife if seminars, presentations, and opportunities for people in midlife to discuss issues that were affecting them were available. Topics that clergy felt might usefully be explored included retirement planning, employment issues, coping with transitions, self-care and use of leisure time. Clergy felt that these matters are rarely discussed in the church despite their relevance to many of their parishioners. Karen (Anglican, 52) was one of a number of middle-aged churchgoers who said that workshops that would be of relevance and interest for people in her age group need not be focused on midlife, nor be promoted solely to congregational members in midlife, but could explore issues which are of relevance to those in midlife and also to people of other ages. She suggested, as an example, that something focusing on coping with change would be a useful topic. Karen said it would be helpful to know that "there's other people going through similar kinds of experiences." She felt it would be useful for church members coping with various transitions to share together and to learn from one another. Other topics for workshops that churchgoers suggested (without any prompting from me) included marriage, divorce, caring for elderly family members, menopause, mental health and retirement planning. Some interviewees noted that Christians in midlife might wish to be better informed about some of these matters for the sake of others within their orbit of care.

Given that most people in midlife have a limited amount of discretionary time and churches have limited resources, it is sensible to question what sorts of workshops or educational programmes can most effectively be offered within particular parishes and when it may be more appropriate for clergy, small group leaders, or pastoral workers to point parishioners in the direction of programmes offered elsewhere. Ministers and priests are often proactive about alerting church members to services provided by agencies such as Presbyterian Support, Anglican Care and Catholic Social Services, and frequently help parishioners to access counselling and other forms of support that are available beyond the local church. It can also be very helpful to parishioners when courses or events offered by other organisations are advertised in church bulletins.

One Anglican churchgoer, Murray (44), told me that he thought that "more community run things from the parish" might benefit churches and individuals. Initially Murray spoke about the potential of social events to provide encouragement to people within the church and the wider community. Then he said, "The other thing I'd like to see happen in the churches is maybe every once in while the different denominations amalgamate and do something together. 'Cause I think there's a whole width of experience there that's not being used." Murray advocated setting up a "universal website" with the other churches within an area so that churches could invite one another to events and find out what is going on in nearby congregations. Murray considered the fact that this was not already happening to be a squandered opportunity. Given that there are so many things that parishes would like to do to provide better support to churchgoers in midlife (as well as to those in other age groups) the suggestion that judicious pooling of time, talents and resources could occur seems particularly constructive.

There are clearly many challenges that can affect people in midlife. In this chapter we have explored ways that churches can support churchgoers who are navigating some of these. Earlier I suggested that another significant factor affecting the engagement of people in midlife can be that the potential for midlife to be a period of discovery and deepening faith is celebrated too infrequently in churches. The three chapters that follow explore this topic. Chapter 5 focuses on shifts in individuals' spirituality and spiritual practices at midlife as they look for "something more" in their faith. Chapters 6 and 7 look at some specific sources of support for individuals in midlife and also at ways that churches might be more intentional about supporting the spiritual development of middle-aged members.

Questions for reflection or discussion

1. In this chapter, did any of the interviewees' stories or comments particularly resonate with you? Did any surprise you? Why?

2. We have looked at some factors that might contribute to some Christians becoming less engaged in the church at midlife. What additional issues concern you?

3. Are you carrying heavy burdens at this time? Is there someone you would feel comfortable speaking to about your situation?

4. How does your congregation encourage and support members who are coping with some of the responsibilities and challenges described in this chapter? What else might be possible?

5. What might you like to pray about, or act upon?

Recommended resources

Aune, Kristin. "Why Women Don't Do Church Any More." *Church Times.* 20 August 2008. <http://test.churchtimes.co.uk/articles/2008/22-august/comment/why-women-don-t-do-church-any-more> (8 June 2017).

Bent, Helen. *Celebration in Times of Grief and Sorrow*. Cambridge: Grove Books, 2018.

Collicutt, Joanna. *Thinking of You: A Resource for the Spiritual Care of People with Dementia*. Oxford: The Bible Reading Fellowship, 2017.

Pontifical Council for Justice and Peace. *Compendium of the Social Doctrine of the Church*. London: Continuum International Publishing Group, 2004.

Theology of Work. <www.theologyofwork.org> (5 September 2021).

5 — Something more

Eternal God,
light of the minds that know you,
joy of the hearts that love you,
strength of the wills that serve you;
grant us so to know you that we may truly love you,
and so to love you that we may gladly serve you,
now and always. Amen.

Collect for the sixth Sunday of Easter
A New Zealand Prayer Book:
He Karakia Mihinare o Aotearoa[175]

In 1948 the influential American pastor and evangelist A.W. Tozer published *The Pursuit of God*. Despite its title, from start to finish Tozer's work celebrates the truth that "we pursue God because, and only because, He has first put an urge within us that spurs us on to the pursuit."[176] All longing for God is initiated by God. This is true not only early in the spiritual life, but also much further on in the journey of spiritual formation.

The priests and ministers I interviewed suggested, both on the basis of their own experience and observation of the needs of parishioners, that a desire for "something more" seems to be characteristic of the spiritual journey at midlife. This theme was also addressed by seven of the ten spiritual directors I interviewed. They explained that this can be the catalyst which prompts people to seek out a spiritual director:

❖ One reason given for wanting spiritual direction is, "I think there must be something more." So it's not that the first half of life hasn't been good and fulfilling – it's been all of those things – but it's like at this point, perhaps with some pause, some space in their lives, they're looking for something deeper, something intimate in their relationship with God. (Louisa, 66)

❖ They usually come with a desire of some sort. And that desire is often connected with, "I know there's more. I've tried this, and I've tried that, and it's not working for me." Those types of questions that they're wrestling with. (Brian, 62)

❖ For many people things happen that throw up questions, or the old ways of praying just don't provide the same nurture, and so I think it's more often in your 30s and 40s that you'll go searching and saying, "Surely there must be more to this faith than this – than what I've experienced or know now." ... Many who come to spiritual direction are looking for something more. (James, 57)

While there are naturally significant differences between individuals, middle-aged Christians who are seeking "more" in the spiritual life often seem to be seeking one (or more) of three things: they want to grow in understanding of their faith, to deepen their relationship with God and to continue to be stretched as they live out their faith. The prayer of 12th century bishop Richard of Chichester, which prefaces this book, neatly encapsulates these three desires: "O most merciful redeemer, friend and brother, may I *know thee* more clearly, *love thee* more dearly, and *follow thee* more nearly, day by day." Similar sentiments are expressed in the prayer which heads this chapter. Learning to love God with all our hearts, souls, strength and minds, and to love our neighbours as ourselves (Luke 10:27), as Jesus extolled his followers to do, is a life-long endeavour.

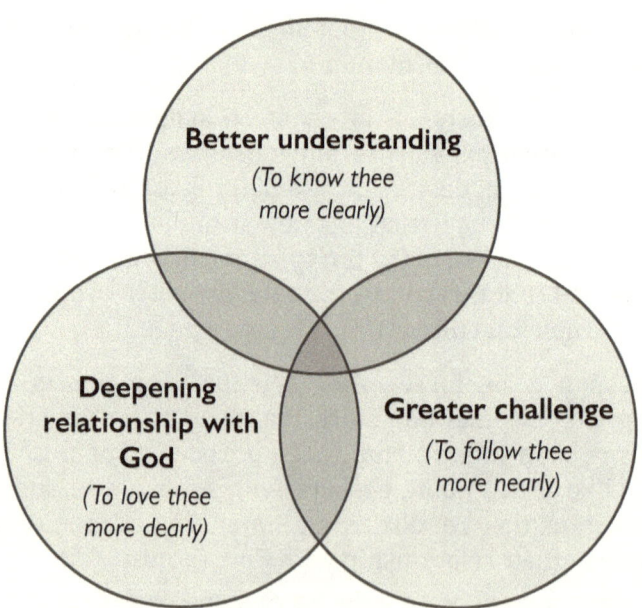

I am aware that this diagram does not fully reflect the integrated manner in which growth in the Christian life actually occurs. Frequently it is in engaging with others and working in various capacities in society that our beliefs and assumptions about ourselves, others, and God are challenged, and we grow in dependence upon God; it is as we seek to love God and serve our neighbour we find that there is a lot more we need to learn. When we seek God in prayer, it is not only our relationship with God but our compassion and concern for other people that is deepened. Furthermore, in loving others, and being loved and supported by them, our appreciation and understanding of God's love, and our courage and will to serve God, are strengthened. This diagram is intended to suggest that these elements of spiritual development are interconnected.

Desire for better understanding

When I interviewed Sally (Catholic, 49), she bemoaned her ignorance regarding aspects of her faith. She said that despite being "born and bred a Catholic, basically" she has learned that she is "still so clueless about everything to do with the Catholic Church." Sally explained why she felt Catholics who are currently in midlife might be particularly appreciative of further education about the church and its practices:

> I was born in '66, so just post Vatican II, and they were throwing out a lot of the old stuff at that point, which we never got taught. And the only reason you realise is because when you go to funerals or the Rosary or the Stations of the Cross all of the oldies know the responses. And I'm saying, "What do you even say?!" And there's one particular part of the Stations of the Cross ... It's not taught anywhere. You know, I try and listen for it, and I can't work out what they're saying. It's amazing! *[She laughs.]* And I think, "Where do you learn all this stuff?"

Sally said that she finds it helpful when certain priests conducting funerals or baptisms explain the meaning behind what is being done and said. Opportunities to "pick up little gems" occur in those contexts but she felt that courses explaining certain aspects of Catholicism could be useful, because, as she put it, "Sometimes you need a refresher." Sally also felt that she didn't know her Bible very well. "That's the sort of thing I would be interested in," she said.

Sally was just one among a significant number of middle-aged interviewees – both Catholic and Protestant – who told me that they would like to have better knowledge of the Bible, of their own denomination's practices and teachings, or of ways that they could bring a Christian perspective to bear on societal issues. Some of the people I interviewed thought it would be good if churches could offer courses or programmes which could deepen their understanding of their faith. Some were already involved in small groups that were helping them to explore their faith. Others had been able to participate in theological education beyond their own churches (and in many cases beyond denominational boundaries) and were enthusiastic about the courses they had undertaken.

Two of the Catholic priests I interviewed told me that some of their parishioners who have been members of the church for some time – predominantly those in midlife – had expressed interest in courses explaining aspects of their faith which they have formerly not had the opportunity to think much about. Bernard (52) and Thomas (54) both felt that within their own tradition there remains "something of a gap" in terms of education for those who have been members of the church throughout their lives because many resources in Catholic education are targeted at primary and secondary schools or towards newcomers to the Catholic faith. The *Order of Christian Initiation*, formerly the *Rite of Christian Initiation of Adults* (RCIA),[177] is a programme about the essentials of the Catholic faith which is offered to those who are new to Catholic teachings and are interested in exploring the possibility of joining the Catholic Church. Bernard told me that some people who had been in the church for a very long time had expressed interest in attending this course because they wanted to receive teaching about some beliefs or practices that they had been brought up with but had never really understood. He said:

> In fact, I hear constantly from people, "We'd like to do that because we have sort of accepted our faith, got it from our parents, but now we actually want to learn about it. We would like to actually know: Why do we this? Why do we celebrate this feast? Who said the church can do that? Or where's the Church's authority for this? Where's that in the Scriptures?" So there's a new sense of enquiry, but we don't have that set up. We do all sorts of camps for young people, "Hearts Aflame" for young adults, we've got sacramental programmes, we've got things for people who want to become Catholics, but we have nothing for people looking to re-examine their faith. Incredible, isn't it?

Thomas told me that he would love to see the focus shift from schools. He said, "People think that education in faith is what happens before you're 18, and we have to come to see that education in faith is what has to happen for me every day that I'm walking on earth."

Clergy from other Christian denominations also perceived that middle-aged members of their congregations would like to "grow theologically," as Russell (Anglican priest, 56) put it. Russell felt that Sunday services rarely allowed sufficient opportunity for that to happen. He said, "There's a whole lot of stuff that we don't have time to do in any depth on Sundays but would be really helpful for people. I think there's a gap there." Russell considered it part of his job to "get some extension going" for mature Christians within his congregation. His church, which is fairly large and very well-resourced, has occasionally run midweek lectures offering theological teaching, which have been well-attended and appreciated. From time to time thought-provoking films are screened which parishioners are invited to see and to discuss. But within Russell's church, and in many other churches, it is in small groups led by lay people that Bible study or exploration of theological questions frequently occurs.

Karen (52) attends a fairly small Anglican church. She joined a home group, which meets weekly, both because she thought it would be good to get to know a different group of people and because she was seeking "more regular study input." The woman who leads the study group accesses resources from a big library at a huge Baptist church nearby which has a resource centre people can borrow from for months. Karen mentioned that her group had completed a mixture of studies including a five-or-six-part video series set in Israel and the Middle East, looking at the history and Biblical context of archaeological sites. The group also used a series about the Psalms by Eugene Petersen, which Karen enjoyed. Karen's group is able to offer continuing education which is flexible. The interests of participants are discussed and taken into account.

Sandra (Anglican priest, 58) has sole responsibility for a fairly small congregation which is spread across more than one location. She told me that quite a number of her parishioners had seized the opportunity to deepen their understanding of Scripture through attendance at an international interdenominational group called the Bible Study Fellowship,[178] which is held at a church not too far from their own. Sandra encouraged this participation and obviously took a close interest in the experience of the group's members, the majority of whom were in the 40 to 60 age range. Although she herself did not attend, Sandra was able to speak knowledgeably to me about the content the group was currently engaged in learning. Sandra considered that for the parishioners who were involved participation was not a small commitment; she described the weekly Bible studies as being quite demanding and noted that the participants were required to complete quite a bit of homework. She felt that the study group was very helpful for the members both because of the fellowship the members found among themselves and because of the stretching nature of the programme.

A number of the churchgoers I interviewed commented on specific courses that they had attended beyond their own churches which they felt had been significant in their faith development at midlife. Some had experienced the benefits of participating in programmes offered through tertiary institutions including Laidlaw College, Carey Baptist College, Good Shepherd College, the New Zealand Catholic Education Office, and St John's Theological College, and they were grateful that these had been advertised within their parish or had been drawn to their attention by clergy. However, it was obvious that a number of other churchgoers who spoke to me were unaware of courses or resources available within their locality, or on-line, that might have addressed areas of need or interest. They simply had not heard of them. For other interviewees, attendance at courses was neither possible nor desirable; they had neither the time nor the inclination to meet in a group to learn about their faith. One spiritual director, Matthew (61), noted that while some of his midlife directees do attend courses, it is usually because they have other reasons for doing so, such as training for ministry or, if they are already in ministry, because they are doing continuing education. For his other directees in this age group, "What would be more common is that they would value suggestions of a reading so that they can do their own personal study, rather than do something formal."

Several interviewees spoke to me about books they had been reading. As an enthusiastic reader myself, I could relate to their appreciation of books and of parish and diocesan libraries, although it was evident that resources held by churches were not always very easy for people to access. One Anglican interviewee, Andrew (44), told me about the library at his church:

> It's under lock and key and it's in the church office somewhere. So, if you want to, you can make an

appointment, they can go and open it for you and they'll stand behind you while you look. *[We both laugh.]* There are plenty of resources there. But we don't really have any inventory system to make it visible, outside of someone actually running their finger down a list of titles on the shelf.

At the Anglican church Nina (44) attends, resources are even more difficult to access. During her interview, Nina mentioned a number of Christian books she had found helpful, so I asked her if her parish had a library. Nina's reply was somewhat startling. She said, "It used to have a library, and then it's disappeared." She laughed, and explained that the church has a new building and Nina doesn't know where the library has gone. Someone culled the old books, but she doesn't know what happened to them. Nina said, "What I notice is that we all buy books, and everyone's got them at home, and we've finished with them and they sit there. Being able to give books to the church, and for others to be able to use them would have been fantastic." She noted, though, that when the church did have a library people weren't actively encouraged to use it, and the books weren't well advertised. "I used it quite a bit, actually, myself," admitted Nina. "It was so good to have resources there." Nina was also appreciative of the fact that a previous vicar had encouraged parishioners to access resources from the library at a local theological college. He provided Nina with a letter that endorsed her attendance at the church, so that she could be issued with a library card. Nina told me how helpful it was to have access to free books because books can be so expensive.

When I asked Patricia (Anglican priest, 58) if churchgoers are easily able to access resources that they might find helpful, she made some interesting comparisons between two parishes she had worked in. She said, "Where I am now, reading material is welcome, is sought, and I can provide some." In her previous parish, one that was serving a low socioeconomic community, that did not work so well and was far less useful to church members:

> It was really the face-to-face talking, making time to see people, perhaps over a number of weeks, or whatever, to support them or go to appointments with them. It was a much more hands-on and relational support because they weren't necessarily readers. That wasn't their way. No internet access, that sort of thing. So quite different. Whereas now reading material is more welcome. But then

people also tend to be more text-savvy and they all Google lots of stuff as well. But in terms of spiritual support, yeah, it's good to have resources.

Patricia went on to talk about a diocesan library, which is open to the public, and which is "full of books" on all sorts of topics. But she reiterated, "Libraries are good, but a lot of people use on-line resources. There's quite a big shift there, in how people use resources."

Churches throughout the world are becoming increasingly creative about using information and communications technology and social media to connect the Christian faith with people's lives. Resources that are offered on-line may be valued particularly by people who cannot readily participate in church activities or groups that are offered outside weekly worship times, including people in midlife. Such resources can help people to remain engaged with the church and growing in faith. It is a common practice for churches to upload sermons to parish websites so that members who are unable to attend services can still be encouraged and informed and remain connected with what is going on in their faith community. Some churches try to ensure parishioners are aware of podcasts, *Facebook* feeds, on-line discussion groups and *YouTube* clips that present issues of potential interest to members. These are becoming increasingly accessible and can be a very real source of spiritual sustenance.[179] In addition, many theological courses are now available on-line. The *RCIA* programme that some practising Catholics expressed interesting in exploring, for example, can be completed through internet tutorials.[180] As Patricia observed, clergy can help church members to grow spiritually by pointing them towards relevant resources they can pursue independently. It makes sense, too, for churches to provide and promote opportunities for parishioners themselves to speak to others in their congregations about resources they have found that may be of interest and help to others. We can be inspired by one another's discoveries.

It is important to remain aware that for financial or other reasons some middle-aged churchgoers will have difficulty accessing books or digital resources, and participation in formal theological programmes will be beyond the reach of many. A limited number of scholarships and grants are available to people who wish to undertake tertiary level courses but not all laypeople want to study at tertiary level and those who do may not be aware of available sources of funding. Literacy or language barriers and the digital divide can also limit individuals' ability to tap into certain forms of continuing education.

There is no substitute for offering one-to-one support to parishioners who wish to deepen their understanding of their faith. It is particularly important to extend this sort of support to Christians in midlife because those who do not find opportunities to explore their faith beyond their involvement in church services can easily feel that their journey of discipleship has stalled, and they may become disheartened. There are opportunities we in the church can seize, as we endeavour to "encourage one another and build up each other" (1 Thess 5:11). In Chapters 6 and 7 we shall look at some ways that churches are offering one-to-one support to parishioners in midlife.

Desire for deepening relationship with God

The spiritual quest at midlife is rarely for intellectual knowledge alone. Many churchgoers in their 40s and 50s want to deepen their relationship with God. These desires are interconnected but not indistinguishable. Here, the focus is on experiential rather than rational knowledge; the desire is not so much to know more about God, but to know God more.

Frances (spiritual director, 70) told me that many people who attend spiritual direction are looking to be "nurtured spiritually in a more meaningful way." Frances described the experience of some of her directees who, in midlife, had begun to question certain church practices and teachings which had formerly sustained them, and then said:

> I think there's a real search for spirituality and they're looking to have, um, not so much beliefs about God but encounters with their spirituality. ... I think it's true of a lot of people in the midlife journey [that] their whole understanding of "who God is" shifts. You know, they discover that what they were taught about God was very limited. And then I think they do question some of the practices that they've held on to.

Within each of the groups of people I interviewed – the churchgoers, clergy and spiritual directors – there were individuals who told me that a significant part of their faith development during midlife had been to explore new forms of prayer and worship. For some people, this had involved changing denomination. Five of the 40 people I interviewed for my doctoral research had changed denominations at midlife. Some other interviewees had not changed their primary church affiliation but had sought to broaden their experience of prayer and worship by attending more than one church, or by attending different types of services within their own parishes. Others told me that, beyond the services, liturgies, and sacraments of their churches, exposure to established spiritual disciplines and a variety of types of prayer was helpful to them as they explored ways to deepen their relationship with God. In the following three short sections we look at experiences of prayer that interviewees described. These are, of course, not the only shifts in prayer that might occur in this life stage.

Simple prayer

A number of interviewees told me that, at midlife, they felt attracted to greater simplicity in prayer. Jane (Anglican, 55) told me that a change she has noticed in her spirituality at midlife is that she has now a much greater appreciation of "prayer that doesn't necessarily rely on me having to come up with the words." She said:

> I'm finding I like repetitive prayers more than I used to. You know, short repetitive prayers where I don't actually have to think very much, but I can still be praying – like the *Jesus Prayer*[181] – you know, that kind of thing. I just feel like there's a point at which God doesn't need me to be constantly looking for ways of saying things. *[She laughs.]*

For similar reasons, Jane is also finding liturgy within her denomination helpful. Her local Anglican church offers a full range of types of service but the service she chooses to attend uses *A New Zealand Prayer Book*.[182] She explained the appeal of this service for her:

> I like liturgy actually. *[She mulls this over.]* Why do I like liturgy? I kind of like not having to reinvent the wheel. I know sometimes people criticise liturgy, because you can just be going through the motions (and you can) but actually if someone's come up with a form of words that you can't really improve on ... *[She trails off.]* And actually I think sometimes liturgy becomes part of you. You know,

you talk about learning things by heart, because that's where they end up if you say them long enough.

Occasionally Jane also attends a church service which is targeted at young people but is very inclusive of people of other ages. Jane told me that one thing she really likes about this particular service is that it includes tangible elements.

> They always have this tray of tea-light candles, and they say at any point in the service you can light a candle for something or somebody that you're concerned for, and at the end we'll just say an all-embracing prayer for the candles – which they always do. And I actually find that a really good way to pray, because, again, it's not like I have to think of the right words for this situation. It's like: Here is the situation.

A further form of simple prayer that appealed to Jane was to use a hymn book during her personal devotions. "Sometimes just starting my devotional time by singing a song or two actually helps," she said. Bypassing the need to always "come up with the words" in prayer was proving liberating for Jane. The use of prayers others had crafted, and the use of tangible elements, were helping her to meet with God at "heart" rather than only at "head" level.[183]

For Bernard (Catholic priest, 52) the sense of "holy repetition" of saying the daily office and saying the Mass is important. He said, "The words gain a new significance, depth and resonance." Although saying the daily office is a consistent spiritual discipline which does not change with age, in Bernard's own experience the plaintive, melancholic psalms "do start to resonate more" in midlife. He said:

> When you read them as a young person you thought, "Come on, get a life!" *[We both laugh.]* When you read them now you think, "Oh, yeah, they're talking about me! I can just feel the Psalmist articulating my own thoughts. Thank you, Lord." But that discipline *[of following the daily office]* stays the same.

Bernard then went on to describe further changes that had occurred in his prayer during midlife:

> I hope my prayer – I think it is – is becoming less active, more passive, more receptive, quieter, less noisy. I feel less a need to articulate my hopes and fears, desires and longings, and more a desire just for the Lord to come. So

in fact the spiritual work becomes not trying to press on the Lord what I think he should know but in fact a sort of clearing of the decks so that the Lord can enter – because he longs to, and I provide the obstacles. I think you get better at that. *[He pauses to reflect.]* Can you get "better" at prayer? I don't know. That's not quite right. You don't get better at it. You get worse at it in a way! *[He laughs.]* And you recognise how bad you are at it. That's what happens.

Jeannette Bakke, who is both a spiritual director and a faculty associate at Bethel Theological Seminary, Minnesota, observes, "At some point highly verbal prayer ceases to be as satisfying as it once was."[184] Even the most talkative of people are likely to be attracted to simpler and "less noisy" forms of prayer around midlife. Matthew (spiritual director, 61) described his midlife directees' preferred forms of prayer as "moving away from kataphatic to apophatic[185] ways of doing things." He elaborated: "It's less about what they're doing and more just about surrender and silence."

James (spiritual director, 57) told me that, for him, discovering the contemplative dimension of faith had been a "hugely significant part of deepening and encountering Christ in a radically more real and personal way, in the depths of being." He described his experience of prayer, at an earlier point in midlife, like this:

> The forms of prayer, and the relationship with God that I'd been given in my evangelical heritage of Bible study and prayer in response to that, were not adequate to maintain a growing spiritual life. I no longer encountered God in a way that was nurturing and life-giving through those forms. I have since returned to those, a long time ago *[he laughs]* – to Scripture reading – but in a different way. I think, for a period of time, creation became a central part of meeting with God. Just going and sitting in a park, early morning, and pondering the beauty of what God has made, rather than meeting with him through his book.

We may recall comments made earlier by Keith (Catholic, 47) who described having a sense of deep gratitude as he drank coffee on his back deck and overlooked his vegetable garden. Simple experiences such as these have the potential not only to point us toward God but to bring us into deeper communion with God.

Michael Mayne, former Dean of Westminster, writes of his "deep belief" that:

> [T]he whole world is sacramental and the whole creation marked with the signature of its Creator, and that the only way to find the holy is in the ordinary; that the ordinary is far more extraordinary than we think.[186]

The experience of recognising "the holy" in "the ordinary" was something that Malcolm (Anglican, 52) described in his interview. Malcolm reflected on a period when he would spend Sunday mornings cycling up in the hills away from the city where he lives and works. This was, for him, a spiritual practice. He said, "I'd go up and speak to God there." Malcolm described road cycling as "quite a meditative thing to do. Working at a steady pace, in a beautiful environment, exposed to the elements, just with your own thoughts ... I found that very good for other than physical reasons. It's so beautiful up there."

Many Christians in midlife describe their growing appreciation and awareness that we can find God "in all things" – even, as Australian cartoonist, philosopher and poet, Michael Leunig attests, in "the invention of the wheelbarrow and the existence of the teapot."[187] "Finding God in all things" is a central concept within Ignatian Spirituality (about which we shall say more shortly) but the fact that individuals can encounter God in the ordinary stuff of daily life is widely celebrated throughout the church. A fun poster, "45 Ways to Encounter God," has been created by the Salvation Army to help people "to connect with God in fresh and unexpected ways – sometimes in the little everyday acts of living and being."[188] It is available in six languages, Te Reo Māori, Fijian, Tongan, Samoan, Spanish and English, and is free to download.

Retreats

People who are attracted to "less noisy" forms of prayer may, at some point, decide to attend a Christian retreat. Judith (Catholic, 60) told me that she had always had the desire for a deeper prayer life and a deeper walk with God. At the age of 35 she attended a week-long retreat (most of which was silent) which was a catalyst for a lot of spiritual change. "It felt as though that everything I had ever believed and had known about God had been chucked up in the air and had come down reassembled. It was wonderful – and scary." Judith explained that from this experience she started thinking more broadly about God. She felt that she did not start believing things that were "unorthodox" but she started seeing God was "far more" than she had imagined. Something else that

Judith considered to be important about her retreat was that she experienced spiritual direction for the first time while she was there. This led her then to seek out a spiritual director, who has provided great support to her over a number of years.

At the time I interviewed Murray (Anglican, 44), he had recently been on a silent retreat for the first time. This was held at the holiday home of one of the parishioners from his church. He said, "It was open to anybody that wanted to do it. A very different experience, actually, being in fellowship and not speaking. And actually it taught me a couple of lessons." After the retreat Murray thought about those lessons, and he was able to apply what he had learned. He was keen to impress upon me that there were practical outcomes from the retreat. He added, "Also when you do a silent retreat your style of worship, instead of being verbal and physical, you know, mentally you're thinking of different ways of doing the same thing. And I think that's a good aspect." Murray said he would certainly go on another silent retreat if one were offered.

Another Anglican interviewee, Malcolm (52) mentioned a seven-day retreat he had attended some years earlier. He told me that he appreciated retreats and "the removal of all that clutter" that they afforded. Like Murray, Malcolm found he had learned some significant lessons in the silence of the retreat. He felt that the retreat helped him to understand the different layers we have as human beings. He said, "To be able to touch that is quite amazing." When I asked Malcolm if he would go on something like that again, he said that he would. In contrast, Grant (Presbyterian, 55) told me that it had been a very long time since he had been on a retreat – perhaps 20 years or more. He added, with a laugh, "I've never been a great retreat person, either. I'd far rather do something else in the weekend." One size does not fit all.

Across denominations, many types and formats of retreat exist. Some include periods of silence but also incorporate individuals' hobbies and interests. A number of the interviewees I spoke to found intimacy with God as they engaged in other pursuits, such as craft-making or tramping. Some stressed and busy churchgoers of middle age, particularly those people who do not feel attracted to more traditional forms of retreat, may be attracted to quiet retreats that include active ways to rest and recharge and to pray. Others find retreats in daily life – retreats during which attendees continue their normal daily activities but commit to prayer and meeting with others – are more accessible and more appealing to them. Bernard (Catholic priest, 52) described a retreat in daily life that was offered in his parish. About 50 parishioners participated in the month-long retreat, which was facilitated by spiritual directors from beyond the parish, and "plenty" of those who attended were in midlife. Bernard considered it to be an effective programme and hoped to offer something similar again.

Yvonne (Presbyterian minister, 58) told me that, in her experience, despite the busyness of middle age midlife parishioners do have the time and commitment to attend retreats – as long as they aren't too long. Women's retreats which have been offered in her parish have sometimes taken place over a day or a day and a half. At times these have involved parishioners leading sessions, based on areas of expertise, and at others a spiritual director or educator from outside the parish has contributed. Yvonne observed, "A good number attend." When parishes are able to offer their own retreats the needs of participants can be taken into account so that an appropriate balance of activity, fellowship, material to encourage and extend attendees, and silent time for prayer and reflection can be provided. This balance will differ depending both on churches' resources and the personalities, circumstances and needs of the individuals involved.

Long-established patterns of prayer

When Jesus' disciples asked him, "Lord, teach us to pray," (Luke 11:10) he gave them what has become the universal prayer of the Christian church, "The Lord's Prayer," also known from its opening words as the "Our Father" (*Pater Noster*). This prayer not only offers a summary of the entire gospel but also provides a solid structure upon which further reflection and prayer may be built. Martin Luther considered the Lord's prayer to be Christ's authoritative guide to the topics we should pray.[189] The prayer book of the Anglican Church of New Zealand, *A New Zealand Prayer Book: He Karakia Mihinare o Aotearoa*, includes morning and evening devotions based on the seven sections of the Lord's Prayer. Whether our prayer is supported by others' written reflections or arises spontaneously as we engage with its familiar words, throughout our lives we can return again and again to the Lord's Prayer and find both solidarity and intimacy with Christ.[190]

When we find ourselves floundering or feeling stuck – which can occur even after years of association with the church – having some sort of structure upon which to build our prayer can enable us to move forward and to persevere. Spiritual directors and churchgoers spoke to me about several frameworks for prayer that they considered helpful at midlife. The two most frequently mentioned by them were *Lectio Divina* (sacred reading) and the prayer of *Examen*. The first encourages listening to God through Scripture by following a series of steps. The second helps people to become more attuned to God's presence and activity in their daily experience. For people who have had, as one spiritual director, Matthew (61) put it, "that background where you just pick up the Bible, wherever, and God speaks to you," discovering long-established patterns of prayer such as these can be transformative.

The contemplative practice of *Lectio Divina* dates back to the fourth century. Traditionally it includes four steps: *lectio* (reading slowly, being attentive to God's word, re-reading), *meditatio* (meditating on a word or phrase or passage that has stood out, chewing it over), *oratio* (speaking with God about it) and *contemplatio* (resting in the presence of God). Christchurch-based Biblical scholar, Kathleen Rushton, argues that a fifth step is essential: "The process of *lectio divina* is not concluded until it arrives at action (*actio*). What has been learnt from the sacred text is applied to daily life, relationships, work, creation and solidarity with the poor, as with Jesus we are invited to complete the works of God (John 5:36)."[191] When we engage with the Bible in this way, asking God to help us to understand the implications of his word for our own lives and for our world, we may experience the fruits of intimacy with God and inspiration and energy to work for his will to be done. "Prayer should move us to action, even if it simply makes us want to be more compassionate and faithful,"[192] writes Jesuit author James Martin.

The practice of *Lectio Divina* encourages us to respond to God with mind and heart, and also to be prepared to act on God's word to us. In other words, it is a process that can help us to know, love and follow God "more clearly, dearly and nearly" – the very things that so many mature Christians desire. It is also a process which can be experienced in a group context. One interviewee, Anna (Catholic, 42) described how helpful it had been to her to participate in a group that had practiced *Lectio Divina* together. Although that particular group no longer met, Anna told me that it was an experience she valued and to which she hoped to return.

The prayer of *Examen*, which Ignatius of Loyola considered to be a tool of such value that he insisted that Jesuits pray it twice daily, can be "life-changing" for people who pray it regularly.[193] It provides a structure within which a person can reflect on all that has happened over the course of a day, and look ahead to the next day, in the presence of God. It encourages attentiveness and gratitude to God as well as raising awareness of areas of life that still require transformation. In *The Psychology of Christian Character Formation* Joanna Collicutt notes, "This pattern of anticipating in advance and reflection in retrospect (holy savouring) is a feature of the corporate daily prayers of all traditions."[194] It is a tool which many people believe is of particular value to people in midlife.

I asked Hugh (52), a Baptist pastor, what motivated him to encourage his parishioners to use the prayer of *Examen*. He explained that it is a tool which encourages people to be more reflective about where God is at work in their lives. He also felt it was important in his own church because Baptists have usually focused on other forms of prayer. He said, "They have tended to be very Biblical people, very book people – the 'quiet time' has been hammered for decades"– but the *Examen* provides another way for God to speak:

> God is engaging with us all the time. The *Examen* encourages us to notice that and to be aware of that, and to be aware of when we are moving away from God. It invites people to think of something else as a place of meeting God – not just the Bible.

For those interested in learning more about the prayer of *Examen*, Jim Manney's little book, *A Simple Life-Changing Prayer: Discovering the Power of St. Ignatius Loyola's Examen*, offers a succinct explanation of this spiritual practice.

With its focus on Biblical narratives and deepening relationship with Jesus through imaginative prayer rather than reason alone, its emphasis on "finding God in all things," its practical teaching on discernment, and the scope for individuality within the clear structure of The Spiritual Exercises, Ignatian spirituality has broad and enduring appeal. Resources relating to Ignatian spirituality are also widely available. Straightforward guides to key themes in Ignatian spirituality are published digitally and in print regularly.[195]

Many New Zealanders, and millions of people throughout the world, now access daily prayers based on scripture through the apps "Pray as You Go" and "Sacred Space," both of which have Ignatian roots. These apps are designed for busy people who want to set aside about 15 minutes a day to engage with Scripture and listen to God. Resources for themed retreats and longer periods of prayer are also suggested. Ignatian retreats in daily life are offered fairly regularly in various parts of New Zealand, and those who attend are often introduced to forms of prayer which can be used on an ongoing basis at home. We shall look more at these forms of retreat in Chapter 7. For some people who are seeking "more," completing The Spiritual Exercises intensively or over a period of nine months can also be an option.[196]

There are other spiritual frameworks within which mature Christians who are seeking to deepen their relationship with God can find support for their spiritual growth and the stability and comfort of knowing that they are following in the footsteps of great saints. Gary Neal Hansen's book, *Kneeling with Giants: Learning to Pray with History's Best Teachers* is a practical introduction to ten figures from church history who approached prayer in different ways.[197] Targeted at people who are "wondering how to get out of a devotional slump" or "longing for spiritual mentors" it is just one example of a resource which could be used by individuals or small groups within a congregational context. Dawn Duncan Harrell's *Ten Ways to Pray: A Short Guide to a Long History of Talking* with God[198] is another practical guide to different forms of prayer modelled by Christians throughout history. New Zealand authors who have published very helpful guides to prayer and traditional spiritual disciplines include Sheila Pritchard and Barbara Sampson. Pritchard's engaging book, *The Lost Art of Meditation: Deepening Your Prayer Life*, introduces readers to contemplative practices which will "revive the soul and rejoice the heart."[199] Although now out of print, it is well worth tracking down. Sampson's *Encountering God*,[200] a six-part study guide for groups, explores images of God, "holy habits" (spiritual disciplines), many types of prayer and ways to read the Bible, and concludes with a study about learning to listen to God. The study guide can be accessed through the Salvation Army online.[201]

Desire for challenge

Some people who have been Christians for decades can find that in middle age the enthusiasm and energy that marked the early stages of their faith may begin to wane, particularly when it comes to what happens at church. In New Zealand it is quite easy (and not uncommon) for churchgoers to become comfortable to the point of boredom. New Zealand hymn-writer Colin Gibson's humorous "Ho-hum Hymn"[202] begins, "Snap us out of it, Lord, we are listless and bored." It goes on to declare, "We're your comfortable sheep, with our minds half asleep, all our pasture is turning to hay; an occasional bleat, or a stamp of the feet, is as much as we dare when we pray." Several members of the clergy, Don (Presbyterian minister, 52), Sung-ho (Methodist/Presbyterian minister, 53) and Hugh (Baptist pastor, 52) spoke to me about the phenomenon of boredom within the church and described approaches that they and their congregations were taking to address it.

Don (52) is the minister of an evangelical Presbyterian parish whose church's vision statement includes reference to living "passionately" for Christ. But Don told me that after a meeting with the elders in his church, all of whom were in midlife, he had been reflecting on the issue of boredom in the faith journey. He said:

> One of the challenges or issues is lack of excitement or fresh passion for the Kingdom of God or the mission of God. I wrestle with this a little bit. … We were having a conversation about this with the elders one time, and I asked them, "Well, does anybody feel bored?" And several of them said, "Yeah, I'm bored." If you've been in church and in leadership for 20 years, or something, like some of these elders have, then they can get to a place where they think, "Oh well, is there anything new?" I would want to critique that a little bit in the sense that part of the answer to that is, in one sense, "No! The gospel is still the gospel." But in terms of new things that God might be leading them to be involved in, then certainly there are new things. That's one of the challenges. A person in leadership, or attending regularly, can just get bored with it all.

Don acknowledged that some people can become tired or jaded even if ministries they pioneered are continuing to meet the needs of their church or community effectively. He felt that, over time, people can and do "lose their passion" and some may feel that they have "done their thing." Don said, "I think this whole issue of 'How passionate are we for the cause of the Kingdom?' is an issue, not in terms of having to sort of 'whip it up' somehow, but in terms of just avoiding boredom." Although his church's leadership team is actively endeavouring to provide opportunities for parishioners to reflect on their life of worship, their roles within and beyond the church, and a number of other aspects of congregational life, Don felt they still had some way to go. When I asked Don what the people in his parish who expressed boredom might be seeking, he said:

> There's a little bit of an uncritiqued "new equals good, old equals bad." So they would be looking for some new thing. I'm generalising here, but I can think of a few examples of that. "A new song is a good song, an old song is a bad song." "A new ministry that's different is a good thing, an old ministry that's been round for years is not such a good thing." There's questions in terms of faithfulness, and stuff we need to wrestle with there, but it's also a helpful thing in the sense that it's quite good to stop something and do something new in its place.

When what was formerly energising in the spiritual life seems "stale, flat, and unprofitable"[203] individuals and congregations can respond in a number of ways, some of which are more likely to be fruitful than others. As Don suggested, some may attempt to "whip it up" by endeavouring to emulate what is happening in churches that are apparently successful in terms of numerical growth. While it can be helpful to listen to and learn from others whose practices differ from our own – which is, indeed, why contrasting case studies of programmes that are seeking to address the needs of midlife churchgoers are included in this book (Chapter 7) – what "works" in one context is rarely directly applicable to another. Nor is it likely that spiritual growth will occur simply because the "old" is discarded in favour of the "new."

Sung-ho (53), who ministers in a church with a combined Presbyterian and Methodist congregation, felt strongly about this issue. Over time, he had become convinced that offering a range of engaging programmes or activities within the church is no guarantee that spiritual growth will occur. He said, "In many cases we feel satisfied, just satisfied. 'I enjoyed it' – that's all. But it doesn't lead to deeper change." Sung-ho admitted that he was still grappling with the fundamental question, "What brings us to transformation? What really makes us grow?" Sung-ho had developed greater appreciation of the importance of learning from the practices and wisdom of Christians from former generations, even if some people considered certain practices to be "bygone and unfashionable." He felt that churches would be helping their members' spiritual development if they regained and tried some of them. Referring to C.S Lewis – who argued that we should not ignore the old in quest of the new but seek to learn from the wisdom of other ages[204] – Sung-ho suggested that by drawing upon some classical spiritual disciplines Christians in midlife would find their faith stretched. Within his own church, Sung-ho observed that spiritual growth was occurring through intentional mentoring relationships, especially when these were focused upon Bible study. The place of mentoring, and its applicability to people in midlife, will be explored in some detail in the next chapter.

Hugh (52) is the pastor of a Baptist church which has a strong community focus. Volunteers and paid employees associated with the church work with the poor and marginalized, offering budgeting services, supporting prisoners and their families, caring for those with mental illnesses, and so on. The church is also involved in ministries overseas. In this church there is no shortage of ways for parishioners to serve God and others, should they wish to offer their time and expertise to these enterprises. But Hugh is well aware that addressing the issue of boredom and the desire for novelty in the spiritual life is not simply a matter of providing more things for people to do. As he spoke to me about midlife spirituality, Hugh reflected on the need for mature Christians to be stretched and challenged beyond their known ability. Linking the concept of "flow" (drawn from positive psychology)[205] to the Christian life, Hugh said, "We are at our most satisfied, happy and fulfilled when there is a mix of challenge and success." He elaborated:

> We are a generation where we have lost that sense of faith-stretching, faith-pushing, faith-engaging beyond the comfortable into the unknown, where we're really at our wit's end but not to the point of failure, to the point of being dependent on God. We are struggling to provide that for a generation of people who see faith as fronting up on a Sunday and singing a few songs. And people aren't doing that for themselves either. We live in a baby adolescent stage when we could be stretched into so much more.

Hugh described how his church was seeking to provide some "stretching points" for mature Christians, emphasising lifelong discipleship and helping members to see themselves as part of influential redemptive communities. The vision shared by members of his church is that churchgoers of all ages will be better equipped to love God, themselves and fellow believers, and to understand and respond to global needs.

The Anglican Church of Aotearoa places this communal prayer at the heart of one of its liturgies:

> God of peace,
> let us your people know,
> that at the heart of turbulence
> there is an inner calm that comes
> from faith in you.
> *Keep us from being content with things as they are,*
> that from this central peace
> there may come a creative compassion,
> a thirst for justice,
> and a willingness to give of ourselves
> in the spirit of Christ.[206]

A prayer associated with the spirituality of St Francis of Assisi, the "Franciscan Benediction," asks God to inspire us to live more wholeheartedly as disciples of Christ, motivated by the "discomfort" God gives us and by the belief that we "can make a difference in this world."[207] A similar theme in the addresses of Pope Francis is that following and accompanying Christ requires us to be "outgoing" – "to come out of a dreary way of living faith that has become a habit, out of the temptation to withdraw into our own plans, which end by shutting out God's creative action." We are to imitate Christ "by leaving ourselves behind and going out to encounter others."[208]

A desire for greater challenge at midlife can motivate us to selfless service. We need, of course, to exercise discernment about what God is calling us to do. Authors Henri Nouwen, Donald McNeill and Douglas Morrison advocate social action motivated by compassion, but include some words of caution:

> In a society that is so keen on new encounters, so eager for new events, and so hungry for new experiences, it is ... important to remain critical of our own activist tendencies. When our own needs begin to dominate our actions, long-

range service becomes difficult and we soon become exhausted, burned out, and even embittered by our efforts. The most important resource for counteracting the constant temptation to slip into activism is the knowledge that in Christ everything has been accomplished.[209]

As we have noted in earlier chapters, we need to recognise that sometimes God's invitation to us, particularly during midlife, may not be to act, but to wait. This can be a difficult call to accept.[210]

I once read of a clergyman who described Christianity, wonderfully, as "the first pool he had stepped into in which he couldn't feel the bottom."[211] In the Christian life there is always more to discover, always the possibility of further personal transformation and deeper relationship with God, and always new ways to serve and love others. Congregations that embrace these truths are likely to be places of grace and nurture for Christians in midlife.

Questions for reflection or discussion

1. In this chapter, did any of the interviewees' stories or comments particularly resonate with you? Did any surprise you? Why?

2. What do you find faith-building at this point in your life? What helps you to pray?

3. Have these things changed or have they remained much the same over recent years?

4. *Understanding:* Where do people in your church find opportunities to learn more about the Christian faith? How are parishioners helped to access resources (websites, books, podcasts, courses) they may find useful? Are there people within your congregation who may have expertise and interest in this field who could be asked to contribute in some way?

5. *Deepening relationship with God:* How can middle-aged parishioners in your church find guidance or support in practising a range of spiritual disciplines? How does (or could) your church facilitate opportunities for people to spend time with God in silence?

6. *Challenge:* How well is your congregation doing in affirming the vocation of midlife parishioners who are living out their faith and using their gifts in their homes, workplaces and in the community? How might your parish encourage individuals to explore connections between their "deep gladness" and the needs of the world? How is God calling your whole congregation to "go out to encounter others?"

7. What might you like to pray about, or act upon?

Recommended resources

Hansen, Gary Neal. *Kneeling with Giants: Learning to Pray with History's Best Teachers.* Downer's Grove, IL: InterVarsity Press, 2012.

Harrell, Dawn Duncan. *Ten Ways to Pray: A Short Guide to a Long History of Talking with God.* Los Angeles: Stone's Throw, 2012.

Ignatianspirituality.com – A useful website for those interested in Ignatian Spirituality

Manney, Jim. *A Simple Life-Changing Prayer: Discovering the Power of St. Ignatius Loyola's Examen.* Chicago: Loyola Press, 2011.

Pritchard, Sheila. *Lost Art of Meditation: Deepening Your Prayer Life.* UK: Scripture Union Publishing, 2003.

6 — Addressing the Discipleship Gap

You then, my child, be strong in the grace that is in Christ Jesus; and what you have heard from me through many witnesses entrust to faithful people who will be able to teach others as well.

2 Timothy 2:1-2

When results from a qualitative study of the ministries and programmes of a prominent church in the United States of America, Willow Creek Community Church, were released in 2007, church leaders were dismayed to find that nearly 25% of its members described themselves as "stalled" in their spiritual growth or "dissatisfied" with what the church was doing to help them grow.[212] The data from the study suggested that the programmes offered by the church were not addressing the needs of mature believers who needed guidance in how to become "self-feeders."[213] These church members said that they would like mentors or coaches who could support their spiritual development, and to whom they could be accountable.[214]

More recently, American author Michelle Van Loon asked readers of her blog who were over the age of 40 if they were more, less, or just as involved in their local church as they had been a decade earlier.[215] Van Loon received feedback from over 500 middle-aged and retired people that revealed that "there's often a discipleship gap for older members."[216] She writes, "Anecdotally, most of the church leaders I'm in touch with admit they haven't given much thought to what discipleship might look like for their older members (especially women) beyond maintaining the spiritual growth from their youth." As a result, people in midlife, who need support and encouragement as they navigate later stages of faith, can often feel "marginalized both as disciples and disciplers."[217]

As I interviewed churchgoers, clergy and spiritual directors in New Zealand I heard similar stories. Tony (spiritual director, 56) echoed many other interviewees' sentiments when he expressed the opinion that in most churches in New Zealand it is expected that Christians in the middle decades of life will "just get on with it." Brian (spiritual director, 62) agreed. He felt that "in this shifting stage I think midlife people are being neglected. So people flounder round." Julie (spiritual director, 60) told me that she thinks it is "important that we don't take for granted or neglect" people in this age group. She said, "Maybe we expect people in midlife to be giving out in particular ways, or helping, but not actually the right formation necessarily being supported."

Grant (Presbyterian, 55) and his wife married young and had a son early in their marriage. Their son has been living away from home for about a decade. Grant told me that once his son left home questions arose for them, like "Well, you know, what do we do now?" You know, "What's the next stage?" Grant talked about hobbies and recreational activities he and his wife were now engaged in, and then reflected on his experience of church. Grant was quite accepting of the fact that resources in his church were directed towards people in age groups other than his own. He described it as "really good" that, in his parish, there's a lot of effort put into children and teenagers, and that there's an environment that kids want to come to. However, he also noted:

> There's that gap in the middle. And then there's the looking out for the oldies, and making sure things are going OK for them. So you do end up with that patch in the middle, where you sorta – if you're not established in a ministry, or working in an area where you feel gifted – then you can drift round a bit. I think personal life's like that as well.

People who have been involved in churches for a long time may be aware of spiritual disciplines they can practise independently, but this does not mean that they are always content to be "left to their own devices," as Karen (Anglican, 52) put it. Many might be glad to receive a little more guidance as their faith develops and changes. In this chapter and the next we shall explore some models of mentoring and spiritual support. First, we need to acknowledge some of the challenges facing congregations and individuals when it comes to addressing the discipleship gap.

Communal and individual responsibility

Ian's story – Part One

I first interviewed Ian (Presbyterian) when he was 41 and had recently married. At that point he was actively involved in home-group and youth leadership, sometimes facilitated Saturday night praise and worship gatherings, and was serving on the parish council at his church. When I spoke to him again, just over three years later, Ian had a baby daughter and was living in a suburb quite some distance from his church. He had found it necessary to give up some of the roles at church that he had enjoyed and found fulfilling, and, as other members of his home group had reached a similar stage as far as family responsibilities were concerned, the group was struggling to find ways to meet together. Ian explained the impact of these circumstances upon the ways his faith was being "fed":

> It's a time-management thing for us, with a new family. Some of the self-reflection things – like *Pray as You Go*[218] and that sort of thing – personal prayer times do get lost. But even when they're there it's important still to have the communal things. For me that includes worship and it includes talking about things at a deeper level. And I think, too, that's where, for me, there's a slight difference between men and women. I think women naturally, when they socialise, tend to talk at a deeper level. Whereas men, or for myself, if I'm just socialising I'm only talking at a certain level. It needs to be an intentional space, like a home group or something, for me to actually go deeper.

Ian reiterated his belief that when his wife catches up with her friends their interactions tend to "go deeper," then continued:

> Mine don't. That's why I need that intentional space. So I think that's what I'm missing out on at the moment. We're at the point where we're just beginning to discuss this with one or two people at our church, but we're sort of wondering is this something that could be changed at church? Or is there something we need to change?

The questions Ian raises are important for two reasons. First, the dilemma Ian describes regarding the balance between the church's responsibility to nurture spiritual growth and individuals' responsibility to "run with perseverance the race that is set before [them]" (Heb 12:1b) is one that has probably been of concern to Christians for generations. Second, the questions troubling Ian affect many people.

In an illuminating article about faith development in the context of church, "Fowler, Faith and Fallout," New Zealand spiritual director, the late Andrew Pritchard observes that individuals tend to become less reliant on the institutional church for support as their faith develops:

> As positive growth occurs, so the balance between the church's primacy in meeting our spiritual needs and our own responsibility for doing so, shifts. That the church no longer meets my needs as fully or as comfortably as it once did is not necessarily an indication that the church has failed me.[219]

Nonetheless, spiritual formation happens in community, not just individually. As Janet Ruffing explains, our "spiritual identity" is "inherently relational." It is "co-authored, co-constructed by theists in their relationship with God."[220] Moreover, we create meaning, not only in the stories we tell ourselves or the stories we tell God in prayer, or even by listening to God who enables us to grow beyond "our self-enclosed ego narrative," but "in relationship to others with whom we share our spiritual journeys and whose lives endow ours with the meaningfulness that results from living intimately with others, contributing to their lives and in serving others in large and small ways."[221] When Ian described his need for an "intentional space" within which he could talk about matters of meaning and significance, then, he was speaking about something of fundamental importance to his ongoing spiritual development.

I asked the spiritual directors I interviewed if they could suggest ways that the church might better support people's spiritual growth in midlife. James (57) said:

> I think we have to provide some teaching around some of the crucial midlife life – and faith – issues. To talk about some of the transitions that happen there, to give input about stages of faith, streams of spirituality. We have to provide places where people are informed and given resources that can help them through midlife life issues and faith issues, and I don't think the church does that very well. I think we are far too geared for early stages of faith, growth and development, and not providing enough for later faith stages.

Matthew (61) told me that directees who have spoken to him about the helpful support provided by their parishes are those who attend churches where "it's OK to bring your questions. Or there's acknowledgment from the front that, you know, that yes, these stages happen, and the doubts can be very helpful if we handle them the right way." He noted that some churches are now introducing members to established spiritual disciplines that have not formerly been widely known, and suggested *Lectio Divina* as one example. Like James, Matthew felt that middle-aged churchgoers can find support when churches offer teaching, or some acknowledgement in regular sermons, that helps them to realise:

> Not all of life is the same, and the spiritual journey is not some smooth path, not some smooth upward incline and you just get holier and holier, but there are earthquakes. There are times when you feel like the wheels have fallen off. And it's OK. This has happened to God's people ever since the beginning.

Matthew gave several examples of Biblical figures, including Job and Peter, whose spiritual paths were notably uneven, then continued, "Without rocking the theological boat too much, we could do more. Churches could help to normalise these experiences and give people some pointers about where they can find help." He added, "I don't think the church needs to do everything, but if they could help people find the appropriate help for what they're going through at the moment, then that would be great."

For this to occur, we need to be aware of the theological and spiritual emphases of our own denominations and parishes, and willing to accommodate and affirm the strengths of other churches' "personality types." Andrew Pritchard explains:

> Mismatch between an individual's own spirituality/ personality and that of the church they attend is one significant factor leading to dissatisfaction and increasing alienation between that person and their church. This is intensified if the church concerned strongly favours its preferred personality. Then people who are different not only feel that they don't fit, they are also made to feel that they are somehow unacceptable to God.[222]

He adds, "When we grow and our spirituality changes, if the church we are a part of is not sufficiently diverse to accommodate this, then frustration and tension result." Pritchard's article, "Your Church's Personality," is available online and is a very useful resource both for clergy who are seeking to support midlife members who need "wriggle room"[223] for their faith and for laypeople who may wish to act as mentors to others.

Ian's story – Part Two

During Ian's first interview, Ian was very keen to tell me about several ways in which other people had played a formative role in broadening and deepening his faith experience at midlife. He told me that he had always really valued regular Bible reading time and prayer but when he was younger he had focused on "me and God" without putting a lot of research into how other people spend time in prayer. This was something that had changed. Ian told me that he had kept a travel diary for a number of years but, over time, this had become a "prayer diary" or spiritual journal. Ian considered this development to be "exciting" and "motivating." In his prayer diary Ian keeps a record of things he is thankful for and blessings he has experienced – a practice which he has maintained for a number of years. Then Ian attended an inspiring workshop run by a local Methodist minister which expanded his understanding of journalling. Ian discovered that journalling could be more than just writing; it could include pictures and art, as well as words. He said:

> I developed an interest in art, which I did before, but I just never felt the freedom to explore it. In a diary, where people aren't necessarily going to see it, I felt liberated to, you know, actually try sharing some of my thoughts and heart and communications with God in a visual way.

Ian also attended some workshops on Christian meditation which he found very helpful. Reflecting on these experiences, he added, "Just in recent years, more, I have come to really value and appreciate input from other people into how I spend my time with God."

Ian went on to talk about another spiritual practice he had discovered as he entered midlife. Ian explained that retreats were not part of his church tradition, and he had no familiarity with them until a work colleague invited him to attend one. Ian was glad to discover "that you could have a retreat time that could take many different forms," both structured and unstructured, from just a morning retreat in someone's garden to something much longer. He really appreciated his first introduction to this type of "quiet time" outside his own "quiet times" of individual prayer. His home group now has an annual retreat. Ian said, in a tone of some satisfaction, "I brought that into our parish." Ian was glad to have been able to share with his peers some spiritual disciplines that had been shared with him. This is a lovely example of mature Christians supporting one another's spiritual development without reliance on clergy or others to organize things for them.

Ian suggested that the wider church could offer workshops that relate to spiritual development, which could be within denominations or inter-denominational. He felt that such workshops would be appreciated by mature Christians because they can "help you with a new idea – plant a seed." Ian said that, in his experience, a lot of workshops that are advertised are focused on other aspects of Christian ministry or leadership rather than personal prayer and spiritual development. He believes that people in midlife would like to explore "not just different ways of being church (because we tend to focus a lot on how to do the Sunday morning church)" but "the ways you can encourage small groups or individuals to have time with God."

There is a lot to ponder in Ian's story. It certainly suggests that a little bit of intentional support and guidance (whether that is offered by clergy or laity) can make a significant difference to people in midlife who might otherwise find themselves "drifting round a bit." Many people in this stage of life are also likely to be able and willing to share with others what they have themselves received.

Mentoring within congregations

Over the 20-plus years I worked as a secondary school teacher, a tried-and-true model of mentoring called "Peer Support"[224] was in operation in many schools throughout New Zealand. Its aims were – and still are – to build confidence and resilience in students who are new to high school and to develop the leadership qualities of the senior students who support them. The programme acknowledges and caters for the different needs of all involved, not just the junior students who might be presumed to be those with most to gain. Activity manuals and training are provided for the senior students who are peer support leaders, and resources and annual courses are offered to the teachers who have responsibility for the peer support programme in their schools. At the heart of Peer Support is the intent to build trusting relationships between students within year levels and between students of different ages. This is a model from which congregations can learn.

Many churches understand the value of mentoring and some have formal programmes within which supportive intergenerational relationships are nurtured. The focus of these programmes is almost always on the needs of younger members. This is understandable. Clergy and churchgoers are rightly concerned about the responsibility to pass on faith in Christ to younger generations and many seek to encourage and assist young people.[225] When the churchgoers I spoke to described supporting people younger than themselves, within their workplaces and families as well as within the church, it was obvious that roles which allowed them opportunities to be "generative" afforded them great satisfaction. They were delighted to be able to share their skills and experience and to offer guidance and encouragement to others.

Phil (53) spoke of the fulfilment he and his wife gain from being able to act as mentors in a pre-marriage course offered in their Catholic diocese. It demands a significant time commitment but Phil feels very glad to be able to contribute to the lives of the people who are attending. "You're actually doing something really amazing," he said. Phil believes that a lot of the people who attend the marriage course would otherwise never have thought about some of the things they talk about there. He felt, "They always end up getting something out of it." Phil is glad that the young couples they have worked with also feel that they have someone they can come and talk to later on. He said, "As we go on, we become that couple that were mentors to us, you know, when we were younger. We're going to be them, in ten or twenty years, or a bit longer. It's so cool." Pastoral theologian Donald Capps notes, "Real generativity reflects an altruistic concern for the care and nurture of others, but also involves the mature adult's need to be needed."[226] Phil's genuine enthusiasm about his mentoring role perfectly illustrates both.

Daniel Levinson, whose work on development in adult life has been extremely influential, claims that "good mentoring is one of the special contributions that persons in middle adulthood can make to society." But he adds, "Given the value that mentoring has for the mentor, the recipient and society at large, it is tragic that so little of it actually occurs."[227] There is certainly some scope for parishes to reflect on the capacity of their middle-aged members to play a more active role in mentoring others. It could be, as was the case in more than one interviewees' parish, that the mentoring relationship has no explicitly religious component but simply involves teaching a younger person a new skill. The relationships that may be forged between people of different ages, through multiple and varied interactions, may be of great value to both parties.

Clearly it can be helpfully stretching to be relied on to draw on one's own life experience, wisdom and skills to assist others. But, as Ian's story illustrated, people in midlife also appreciate and need the encouragement and example of wiser counsellors and friends to help them move forward in their own journey of personal development and spiritual formation. Debbie (Catholic, 51) was one of a number of interviewees who stated that while it can be wonderful to have opportunities to act as mentors, Christians in midlife need to have "people who are further along" to support them. As she put it, "We need both in our lives – we need people we look to and respect and admire, and those who we encourage."

Almost half of the midlife churchgoers I interviewed stated that they valued the relationships they had with parishioners who were in a similar stage of life to themselves because they felt that people around their own age could readily understand and identify with their experiences. Together they could share their stories and feel accepted and supported. But even more interviewees – in fact, 80% of the middle-aged churchgoers who spoke to me – said that they valued the opportunities that being involved in the church gave them to mix with and learn from people who were older than themselves. They were extremely appreciative of the wisdom and guidance older parishioners and elderly clergy offered them. They found reassurance in being able to speak to people who had "been there and done that" and, importantly, could now spare time to listen.

I found it striking that so many of the women I interviewed told me that they drew support and guidance from a close friendship with an older woman. In most cases these formative relationships had arisen spontaneously within the church context and had developed gradually. Nina (Anglican, 43), spoke with great affection about an elderly woman she had met at church, with whom she had spent a lot of time. Her 86-year-old friend, who is an avid reader, had given Nina books such as commentaries and study Bibles. Nina told me how grateful she was that she has been exposed to "good authors." (She mentioned Tom Wright, Richard Rohr and Henri Nouwen.) The same friend had also introduced Nina to retreats. Nina said, "So she's sort of opened a new world for me. She's opened a new doorway which is quite different to what happens at church." In return, Nina has shared YouTube clips with her friend – of authors speaking, for example – and her friend "just loved it." Nina told me that she feels very blessed to have this relationship, but her friend says that she feels it is the other way round. Nina's friend enjoys hearing about what is happening in the workplace and in the world, now that she has retired, and she has been very supportive when Nina has been dealing with workplace issues such as restructuring. She has prayed with Nina. It's "been very lovely," concluded Nina.

Alison (Presbyterian, 59) expressed sincere gratitude for the support of an elderly parishioner with whom she had prayed regularly for approximately a decade. This friendship was particularly important to Alison as she had been widowed at the age of 41. Alison also considered her prayer partner's husband to be a supportive, prayerful friend. She said:

> This person, she's older than me and like, you know, they're the saints of the church. Her husband was an elder and they've been there, done that, got the T-shirt. They're just the most wonderful people. ... Sometimes it just all gets too much, and I'm the only person that knows the Lord in my family now, and they are rocks, absolute rocks.

Later in her interview Alison pointed to the significant role other people in her church had played in encouraging her to recognise, develop and use her gifts in Christian ministry. She was approaching the age of 50 when members of the clergy encouraged her to pursue theological training at tertiary level, a decision that led to a career change. Alison was also invited to participate in a programme at church called *StrengthsFinder*,[228] which she found built her confidence not only in identifying her own gifts but in appreciating the complementary gifts of her colleagues. For Alison, the active guidance and support of mentors within the parish had helped her to take some professional and personal risks at midlife. These strengthened her commitment to the church and played a significant part in her spiritual development. Alison saw herself as someone who had grown into her capacity to be a mentor to others. She told me that "the key people" in her own life "at pivotal moments" had been Christians in the 40 to 60 age bracket. She now realised, "My last ten years have been about God using me to be that person in others' lives."

Some of the spiritual directors I interviewed felt that not all older Christians have the breadth or depth of faith experience to be well equipped to support others in their faith journey. James (spiritual director, 57) spoke of a scarcity of older folk within his parish "who have done the deep journey." He has sought to address the discipleship gap in his church by establishing a mentoring system based on Jesus' model of working with twelve disciples. Louisa (spiritual director, 66) also suggested that groups could play a significant role in supporting spiritual development for those in midlife. She felt that there could be a place for small groups that are willing to encourage "almost in-your-face accountability" by posing very direct questions, as John Wesley did when he opened meetings by asking, "How is it with your soul?" Louisa considered "those kinds of questions that we don't ask so directly now but can get to the very heart of the matter" to be very constructive. She mentioned some materials published by *Renovaré*[229] which she thought could be helpful in supporting this model of discipleship in a group context.

In some Anglican dioceses in New Zealand *Cursillo* programmes are offered. *Cursillo* is a worldwide discipleship movement which originated in the Roman Catholic Church in Spain in the 1940s. During a three-day residential programme of testimonies, talks and group discussion, participants are invited to reflect upon core Christian values and spiritual practices, and encouraged to commit to taking what they have learned back into their daily lives. Cursillo relies heavily on peer accountability; those involved are encouraged to continue to meet regularly with other "cursillistas" in small groups and at wider gatherings so that they may support one another as they build on their commitment to Christ together.[230] "Fourth Day" meetings follow a prescribed structure of prayer and mutual sharing around the themes of piety (spiritual life), study and action.[231] For some mature Christians participation in Cursillo provides a boost to motivation, and provides direction, at a point in life when "the cares and riches and pleasures of life" (Luke 8:14) can so easily cause people to falter or become discouraged. Other denominations offer short-term courses or events which have similar aims.

Spiritual Direction

Spiritual direction is a ministry which is totally focused on supporting people as they journey in faith. It has been described as "a gift for midlife."[232] I asked the spiritual directors I interviewed to reflect on the particular attraction of spiritual direction for people in their 40s and 50s. They "want to go deeper into God," one spiritual director, Carol, observed. They "want to grow in their relationship and understanding." Others who are drawn to spiritual direction may feel that they have reached a "stuck place"[233] in their faith, when spiritual practices which had formerly provided effective nurture and nourishment no longer seem to be so helpful. Spiritual direction can be of particular value for those who find themselves at growing points such as these in their spiritual journey. Frances (70) captured the flavour of many of the spiritual directors' comments when she said:

> A lot of people question their faith in midlife and their spirituality and their values, and what they want to hold onto and what they want to let go of, and what they want to reclaim in a new way. I think having someone to listen to them, you know, and to tell their stories to, is probably the greatest help.

For some people, external events can precipitate a search for meaning and deeper authenticity at midlife. Brian (62) felt that, through a range of circumstances including burnout, loss, failure, illness, crises in relationships, and workplace disappointments, "People come to the end of themselves. That really just means that they come to realise that they're not in control. Circumstances happen to them that are outside my control – that's not unusual at midlife." It can be at this point, also, that:

> People notice things about themselves that they don't like, and that's when they'll look back to see what's the root of that. I think that probably in this time – midlife – people are quite serious about becoming who they are and sometimes there are things in their lives that block that. So that's when they want to look back, you know. They want to find out, "OK, why am I like this? Why do I get anxious about this? Why am I always having broken relationships? Why am I always struggling with intimacy?" You know, those types of things are really important.

Brian added, "Sometimes with people there's a knowing that they are not living fully yet – that they could be – so they really want that."

Maureen (56) noted that the journey of self-discovery that some people embark on during midlife can be "unstabilizing." For some, the discovery that "I'm not who I thought I was" is part of a "movement toward truth." Maureen described this process as the discarding of parts that are not quite the truth about who we are, then facing the question of, "Without that there, who am I?" Engaging with these questions and becoming comfortable with the answers may be painful, as Raymond Studzinski, author of *Spiritual Direction and Midlife Development*, points out: "Letting go of certain images of self, defective ideals, and unrealistic expectations constitute losses for people at any age. At midlife the sense of loss may be especially great because so much energy has been spent in the first part of life in the service of these ideals and images."[234] But, as one spiritual director I interviewed, Tony (56), put it, for some individuals in midlife it can be liberating to discover that "they don't have to be constrained by who they have been. You know, God is infinitely creative and still creating."

Matthew (61) described "a variety of precipitating factors" such as relationship issues or an unforeseen end or interruption to a person's career or ministry which could prompt a person to question their faith and relationship with God, then continued:

> The key issues usually are, "How do I make sense of what God's up to, here?" And changes in their image of God, and often changes in their pattern of spiritual practices because they feel, you know, that what they were doing is now inauthentic. And those two things go together. You know, "Who is the God I'm praying to? If I don't know, how do I pray?"

Sociologist and spiritual director Susan Philips notes that spiritual directors can "extend the gift of memory" to people experiencing disequilibrium in their faith. Speaking with someone who recalls "the ups and downs of the path we have walked, and continue to walk"[235] can have a stabilizing effect and be very reassuring. At times of uncertainty or upheaval, a spiritual director can gently remind us that God has been with us in the past, is with us now, and that God's faithfulness "endures forever" (Ps 117:2).

A further attraction of spiritual direction for people in midlife can be that it affords the opportunity for attendees to expand their spiritual horizons. Spiritual directors can be "invaluable in assisting with resources for the journey" as they are often very well resourced, keeping up "a regular intake of books, articles, courses, tapes of speakers, visiting speakers, retreats, and their own growth in Christ," Andrew Dunn points out.[236] Exposure to resources and spiritual practices which have proven helpful to other believers can be really beneficial for people who have been going to church for some time. Spiritual direction also affords the opportunity for people to talk about the resources and practices they have come across themselves and are wondering about. Tony (56) observed that spiritual direction provides space for "tentative exploration." He told me that he sometimes suggests to his directees, "Why don't you go away and try that, and let's talk about it next time?" Liz (Anglican priest, 55) also described spiritual direction as a context within which "a lot of people" in this life stage can have "great fun exploring things." She added, "And I am too! Often, when there are so many demands, that actually that chance to go in new directions, new places, permission-giving to have a bit of fun and to explore is really freeing."

Experiences of spiritual direction at midlife

A number of the churchgoers I interviewed had spoken to a spiritual director either on a short-term basis (perhaps once or twice when attending a retreat) or over a sustained period. All of those who had received spiritual direction felt that it had been beneficial to them, particularly during times of transition, but not all had the opportunity or the inclination to attend spiritual direction on an ongoing basis. Some felt that attending spiritual direction was useful for a short time or under certain circumstances. Other interviewees had never heard of the ministry of spiritual direction.

Linda (Anglican, 58) was one of a handful of interviewees who attended spiritual direction regularly. Linda has a paid position in her parish and she attends both spiritual direction and supervision. Given her work role, Linda considers attending spiritual direction to be "vital." She explained why. First, Linda distinguished between the relationships she had with what she called her "sister-type friends" and her experience of spiritual direction. "The soul friends, the sister friends, it is listening to both (not just you sitting doing the whole talking) and being a little bit more discerning and not coming in with your own story." She added, with enthusiasm, "In spiritual direction you've got the floor!" Linda then told me that spiritual direction provides a place where she can share the "intensity and the depth of the layers" that can happen within four weeks, between visits, and feel totally safe. She concluded, "I could not do the job without it."

Many people who hold positions of responsibility, especially within the church, appreciate the safe space that spiritual direction provides for them to talk about whatever they wish. Others are simply grateful to find a context within which someone is willing and able to give them their undivided attention. Raewyn (Presbyterian, 47) attends spiritual direction regularly. I asked her if she could explain, in general terms, how the experience of spiritual direction had been of use to her. She said:

> The thing that I have enjoyed has been – this sounds a bit selfish, but – is time to talk with someone about different thoughts and issues. To have someone just to give their time up to listen to me is just amazing. I haven't had that before, so that's been quite, yeah, precious. *[There was a long pause before Raewyn continued.]* It's a bit of an anchor, really. Sometimes I might think, "Am I silly thinking that?" or "Is that dumb?" It helps clarify things a bit, talking to someone else, 'cause I don't tend to do that. Yeah.

Later in her interview Raewyn said, "I do find that it really is quite grounding to have a wiser person to talk to." She expanded on her response, saying, "She's good because, like, she challenges me if she thinks I'm being, you know, stupid." Raewyn laughed, then added, "She doesn't say that, but you know! It's good. I appreciate that."

Judith (Catholic, 60) has received spiritual direction for over 20 years. This has sometimes occurred through letters rather than in face-to-face meetings. Judith said that spiritual direction had been invaluable in helping her to understand an Ignatian approach to discernment, in identifying "consolation and desolation" and preventing "emotional derailment" at times – "in a lovely way" – and in "encouraging prayerfulness and hanging on to Christ in the storm." Spiritual direction helped Judith through some very rocky times in her marriage. Judith also identified some of the forms of Catholic spirituality she was introduced to through spiritual direction as being "life-giving" for her. When asked for suggestions about further support that could be offered to people in midlife,

Judith reflected on the role professionals might play in facilitating support groups for people navigating midlife issues. She said, "Probably if there'd been a support group like that, not aimless, but with an actual facilitator, I think I probably might have gone to something like that." But Judith then said that actually one-to-one spiritual direction was what she had needed more than a group. In addition to receiving spiritual direction Judith went to "a tiny bit of counselling" and probably would have gone to more if she'd had more money. Judith pointed out that counselling, including marriage counselling, can be very helpful but is not accessible to all.

Cost can certainly be a factor preventing people seeking counselling or spiritual direction, and this was an issue that was also mentioned by both spiritual directors and clergy. Another difficulty can be that people do not know very much about spiritual direction, let alone how to find a spiritual director that they feel is suitable.[237] Nina (43), who attends an evangelical-charismatic Anglican church, raised both of these issues as she described her experience of spiritual direction, which she had attended for a period during her 30s. Nina told me that she felt blessed that she had been able to afford to attend spiritual direction, especially as her spiritual director was female when (at the time) all the members of her church's leadership team were male. She was glad that she had an older woman she could talk with, but said, "It kind of saddened me that I had to pay for it." She added that she would have appreciated having someone available at church to talk to occasionally. Later in her interview Nina told me that she was "so shocked" to mention spiritual direction to people at church, only to find that they had never heard of it. "I had just taken it for granted that everyone knew," she said. Nina added that when she talked about silent retreats people were quite interested in them and were curious about what happened there, but when she talked about spiritual direction "the conversation ended shorter!"

One aspect of spiritual direction that Nina particularly valued was that her director was willing to challenge her about some of her thinking about God. Nina said, "I really appreciated being challenged, because no-one else would really challenge me, actually, in the church setting." Nina felt that, "In church we don't want to offend someone, or we don't know how to challenge someone in a way that is respectful and loving. We don't necessarily see that modelled." Nina was happy to have that happen in the context of spiritual direction, where she was talking with someone she trusted.

It is not only what happens during the time of spiritual direction that can be helpful. The preparation that people may make beforehand and the reflection that occurs afterwards can also be significant, as both Jane and Richard pointed out. For Jane (Anglican, 55), attending spiritual direction is a fairly new experience. She told me that she had initially found it difficult to work out what it was that she was supposed to talk about to her spiritual director. But Jane now appreciates having "somebody asking the fairly searching questions" that she otherwise "could just coast along and might not reflect on very much." She said:

> I think it's helpful. I feel like it's taken me a bit of time to get comfortable with, but I find it good to have the accountability as much as anything, really. If I know I'm going to talk to someone in a few weeks then that motivates me to be thinking.

For Richard (Catholic, 48) a "very basic question" of spiritual direction is, "Where is God in this stuff that's happening here?" He considered that to be "a very good question." Richard told me that he found attending spiritual direction and the reflection that happened afterwards really helpful "because it's hard to see God at times."

Although a number of the middle-aged churchgoers I interviewed had some awareness or experience of spiritual direction it remains the case that in many New Zealand churches the ministry of spiritual direction is neither widely known nor very well understood. Tony (spiritual director, 56) felt that spiritual direction somehow needs to be "normalised" so that people can say "of course" they are attending spiritual direction:

> The more ministers, pastors and priests that have experienced it, the more likely they are to talk freely about it, and to offer it, or train for it, or encourage it in their second or third level leaders, and just ordinary folk of the churches. That would be wonderful. ... If it's seen as part of discipleship for people who've been around for a while then I think that would benefit a lot.

Elements of spiritual direction that can appeal to Christians in midlife

- ❖ Someone will listen!
- ❖ The listener is not directly involved (in my church or work or relationships)
- ❖ Confidentiality
- ❖ A sense that this time and space, set apart, is holy – God is present
- ❖ I am helped to discern God's presence in my life
- ❖ Accountability
- ❖ I feel supported during transitions in life or faith
- ❖ My confidence to face difficult issues is increased
- ❖ I am encouraged and helped to explore different forms of prayer

- ❖ I can raise questions I might not talk about elsewhere
- ❖ I may be introduced to resources which are relevant and useful to me
- ❖ Replenishment
- ❖ Preparing for my appointment is a helpful process in itself
- ❖ Reflection on what arises at spiritual direction contributes to my faith development
- ❖ Someone remembers my story and can remind me of God's faithfulness in the past
- ❖ Challenge

Many Christians who have "been around for a while" – namely those who are in midlife or older – clearly find it helpful to speak to someone in confidence about their spiritual life. However, spiritual direction does not appeal to everyone. Several of the midlife churchgoers I interviewed who had heard about spiritual direction were dubious about its value and its applicability to them. Grant (Presbyterian, 55) said, "It's not part of my make-up really." He told me that if he had something he needed or wanted to talk about he would go and see his minister or a member of the pastoral team, or one of the men in the parish that he knows well. Debbie (Catholic, 51) has never attended spiritual direction. She knows people who do go to spiritual direction but she told me that as she shares everything with her close women friends she can't understand the need to speak to someone else.

Given the limited accessibility of spiritual directors and the demands already placed upon clergy, it is important that individuals within congregations can turn to one another and be heard. Being able to talk about our questions can strengthen our faith during times of disequilibrium. Sharing the anxieties of parenting, or the sense of inadequacy and grief that may be part of caring for a sick spouse or a frail parent, or the pressures of work, and/or many other situations that are part of midlife experience, lightens heavy burdens. It is also wonderful to be able to share moments of joy and discovery and achievement. Debbie explained, "All of the questions to do with the big changes in our lives, when you can talk to someone else about it – it helps."

In endeavouring both to support church members and to extend God's love to others in our communities, churches can be very busy places. Running an activity or programme can sometimes feel more constructive than sitting quietly listening to someone speak about their life and faith. But Thomas Hart, who teaches theology at Seattle University and is a therapist in private practice, writes, "There is probably no service we can render other persons quite as great or important as to be a listener and receiver to them in those moments when they need to open their hearts and tell someone their story."[238] Upon his retirement, Michael Mayne, the former Dean of Westminster, identified "six great truths" he had learned from a handful of people who had influenced his ministry. Mayne admitted that he was slow to learn the lesson of "the value of silence and the need for inner space" but he had come to realise that "what people need of their clergy most of all (in the midst of our busy lives) is stillness and the readiness to listen."[239]

Henri Nouwen describes listening as "a form of spiritual hospitality" which allows those who are listened to "to start feeling accepted, start taking their words more seriously and discovering their own true selves."[240] It has certainly been my observation (and experience) that when people within the church really listen, churchgoers in midlife feel valued and well supported.

Questions for reflection or discussion

1. In this chapter, did any of the interviewees' stories or comments particularly resonate with you? Did any surprise you? Why?

2. Can you recall a time when you received meaningful support or guidance from someone (or from a group of people) within your church?

    • What was that like for you?

    • What did that person (or group) do?

    • Why or how was that helpful to you?

    • What might you learn from that?

3. Do you perceive that there is a "discipleship gap" for people in midlife in your own church? Does this matter? If so, what ideas raised in this chapter might you or your congregation begin to explore?

4. What might you like to pray about, or act upon?

Recommended resources

Dunn, Andrew. "Spiritual Direction." *Candour: News and Views for Ministers* (February 2011): 17-20. <https://www.presbyterian.org. nz/sites/default/files/candour/Candour_February_2010.pdf> (23 May 2020).

Hart, Thomas N. *The Art of Christian Listening.* Mahwah, New Jersey: Paulist Press, 1980.

Maccaulay, Martin. "Take it Personally – Discipleship as Personal Interaction rather than Programme." *Candour: News and Views for Ministers* (April 2011): 10-11. <http://presbyterian.org.nz/sites/default/files/publications/candour/Candour_Apr_2011_lo-res.pdf> (28 May 2017).

Andrew Pritchard, "Fowler, Faith and Fallout," *Reality Magazine*, Issue 33 (1999) <http://www.reality.org.nz/articles/33/33-pritchard.html> (18 March 2014).

_____ "Your Church's Personality," *Reality Magazine*, Issue 45 (2001) https://www.reality.org.nz/articles/45/45-pritchard.php

Studzinski, Raymond. *Spiritual Direction and Midlife Development.* Loyola University Press, Chicago, 1985.

7 — Two case studies

We need laypeople who are formed well, who are animated by a clear and sincere faith, whose lives have been touched by a personal and merciful encounter with the love of Jesus Christ. We need lay people who take risks, who soil their hands, who are not afraid of making mistakes, who move forward. ... And we need laypeople with a taste of the experience of life, who dare to dream.

Pope Francis[241]

As I visited churches in Auckland, Christchurch and Dunedin, I came across a number of programmes that were offering meaningful support to Christians in midlife. This chapter focuses on two such programmes. I have chosen to describe these two because although they are in many ways quite dissimilar they share some features which contribute to their appeal and to their effectiveness for people in this stage of life. The interviewees who had were leading these programmes – Hamish Galloway (Presbyterian minister and Moderator of the General Assembly of the Presbyterian Church of Aotearoa New Zealand) and Kevin Gallagher (a lay-person who is a member of the leadership team of Ignatian Spirituality NZ) – have agreed that I may use their real names in this chapter.

The first initiative was conceived and offered within a large Presbyterian church in response to the perceived needs of parishioners approaching retirement. Individuals participating in this programme received education, training and one-to-one support as they reflected on the transitions of late midlife, explored their gifts and considered how they could continue to grow in faith and in service of others. This project was specifically targeted at churchgoers in late midlife.

The second programme might be described as "tried and true," as it was based on spiritual practices that were modelled and taught by Ignatius of Loyola approximately five hundred years ago and which have been replicated and developed by others ever since. As we noted in Chapter 5, "retreats in daily life," adapted for a modern context, are now used in a number of Catholic parishes in New Zealand. Demand for them is increasing. Although these retreats are open to people of all ages a lot of people who attend them are in midlife.

I would like to emphasise that these two case studies are included not so that others may replicate these programmes but to illustrate that it is possible for churches to respond to the needs of their midlife members in quite different but equally effective ways. One size does not fit all. Individual Christians will be attracted to different sorts of opportunities for spiritual formation according to taste and temperament, life and faith experience, and personal circumstances.

The Moses Project

The Moses Project began in a large and rapidly-growing evangelical Presbyterian church. The programme was targeted at parishioners who were moving towards retirement and those who had recently retired. At the time I conducted interviews with the founder of the programme, Hamish Galloway, and with four churchgoers who had participated in it, approximately 40 people had been involved in the project. Most of the participants had been in their 60s. The programme was first offered in 2011 and with some modifications was run twice more over the following five years.

At this point I should acknowledge that since researching the Moses Project I have shared in developing and offering another programme, with Hamish Galloway, within the wider Presbyterian Church of Aotearoa New Zealand. The Pathways programme (as it has now become) differs in content and is broader in scope – it is not targeted at specific age group as the Moses Project was, for example – but it shares some similar aims and is run in a similar way. At the time of the interviews cited in this chapter, though, I had no personal connection with the Moses Project and I knew none of the leaders or participants within it.

The inspiration for the Moses Project arose from three sources, as Hamish explained:

> The ultimate inspiration was one day when I was biking back to church and thinking about the sermon for Sunday, which was around Moses's call, and the fact that he was 80 at the time. And [I was] just thinking about how many people we've got in church who are at that phase in life where they are just transitioning towards retirement. They're going to have a lot more discretionary time on their hands. What can we do for them to help them continue to

grow in their faith and to serve well? So that was one thing. That was kind of an inspirational moment.

Hamish had also been teaching a course which included a module on Erikson's theories of human development. Erikson's description of the tension between generativity and stagnation at midlife intrigued Hamish and prompted him to reflect on how Christians in late midlife could be more helpfully encouraged and equipped to serve. At about the same time he came across the research conducted by Willow Creek Community Church[242] (referred to in the previous chapter) which revealed that mature believers might be seeking greater challenge and guidance and accountability in their faith. Hamish decided to implement a "pretty simple little project" to engage with people around retirement age.

Although the project has evolved over the years its essential components have remained the same. After the programme has been advertised, and individuals have also been approached and encouraged to attend, a member of the leadership team meets with each parishioner who has expressed interest in participating. At this interview the project is explained to them and people have the opportunity to talk about their own situation. Next a day-long workshop, led by several members of the church's leadership team, is held. Hamish described the workshop:

> There's a wee bit of homework for them to do before it. We give them a spiritual gifts survey. We get them to do the *StrengthsFinder* programme.[243] We pay half of that. They pay the other half. And then we talk about that – how they're wired to serve. We have a session on transitions. They love that. Where are you at now? What does the next five years look like for you? And we talk about how they're going spiritually. What's helping them to grow, where are they stagnating, what do they need? So that's the day workshop.

Following the workshop each participant has "a one-on-one debrief and follow up regarding next steps" with Hamish (or occasionally another member of the leadership team). Notes from the conversation are later sent to the participant. This follow-up interview provides participants with the opportunity to speak in a confidential environment with the senior pastor of the church about their strengths, gifts, passions and personality, and to consider opportunities for meaningful service within and beyond the church. Not everyone who participated in the Moses Project chose to engage in further voluntary service, but those who did offer to contribute their time and talents to the work of the church did so in wide-ranging fields. One gardened for the church and propagated plants for parishioners, another served as an "area pastor" caring for church members who did not belong to any of the small groups within the parish, someone else offered transport for isolated people in the community who attend a mid-week church service and morning tea, and another connected with a group for people with intellectual disabilities. It was clear that participants who offered their services in these ways felt that in doing so their gifts and talents were recognised. They were not being coerced into undertaking roles that were too onerous or were outside their field of expertise or interest. Those who did take up new forms of service were really enthusiastic about the things they chose to do.

A key element of the follow-up interview was that participants were able to talk about what was happening for them spiritually. They were encouraged to explore and build on specific spiritual practices that could enable them to continue to grow in faith. A number of participants already had established rhythms of prayer and Bible study and they were affirmed in what they were doing and encouraged to continue these practices. A number of those involved in the project had gone on to do courses in theology beyond the church. A few joined groups within the church. At least one person signed up to go on a retreat. I asked Hamish if people were keen to participate in the follow-up interviews. He said:

> People really appreciated it. They felt like it was relevant, really focused pastoral care. "Someone's interested in me." And from my perspective, while going and having a cup of tea with someone and talking about how they are in general terms, and how their family is, is fine, sometimes you think, "What am I really achieving here, other than being a friendly face?" This is very focused in key areas of Christian discipleship and spiritual formation – which should be the focus of pastoral care.

Several months after the day-long workshop, Hamish was intending to go back over the notes from follow-up interviews with people who had attended the third course so that he could "get a feel for where they are up to now, and encourage them to keep going with it."

The first iteration of the Moses Project differed quite markedly from its successors because its focus was very much on equipping people to use their gifts and life experience as volunteers within the church, and those who chose to take on voluntary roles signed a formal contract. Later this group also had some follow-up meetings that included further training. The feedback Hamish received from the first group indicated that this approach was too structured for some people. The programme was adapted accordingly. But Penny, who was (at the age of 68) a participant in the first programme, told me that she liked the formality of the process she had to go through. She explained that to be accepted she had to fill in an application form and attend an interview. "It gave it an official standing, which I liked." Penny missed attending the initial workshop but she did complete the *StrengthsFinder* programme, which she found very helpful. She also had a meeting with a *StrengthsFinder* coach and on the coach's recommendation read some books in the church library. Penny felt empowered and supported as she took on an unpaid pastoral care position in the parish.

Four key elements of the Moses Project particularly appealed to Penny. First, she liked meeting with other people in the same age bracket who had similar goals. She said that this gave her a sense of "comradeship, unity and purpose-sharing." She also liked hearing about what other people were doing. She pointed out, "It's so easy to do voluntary work and be isolated. With the Project Moses team you weren't isolated." Second, Penny appreciated the fact that participants in the project did not all have to do the same things but could choose what they wanted to take on. As she put it, "It's an area of service, but there are lots of strands within it." Third, once Penny had agreed to take on the pastoral care role she was offered regular supervision. Her supervision meetings followed a format suggested by Hamish. Penny told me she was asked questions like, "How's it been going? What's been good? What are you concerned about? And how's your walk with God?" Penny really appreciated meeting with a supervisor. She said, "I think it's kept me accountable." Finally, Penny said that she liked having a three-year contract. "I'm not sure that a contract was necessary," she admitted, but she felt that having a contract made clear what the responsibilities were on both sides. She said, "The volunteer is contracting to do this, but the church is contracting to support the volunteer in that. I think I liked that, because it was formal." At the time of her interview with me it had been more than three years since Penny had signed up to be part of the Moses Project. She no longer had a formal contract but was still working in the pastoral role for which she had volunteered.

Christine (65) was a member of the third group to participate in the Moses Project. Her experience of the programme was in many ways quite different from Penny's. Christine had been retired for one month when the opportunity to participate in the Moses Project arose. She explained that the opportunity was particularly timely for her because she had retired more suddenly than she had expected and she thought she might be "floundering a bit" being at home full time. She was attracted to the course because "it sounded as though it was going to give you some direction." She also liked the idea of being in a group of people who were in a similar stage of life to herself.

Christine gained a lot from attending the initial workshop. She liked the fact that it was offered over a full day as she thought it would lose continuity if it were broken into two. She also felt that having four people presenting different sessions during the day was helpful because they were "coming from different angles, and different backgrounds and perspectives." Christine was particularly struck by some key metaphors used by presenters and she referred to these at a number of points during her interview. For example:

> We talked about being a tree growing and that's never going to stop growing. Because sometimes you do think, "Well, I've done everything, I've been everywhere, there's nothing more for me to do," but when you think about that [the image of the tree] it was, for me, a really good analogy. You keep growing. You don't stop.

For Christine, the session entitled "Exploring Transitions in Your Stage of Life" was particularly meaningful. Project Moses participants were invited to look at where they were financially, emotionally and spiritually. Christine found this part "really good." She said, "It really made me look at where I was at, and what I could do to build more on the spiritual side of things now that I had time on my hands." The whole day helped Christine to reflect on her life experiences and to understand that she could sometimes share with others what she had learned from them. She told me that she had come to realise that she was "not useless" but had "lots of things to be able to give." At the workshop Christine also appreciated hearing about why other people were there, what they had done, and where they thought they were going. She said, "Everybody all felt that they still needed to grow spiritually, which was a really good thing to hear. A really good thing to hear."

Christine had not realised that the Moses Project participants would be encouraged to have a follow-up interview with one of the four leaders and she was initially nervous about this prospect. But the follow-up interview turned out to be a very positive and helpful experience. Christine liked having three weeks prior to the interview so that she could go over the course notes and reflect on what she wanted to talk about. She identified that she would like to read the Bible more and become more involved in prayer. When she met with the leader, Christine was asked what help she needed and she was provided with some relevant resources. Christine had been putting off joining a prayer group despite being asked to go along a few times by a friend. She said, "I hesitated to go, because I don't know what they do; I don't know if I will say the right thing." She discussed this in the follow-up interview and with the leader's encouragement she decided that she would attend. As she explained, "It gave me the confidence to go, and if I don't like it I can go, 'This is not for me.'" Christine said, "And then I found that I actually really enjoy going to the group. … And a couple of others who were at the prayer group did the Moses Project too. So I felt like, yeah, coming home!" Christine told me she was really looking forward to having another appointment with the same leader from the Moses Project, six months after her first follow-up interview.

I asked Christine what the outcomes from the Moses Project had been for her. She said:

> For me, it's been that I now look forward. And I know that where I am now is because of what happened in my past, but I want to continue growing. It's made me much more aware of my spirituality and how I can grow that. And I can enjoy it. And it's OK to take time to be me. I don't have to be rushing around doing things. … I learned, you know, that, yep, you're always forever growing and you've just got to take it slowly. You don't have to get there tomorrow. *[She laughs.]*

Owen (71) had participated in the Moses Project at the same time as Christine. When I went to visit him I discovered that his wife, Eleanor (71) had also been involved in the programme. Owen and Eleanor were happy to be interviewed together. A dominant theme in Owen's feedback about the project was that at no stage had he or Eleanor felt under any pressure to do anything beyond "just coming and taking part and seeing." During the interview it emerged that both Owen and Eleanor had become exhausted after being "over-active" in a small parish to which they had previously belonged. Eleanor said, "We sort of felt like we did everything. We were absolutely worn out by the time we left. That's one of the reasons why we left. So we decided we'd just sit quietly and wait until we were approached – if we were – before we offered to do anything." They decided to take a year's break from taking on any responsibilities at their new church, and, as Eleanor put it, they "just sat back and enjoyed being people, as it were, with nothing else to do." But by the time the Moses Project came up they were ready to get involved again. Eleanor said, "The timing was perfect for us."

Owen and Eleanor both enjoyed the day workshop. Owen liked participating in a small discussion group at regular intervals throughout the day. He observed, "They seemed to go very well because they had to call the participants back from the groups, so they were obviously well received. People contributed to them rather than having to stand up in the whole meeting." Once again he noted, "There was no pressure. You could contribute as little or as much as you wanted, as time allowed." Eleanor commented on the fact that everyone who attended was encouraged to think about service in terms of what they were passionate about. "What you are passionate about is where you should be serving. That was the thing that I appreciated most." Neither Owen nor Eleanor saw any need to complete the *StrengthsFinder* course which was offered within the programme and there was no pressure for them to do so.

By far the most important component of the Moses Project, from Owen and Eleanor's perspective, was the follow-up interview they had with Hamish two or three weeks later. Hamish spent a morning with Owen and Eleanor and "talked through a lot of stuff" with them. He made notes and then emailed back to them what they had talked about. Eleanor found this "very helpful, personally." She said, "We've got a copy of what he sent through to us, which is great. He'd taken a lot of time and trouble over it." Owen said:

> It was important because it was one-to-one. You were able
> to share what was on your heart. The other thing that I was

impressed with was here was the senior pastor of a church with a thousand members taking time to come and talk to us. And it made you feel, well, important, I s'pose. And he'd obviously done his homework before he came. That was really encouraging. And then the fact that he emailed the feedback.

Eleanor agreed:

And he made sure it was correct. He didn't just type stuff into his computer while he was sitting there talking to us. He would say it back to us to make sure that he got it right. It was good. And I think if we hadn't had that, we might have just walked away and said, "Oh, that was a nice programme," and then not done anything else about it. But he spent a long time with us, more time than we expected. It was a couple of hours. He was very thorough.

Owen then explained that as a result of the Moses Project he and Eleanor had decided to take on two roles within the parish. Or, as Owen expressed it, "We got two jobs out of it!" They are now sharing leadership of a home group with another couple and assisting with prayer ministry. Owen considers that these jobs are "not overly burdensome." He added, "The things we have been given to do are our passions. There's nothing more disheartening than being asked to do something that's really not your passion, and you do it because nobody else will. But if it's your passion it's not really onerous." Owen and Eleanor have now met a lot of people also involved in similar ministries. Both feel very committed to the parish. Eleanor said, "I believe the more you are invested in something the more you take ownership of it. As far as going to the services go, we wouldn't miss it."

Later in this chapter we will reflect further on the Moses Project and consider specific aspects of the project which are helpful for people in midlife. We now turn to a programme which is quite different from the Moses Project – both in its focus and its delivery – but is also proving to be beneficial to Christians who have been journeying in faith for some time.

Ignatian Retreats in Daily Life

Retreats in daily life are not new. They have been offered in various forms for many years. One format of retreats of this type is that participants meet initially in a group for a day or part of a day, commit to a programme of individual prayer throughout a week, then meet again with others a week later. Often the opportunity for retreatants to meet daily with a spiritual director is offered. This form of retreat in daily life is popular throughout the world. Such retreats can provide very helpful guidance and encouragement for individuals, some of whom may never have had the opportunity to speak one-to-one with someone about their experiences of prayer. But for many people it is quite a big commitment to go to see a spiritual director every day for a week, and some may find doing so in an unfamiliar environment quite daunting.

With the support of a team of trained spiritual directors, Kevin Gallagher has been leading retreats in daily life in Catholic parishes for several years. Some take place over one week and include several opportunities for groups to meet in person or via Zoom. In the retreat described in this chapter, though, members of a particular congregation met together at their own church one evening a week over five weeks. Kevin explained what happened on each of the five evenings attendees met. Participants were led through an experience of guided prayer based on a Scripture passage and provided with some quiet time to reflect on that experience. Some people chose to write in a journal during this time. They then moved into small groups, each of which was guided by a spiritual director. In these groups each person had an opportunity to share for a few minutes while others listened without commenting, and after everyone who wished to speak had done so, "spiritual conversation" (discussion of points that had arisen) could occur. In Kevin's experience, this process works well. Everyone came back together for half an hour at the end of the evening and they could share a word or image for their experience if they wished to. "It's like a review," explained Kevin. He continued:

> We keep to that pedagogy of the context of people's daily life, the preparation and the led experience, the reflection on the experience (in several levels, like their personal reflection, their writing, their sharing, their listening) and then an evaluation. And then there's the action. How's this going to impact on my relationships in my life? How's it going to impact on my life? What is it calling me into?

Retreat participants were also provided with materials to pray with during the week. In some cases they were encouraged to use symbols such as soil and water as part of their prayer, but the main focus was on praying with Scripture. Kevin ended his description of the retreats by saying, "We don't preach. We don't tell people how to pray. It's experience-focused learning, commonly known as the active-reflective process of adult learning. The way the retreat's run leaves room for everybody to be different. Your relationship with God is unique."

At the time I interviewed Kevin, he and his team had offered three themed retreats based on a book by Michael Hansen, *The First Spiritual Exercises*: "Inner Peace in Divine Love," "Inner Peace in Darkness and Light," and "Inner Peace in Friendship with Jesus."[244] However, the form of retreat described in this chapter is not dependent on the use of any particular text. Over time Kevin has adapted and simplified Hansen's suggestions for prayer and has also offered retreats on a range of other themes. In one year Kevin's team led five retreats in five Catholic parishes. Most retreats accommodated 30 to 40 people, but in at least one instance the number attending was closer to 80. Kevin said:

> I am completely amazed at the hunger. What I'm finding is that there's a desire for people – a real, earnest, sincere desire for people – to discover meaning and purpose in their lives. ... Where does that hunger come from? Well, the hunger I believe comes from God, it comes from the Spirit. And people's own search. Somehow in parishes in this time, this is meeting that hunger, for some people.

I asked Kevin what proportion of those attending would be in midlife. Reflecting on the retreat he was leading at the time of his interview, Kevin estimated that the youngest participant would be about 40, about 50-60% would be aged between 50 and 65, and over 25% would be older than 65. Kevin observed that people in midlife seemed particularly affected by the retreat experience because they were "really searching." People in this age group were also often very committed to following the daily pattern of prayer that was suggested.

According to Kevin, several kinds of "fruit" are emerging from the retreats in daily life. First, participants are discovering new ways of praying. They are opened to not just "saying prayers" but allowing Scripture to speak to them and to take them into a deeper relationship with God. Second, people are sharing their faith with one another. Each week, in the confidential context of their small groups, people share openly with others about what is happening for them in prayer. Kevin said:

> That is a major one in our Catholic communities because quite often on a Sunday we'll go to Mass, we'll say a quick hello to people as we go out, and it's not that *usual* for us to share our faith with each other. When that happens it deepens communal life extraordinarily. It helps people know what's going on in other people's lives. It helps them to support each other.

Third, in some churches small groups are formed after the retreats so that those who wish to do so can continue to meet regularly. "Christian Life Communities"[245] and other comparable groups use Ignatian-based texts[246] and follow a similar pattern of reflection and discussion to that used in the short retreats. Kevin believes these groups "satisfy something of their desire for community and desire for help with their own prayer journey." Fourth, parish retreats provide "an access point" for individuals to explore longer retreats of three, six or eight days. Some may also choose to work through the Ignatian Spiritual Exercises in daily life over a number of months. Others are attracted to retreats that are available on-line.

I interviewed two women and one man who had been involved in one of the retreats led by Kevin's team. Each had benefited in some way from participating in the retreat but their perspectives on their experience were quite different. Some elements of the programme that appealed strongly to one interviewee proved problematic for another. Even aspects of the retreat that all three interviewees appreciated were helpful to them for different reasons.

Anna (41) attended the Ignatian retreat entitled "Inner Peace in Friendship with Jesus." She had mixed feelings about the experience as although she found some of the content of the retreat confronting she also felt that the retreat helped her to establish some close relationships and develop skills of enduring value. She described aspects of the experience as "empowering" but told me that she would be unlikely to do the same kind of retreat again. Anna explained what the retreat involved:

> You went along on Tuesday night for a couple of hours. They started with some prayer. They took you through imaginative prayer. So you had to imagine yourself within

the gospel. That was very lovely. They often had reflective music and down time. They encouraged you to keep a little diary in a small booklet, if you wished to. After that they then did small group work. It was the same five or six people in the small group each week, and you discussed anything around your diary, how your prayer went for that week, anything else that came up. There was a very good emphasis on listening to the speaker and not being able to say anything. And then at the end of that I think there was a little bit more prayer time, and then you went home.

They also gave you a handout each Tuesday which extended for the next week and showed you what to do for your prayer every night – around about 30 minutes. It took you through step-by-step the gospel, some reflective time, writing in your diary, and then usually an activity. For example, the first activity was go outside and get some dirt from your garden and then sit there and think about it. Yeah. And then there was a little bit from a retreat book. It sounds like a lot but it wasn't really. And you had Sunday or Monday off. It was the same pretty much every time for those number of weeks.

Anna (who has a young child) admitted that during the five-week retreat she only managed to pray for the suggested time of half an hour once, but she didn't feel pressured to try to meet that time. She also told me that some of the written reflections after the gospel reading didn't sit well with her. She disagreed with some and felt they "weren't very Catholic." She only wrote in her diary a few times. What drew Anna back to the retreat gatherings each week was her small group, which she loved. She described the group as "nice and gentle" and "respectful." There were two aspects of the group experience which Anna dwelt on in her interview. The first was the listening process which group members were taught. The second was the depth of sharing that occurred within the group.

The groups were taught to listen attentively to every individual who wished to speak, in turn, before anyone offered any comments or feedback. The leader would thank each person who spoke and then it was somebody else's turn, if they wanted to speak. Discussion only occurred after everyone had shared. Anna was disarmingly frank about finding this a challenge. She said, "That's actually really hard to do! Because you want to butt in and say, 'Oh, I've got a relatable story. And I'm going to tell you right now!'"

Anna laughed, then added, "And we all tend to want to do that." The members of Anna's group had discussed the listening process among themselves and all had agreed that they found it a valuable learning experience. Anna told me that she has been trying to carry on that sort of listening in her daily life.

Other aspects of the small group experience touched Anna, too:

> It was lovely. I really really enjoyed that. Just the sharing. ... It was interesting, everybody came with quite a deep and sad or profound thing that had happened to them in their life, and we were all able to share that. And through that you sort of thought, you know, "It's not just me." Sometimes you get into your own little bubble and this has happened to you and it's awful and terrible, but actually everyone's got a little story. And I think that was valuable.

After the retreat had ended Anna would have liked to have continued to meet with her small group (all of whom were women) for a little bit longer. Some other retreat participants did form a prayer group which is continuing to meet regularly.

Anna had previously belonged to a *Lectio Divina* group, and she had attended other retreats, including a women's retreat and a marriage retreat, which she enjoyed more than this Ignatian retreat. Although she could do the imaginative activities she did not think it likely that she would continue with that kind of prayer. She said, "It was not up my alley." Nor did she find the use of symbolic items during the retreat helpful. These were a bit too "fluffy" for her. "I'm not that kind of person," Anna said. "I'm a bit more black-and-white. But I know there was another person who loved it." Anna felt sure that in attending the retreat "everyone would have found something that they enjoyed or took something from." She reiterated that the main thing that stood out for her from the retreat was the experience of listening in a very focused way. "I'm trying to take better listening skills out of it," she said. Attending the retreat had also prompted Anna to think about returning to her former prayer practice of *Lectio Divina* which she had found so helpful.

For Kay (62) "Inner Peace in Friendship with Jesus" was the second experience of an Ignatian retreat in daily life. She described these retreats as "an amazing way of deepening your faith, of exploring your personal faith and where you are at with God." As I had done with Anna, I asked Kay to tell me what the retreat involved.

Naturally most of Kay's description of what occurred was very similar to Anna's, but the differences were striking.

Kay began by describing a "guided relaxation" which Kevin led at the start of each evening to help people to become aware of God's presence. "And after that he would allow a time of silence, which was lovely. And you just quietened right down," she said. On each evening there was also a physical element to consider – Kay mentioned a lit candle, stones, and water – which represented the theme of that week's session. Kay then described the Bible reading, the time of reflection, and the small group discussions, all of which Anna had mentioned, and which Kay also enjoyed. But for Kay one of the most meaningful aspects of each evening occurred towards the end, when the whole group was present. The element which had provided a focus for prayer at the start of the session was passed around. She explained:

> So, if it was water, we were invited to wash our hands. One that stood out to me was oil. We were asked to anoint each other's hands and say a prayer over that person, and then pass it on. That was really lovely. *[She pauses.]* It was something concrete. I like my symbols and things. That spoke to me very strongly.

The use of physical symbols was also important to Kay as she prayed during the week. The theme of the first week of the retreat had been creation. For Kay, collecting a bowl of soil and contemplating it, in conjunction with the Bible readings, had been meaningful.

Another aspect of the retreat that Kay found particularly helpful at home was journalling after the time of reading and contemplation. She said:

> The journalling part's quite important – that you are actually capturing what's happening for you. ... My mind just goes every which way. Whereas when I come to journal, that's when it all comes out. That's when I find out what I've actually been contemplating! *[She laughs.]* It wasn't yesterday's lunch and it isn't tomorrow's washing! *[She laughs again.]* This is what I've actually been thinking about, or what God's been talking to me about.

Kay has prayed with Scripture on a daily basis for some decades and journalling is usually part of her devotional time. One result of attending the two Ignatian retreats in her parish is that Kay had chosen to undertake a 34-week Ignatian retreat on-line.[247]

The third participant in the Ignatian retreat that I interviewed was Peter (73). Peter and his wife had attended a shorter retreat run by some of the same team members before. They were glad to be able to attend another one partly because they knew some of the leaders and some of the other participants but primarily because they were "looking for more formation." Peter, who has been involved in the Catholic church and in the Catholic education system for most of his life, said:

> One of things we found going around, depending on what parish you're in and what diocese you're in, there wasn't a lot of ongoing adult formation in the Catholic church, not quite the same as there might be in some of the other churches, you know. And just "paying one's dues" *[Terry uses air quotes]* on a Sunday just doesn't cut it, so to speak. You know, if you're supposed to have a personal relationship with the Lord then you've got to have a personal relationship. So it was one of those things we wanted.

Peter also felt that other parishioners who attended were looking for the same thing. He and his wife wanted to meet with "like-minded people, all searching for something to carry on their adult formation."

Peter identified several aspects of the organisation of the programme that appealed to him. As he was still working part-time he appreciated the fact that the retreat was held during the evenings rather than during the day. He also considered that the programme was "well run." Peter commented specifically on the "very good" weekly notes that were issued:

> You had a weekly theme. You had sort of weekly homework. There were several readings from both the Old and the New Testament and you could concentrate on the ones that sort of vibrated with you, you know. Which is the one that catches your attention? Which is the one that you want to concentrate on?

Peter appreciated the discipline of having weekly homework but he did not always do all that was set. He told me that he felt under no pressure to do so. He said, "I'll do what I can do."

When I asked Peter what had stood out most for him from the retreat he identified several components that he considered were valuable both at the time and afterwards. First, he described the importance of the opening period of silent prayer at each of the evening gatherings. He said:

> I always liked the part where, you know, once you've come together, it's that quiet time. It's that grounding yourself. It's that remembering that you're always in God's presence. That he's looking at you, you know? That was really one of the things that came home. That it doesn't matter what time of the day or night it is, what sort of mood you're in, what sort of pressure you're under – you're here now.

Peter said that this aspect of the retreat had a flow-on impact for him because it has helped him to enter more readily into prayer when attending Eucharistic Adoration. He said, "That part *[of the Ignatian retreat]* certainly helped that grounding."

Second, Peter appreciated being able to participate in a small group during the retreat. He enjoyed "getting to know different people" and "listening to part of their life story, and what had brought them to it." He also valued the insights that others shared about the various readings and prayers. Peter said, "Just listening to what other people have got out of it you think, "I missed that! Wow! That's a new take on it."" After the retreat finished a prayer group was formed which Peter and his wife decided to attend:

> This is what I think we need within parishes. When you come together as several hundred people, yes, that's great, but you can't get to know all those people, and you can't share with all those people on a deeper level. That's why you need to come into smaller groups. And this was a good way of starting it off.

Finally, for Peter the retreat engendered optimism about the future. It provided guidance in forms of prayer – some of which, such as the prayer of *Examen*, he admitted he was still struggling with – and, as he had hoped, the retreat assisted and encouraged him in his ongoing formation as a follower of Christ. "That's what it was all about. It was opening yourself up to the possibilities of what God can still do in your life. Because he's not looking at you and saying, 'You're in your mid-70s, you should ...' No! You're just another one of the disciples."

Anna, Kay and Peter's experiences of "Inner Peace in Friendship with Jesus" differed markedly but each said that attending the retreat had been beneficial in some way. All felt that they had learned from the retreat and each spoke of forms of prayer they were committed to continue engaging in regularly. Kay and Peter were clearly more enthusiastic about the Ignatian retreat than Anna. At the conclusion of her interview Kay said, "I would really encourage anybody to do one because it opens a doorway. It opens a doorway for God to come in and show you bits of yourself that you had hidden away."

Retreats in daily life can be offered in a variety of ways. An on-line component can easily be incorporated into a retreat such as the one described here. Whether this involves individuals speaking to a group leader one-to-one, or group members participating in discussion together via Zoom, meeting virtually can be helpful for middle-aged participants who might otherwise find it difficult to incorporate a retreat into their daily lives.[248]

Points of commonality

The Moses Project and Ignatian retreats in daily life are programmes which differ in many obvious respects but it is in considering what they have in common that we may gain some very useful insights. By focusing less on the specific content of each, and more on the elements and outcomes which were of value to those who attended, churches may be enabled to develop other ways of engaging middle-aged members and supporting their spiritual development – ways that will be appropriate within their own contexts. The points that follow are numbered for ease of reference rather than to suggest a hierarchy of importance. In addition to the points explored here, other factors which helped the participants to benefit from these particular programmes could be considered.

1. *Each programme is focused on supporting individuals in their spiritual journey*

The leaders of the Moses Project and the Ignatian retreat in daily life were very intentional about wanting to help participants to deepen their relationship with God through prayer and through service. The programmes recognized differences in people's backgrounds and aspirations and celebrated the uniqueness of each person's spiritual journey. Flexibility within each programme allowed individuals to opt in or opt out of aspects which they did not feel were applicable to or appropriate for them. Participants also felt free to choose how they would apply what they had learned or experienced after the programmes had finished. Kevin, who led the Ignatian retreat, told me that he hoped that those who attended would be empowered "to get on with it themselves and see what God has got in store for them personally." Christine said of the Moses Project:

> The thing was they didn't actually say, well, you know, you can go and join this group to do this, or you can come to church and get involved in that. It wasn't about that. It was actually about you as a person, and your growth and your development. I'd thought that they maybe would have offered, you know, "Well we've got this group that needs somebody more to come along," or something, but I'm glad that they didn't because it would have detracted from the whole process, I feel. It was about each person as an individual, knowing that they could keep moving forward.

To be assured that "they could keep moving forward" had a profound impact on some of the participants, particularly those who were experiencing or anticipating significant transitions in midlife. Both programmes offered hope and a sense of direction to those who attended.

2. *Participants are helped to 'process' or reflect upon whatever arises for them during the project or retreat*

We know that a characteristic of midlife is that people need to be able to reflect on the meaning and significance of the activities that engage their energies and to take stock of where they have been and where they are going. Both the Moses Project and the Ignatian retreats provided opportunities for people to pause, to re-examine their lives and to renew their commitment to God. Author and educator Parker J. Palmer insists that "inner work" is as real as "outer work" and "involves skills one can develop, skills like journaling, reflective reading, spiritual friendship, meditation, and prayer."[249] Churchgoers attending the Moses Project and Ignatian retreats were offered opportunities to practise and develop some of these skills as they engaged in "inner work." Moreover, the structure of each programme implicitly recognised that inner work cannot be hurried. Participants in the Moses Project had several weeks to ponder and pray about what they might do or be involved in (if anything), prior to their follow-up meeting with a member of the church leadership team. Even then, no-one felt pressured to make decisions. Participants in the Ignatian retreats in daily life were guided through silent, spoken and written forms of prayer and reflection and provided with tools they could choose to use in private on an ongoing basis.

3. *The experience is shared with others*

Parker J. Palmer insists that "inner work, though it is a deeply *personal* matter, is not necessarily a *private* matter: inner work can be helped along in community. Indeed, doing inner work together is a vital counterpoint to doing it alone."[250] While the focus of the Moses Project and the Ignatian retreats was on individuals' ongoing spiritual development, participants in the programmes really valued the depth of the interactions they had with others. Respectful, attentive listening was a fundamental component of both programmes. Interviewees spoke from the heart when they told me how supported and valued they felt when others took the time to really listen to them. They also counted it a privilege to hear other people's stories. They drew comfort and encouragement from the realisation that they were not alone in some of their struggles or in their desire for continuing growth in the spiritual life. In the parishes where the Moses Project and the Ignatian retreats were offered the connections established between participants also had a flow-on effect in encouraging closer, genuinely supportive relationships between congregation members after the programmes had finished.

4. *The demands of each programme are not overly burdensome for participants or leaders*

Each programme ran over a finite (and fairly short) period and those who signed up were clear from the outset about the time commitment required. This was clearly appreciated by the midlife churchgoers and was a factor they considered before registering. Some people went on to commit more time to prayer, or to groups or voluntary service that emerged from the programmes, but no-one felt that they had to do so. None of the churchgoers I interviewed considered that the core demands of the programme they attended were unrealistic. Moreover, as they explained, each person was encouraged to complete activities they felt were of value to them rather than being made to feel that all activities were compulsory.

It is also worth noting that the leadership of each programme was shared, thus reducing the burden of responsibility to be shouldered by individual team members (a number of whom were also in midlife). The shared-leadership model was also appreciated by participants as they felt they benefited from the variety of attributes, expertise and life experiences the team members contributed.

In neither programme was cost a barrier to participation. Expenses were largely covered by the parishes involved, although a part charge was made to those who undertook the *StrengthsFinder* course as part of the Moses Project, and a small materials fee was paid by those who attended the Ignatian retreat in daily life.[251]

5. *Accountability can be helpful*

There were participants in both the Moses Project and the Ignatian retreat who told me that accountability to fellow group members or to the clergy or lay leaders involved in the programmes was a significant aspect of the programme for them. Penny, who was the only Moses Project interviewee who had signed a formal contract, relished the opportunity to attend supervision provided by the church once she was employed in a voluntary capacity as a pastoral worker. Kay, who participated in the Ignatian retreat, felt that following a guided programme of prayer, whether within the parish or on-line, boosted her confidence. She said:

> For me, I can't just do it by myself. I need someone to be showing me and guiding me. I've got to have a bit of a structure around it. I get lost in my own space. Mmm. That's probably a bit of fear, that I'm doing it wrong. So I like the comfort of knowing that I've got someone around me to point me in the right direction.

Their experiences serve to remind us that churchgoers of all ages benefit from sharing their spiritual journey with others who will help them to keep their eyes fixed on Jesus, "the pioneer and perfecter of our faith" (Heb 12:2).

Further thoughts to ponder

In Chapter 2 we noted one spiritual director's suggestion that in order to accommodate the needs of people who are dealing with the sorts of issues that can arise in the second half of life the church might need "*Beta* to go with *Alpha*." The Moses Project and Ignatian retreats in daily life may be considered *Beta-style* programmes. The impact of these programmes on many of the people who participated in them demonstrates that it is possible for parishes to offer intentional, meaningful support to parishioners in midlife who are seeking "something more" in their faith. There are, of course, other programmes that have similar objectives and sometimes include similar components.

These help participants by:

❖ providing them with time, tools and encouragement to reflect on "the religious dimension of experience"[252]

❖ celebrating God's unique relationship with every person

❖ emphasising that faith development is a life-long process

❖ inspiring and equipping people to engage in diverse forms of prayer or service

❖ strengthening relationships between Christians within congregations

While the Moses Project was designed to respond to the needs of churchgoers who were in a period of transition to retirement it has subsequently been adapted quite easily to cater for people in other age groups. This suggests that churches can provide support for middle-aged members alongside parishioners of other ages as long as programmes are flexible and do not require individuals "to go back in some box that they feel they can't go back into theologically or personally," as Matthew (spiritual director, 61) put it. Given the limited resources of most church communities, this is good news.

Growth in understanding, a deepening relationship with God, and increased willingness and capacity to care for others are gifts that many people hope and pray for. We have seen that development in these areas can occur when individuals are able to share their stories, learn from others, and receive encouragement and guidance as they set aside time for personal reflection and prayer.

Questions for reflection or discussion

1. In this chapter, did you identify with any of the interviewees' stories or comments? Did any surprise you? Why?

2. What elements of the programmes that were described in this chapter appealed to you? What elements did not appeal to you? Why?

3. What other programmes are you familiar with that offer support to Christians who have been journeying in faith for some time? Have you participated in any? What do you consider to be the most helpful components of these programmes?

4. What might you like to pray about, or act upon?

Recommended resources

Baab, Lynne. "Beating Burnout by Building Teams." *Congregations, Fall 2003*, 6-9. <https://www.lynnebaab.com/articles/beating-burnout-by-building-teams-> (10 June 2021).

Gallagher, Timothy M., *Meditation and Contemplation: An Ignatian Guide to Praying with Scripture*. New York: Crossroad Publishing, 2008.

IgnatianSpirituality.com. <http://www.ignatianspirituality.com> (12 June 2021).

8 — Observations and next steps

Lead us, heavenly Father, lead us
o'er the world's tempestuous sea;
guard us, guide us, keep us, feed us,
for we have no help but thee;
yet possessing every blessing,
if our God our Father be.

Hymn, James Edmeston (1791-1867)[253]

Throughout this book it has been my intention to raise more questions than I have attempted to answer. This approach is partly attributable to the fact that I am keenly aware of the limits of my knowledge and understanding, but also stems from my conviction that there is great value in sitting with questions which help us to make sense of our experience, values and beliefs. Without now diverging from this approach, in this short chapter I would like to draw together some of the key themes raised by the churchgoers, clergy and spiritual directors I interviewed, and suggest some next steps that individuals or congregations might wish to consider.

Churchgoers in midlife

The interviews I conducted with churchgoers aged between 40 and 60 confirmed that midlife is a period of complexity and contrasts. Among those I interviewed there were people who were juggling the conflicting demands of work and family life, caring for those who were younger and/or older than themselves, and coping with significant personal transitions. Some were adjusting to the departure of children from home or to the death of loved ones. Some of the interviewees who were in later midlife were adjusting to having more flexibility of time and resources than they had ever had before. The desire for "balance" in these and other aspects of life emerged as a recurring motif in the interviews. Interviewees also acknowledged that busyness, stress, anxiety about the future, awareness of personal limitations (including physical limitations) and increasing consciousness of the inevitability of death, were, or had been, part of their experience of midlife.

Many of the middle-aged churchgoers I spoke with were aware of some changes in perspective and in their faith. In most cases these changes were considered by interviewees to be gradual shifts rather than seismic upheavals. Few interviewees used the word "crisis" to label their midlife experience, but tears surfaced in some interviews as people shared stories of bereavement, loss and trauma, or spoke of some significant pressures and struggles that had been, or were still, part of their midlife journey. I found it humbling to hear these stories, generously communicated for the potential benefit of others. While acknowledging that some aspects of midlife were extremely difficult, many of the people I spoke with also perceived that there was much to celebrate about being in this life stage. A number stated or implied that in the midst of change they derived a sense of security from their relationship with God and their experience of God's faithfulness to them in the past. The ability of these midlife churchgoers to derive meaning from their life experiences and "to give thanks in all circumstances" (1 Thess 5:18) was linked to their faith.[254]

All of the churchgoers I interviewed could identify elements of church involvement they valued. These were described in some detail in Chapter 3. Many interviewees spoke with gratitude about the impact of individuals who had offered them timely support and encouragement in their faith journey, by encouraging them to explore and utilise their gifts or by introducing them to spiritual disciplines they had formerly not encountered. Interviewees who were beneficiaries of this kind of mentoring, whether it had occurred informally or in formal contexts such as in spiritual direction, spoke with real energy and enthusiasm about developments in their faith. Some who felt their parishes had left them to "drift" in midlife, on the other hand, had a diminished sense of connection to their churches. A significant number of the midlife churchgoers described the fulfilment they experienced in being "generative" – in being able to care for others in a wide range of ways and in a variety of contexts – although some also recognised the need to step back from certain roles within the church, for a time. Almost all interviewees described ways that they were conscious of God beyond the church, in creation, during times of leisure, or in their work.

At the start of this book I quoted an interviewee who said, "Stories are good because they either trigger off things you haven't thought about, or they are helpful because you realise 'it's not just me'." I hope that readers from a range of church backgrounds may have been able to identify with at least some of the stories shared within these pages. Knowing that aspects of our experience are shared by others can be immensely reassuring. Being aware, too, that faith at midlife may look or feel somewhat different from faith at earlier life stages can help us not to panic, but to pause, notice, attend to what we might learn, and to move forward with optimism. Recognising the value of ways we are already relating to God or serving others may increase our confidence. Developing our awareness and understanding of spiritual practices that other people find helpful, too, can inspire and motivate us. We can be encouraged not only to persevere with forms of prayer, worship and service that are important to us, but to move beyond what is familiar and comfortable, so that our faith is stretched and our relationship with God is deepened. I hope that this book has helped churchgoers by offering these forms of support and encouragement.

Clergy

The members of the clergy I interviewed were quick to identify significant challenges in their own or others' midlife journeys, and demonstrated empathy and concern in reflecting on the needs of their parishioners in this life stage. They admitted that, as far as ministry within their parishes was concerned, they had not previously given these issues a lot of thought. Their genuine interest in my research may have been partly attributable to the fact that they were themselves in midlife, but also appeared to stem from the novelty of the questions they were being asked to consider and the possibilities for more effectively reaching out to midlife parishioners that emerged as they spoke. Their responses tended to be both philosophical and practical. As they reflected on the universality and significance of inner shifts at midlife and the connection between these shifts and faith development, clergy provided specific examples of initiatives they had offered or been involved in, and (while respecting the anonymity of their parishioners) shared anecdotes about the impact of these on individuals. They had no difficulty identifying ways in which churches currently assist midlife parishioners to connect with God and one another. As we have heard, they were also easily able to generate diverse and numerous realistic suggestions about further forms of support that might benefit people in this age bracket.

Several of the priests and ministers I spoke to stated that they felt there was scope for personal and professional development in discussing midlife issues with other clergy. Anglican priest, Patricia (58) said:

> I think this *[the interview time]* has been really great. And I think it would be wonderful to have some specific focus in ongoing formation workshops for clergy, discussion points, you know, to get together and actually specifically look at it. ... I think some really interesting stuff could come out of that. It's stimulating.

Many clergy and church leaders are in midlife. They, too, need opportunities to stop and take stock of where they find themselves relationally, vocationally, physically and spiritually.

Given all the expectations placed on clergy and other leaders – and the staggering range and magnitude of needs in our communities and the wider world – the suggestion that yet another issue merits attention might seem rather discouraging. I hope that I have demonstrated that it is possible for parishes to be intentional about providing pastoral and spiritual support to people in midlife without placing unrealistic demands upon clergy or congregations. First, we have seen that it is possible to help people in who are in midlife while simultaneously extending support to people of other ages. In fact, multi-generational groups or events can be particularly beneficial for individuals in midlife because they afford opportunities both to receive and to offer care. Second, we know that very simple forms of pastoral and spiritual support can have a big impact upon people in this stage of life. An open church, a listening ear, an offer to babysit so that parents may participate in a small group or attend a retreat, regularly affirming the value of people's weekday work – these and other small acts are not complicated or costly to implement, but each demonstrates compassionate awareness of the needs of people in this demanding period of life. Third, the stories that interviewees shared revealed that God's call to individuals extends well beyond the "aviary walls" of our own parishes. Opportunities to deepen in faith and to serve God and others can be found everywhere. It is true that walking alongside individuals as they explore a range of opportunities, resources and tools for the journey – and equipping others to share this responsibility and privilege – requires time and discernment. But, as several members of the clergy observed, this is a shared call, and one which depends less on our abilities than our willingness to "look at what God is doing and joining in."

Spiritual directors

The spiritual directors I interviewed focused most closely on the inner journey of midlife and aspects of spiritual formation that often arise in this life stage. A number of them linked the journey inward to a desire for greater authenticity, greater wholeness, and integrity – for what Parker J. Palmer calls "deeper congruence" between the "inner and outer life."[255] All of the spiritual directors identified midlife as being a period of change and a period of growth. Some spoke of faith stages and transitions. Those who did so stated or implied that churchgoers who have been Christians for many years are not always well prepared to anticipate and negotiate such changes.

The spiritual directors were able to comment on the experiences of churchgoers who felt their faith was well supported by their church communities and also on the needs of individuals who felt somewhat distanced from, or even disaffected by, the church. They noted that, at midlife, some churchgoers require pastoral and spiritual nurture that is different from the forms of support that have been helpful to them in earlier life stages. Like the clergy I interviewed, the spiritual directors acknowledged that it is not always easy for churches to cater for those who are questioning aspects of theology or spirituality, especially if these matters are not of concern to the majority of members in a particular parish. Several also addressed the issue of burnout among midlife churchgoers. Given the nature of the ministry of spiritual direction it was not surprising that these were issues that spiritual directors raised.

The spiritual directors I interviewed drew freely on a wide range of resources, images and metaphors to explore some of the deeper questions of faith that their directees shared with them. A few alluded to the fact that the balance between the church's responsibility for parishioners' spiritual nurture and individuals' willingness to embrace opportunities to deepen in faith and understanding is likely to shift during the middle decades of life. One reason that spiritual direction can appeal to people in this life stage is that it affords the opportunity for attendees to expand their spiritual horizons.

Denominations

It was personally very important to me to include the perspectives of people from Presbyterian, Anglican and Catholic churches in this book, as my life and faith have been greatly enriched by my involvement in these three denominations over many years. Across all three groups of interviewees, denominational affiliation made less difference to people's experiences and perceptions than other factors, such as age, gender, marital status and familial situation. Denominational differences that did arise were generally predictable. For example, some interviewees from Anglican and Catholic churches commented on the centrality of the Eucharist in the practice and experience of their faith, whereas those from Presbyterian churches (in which the observation of communion usually occurs less frequently) did not. What was perhaps a little more surprising was that many similarities in perspectives were shared by people from quite different sorts of parishes, both within and across denominations. For example, midlife churchgoers from all church types – whether evangelical/charismatic, Anglo-Catholic, Catholic, or traditional or non-traditional Protestant churches – considered intergenerational relationships within congregations to be a particularly positive and important aspect of their parish involvement. Interviewees from parishes that were quite dissimilar also expressed genuine appreciation of opportunities for shared silent prayer and occasional retreats. It was noteworthy that midlife churchgoers appeared to value exposure to these forms of prayer even if they were not a part of their faith communities' normal practices.

The people I interviewed came from just three Christian denominations but the churches they attended were very different in character, and the individuals who spoke with me expressed their faith in quite varied ways. In the wise words of Pope Francis:

> In the church there are a variety of ways and a variety of spiritualities. What is important is to find the way best suited for you to be with the Lord, and this everyone can do; it is possible for every state of life.[256]

Next steps

In considering next steps, some readers may find it helpful to return to the questions posed at the end of an earlier chapter. Other individuals may wish to reflect upon one or more of the following questions:

❖ Are there images, concepts, stories or statements shared in this book which have remained with you? Why do you think this is?

❖ If you are in midlife, what challenges and opportunities are part of your present experience? Might it be possible for you to set aside some time to pray about these things?

❖ As you reflect on your faith, for what are you most thankful at this time?

❖ If you attend church, think about your involvement there. What do you value? What do you contribute? How do you feel about that?

❖ What helps you to be conscious of "the religious dimension"[257] of daily life?

❖ Are there spiritual practices described in this book (whether familiar or not so familiar) which particularly appeal to you? Is there something you would like to explore further?

❖ Remembering the importance of the communal dimension of the Christian life, is there some form of service within your church or community you would like to join with others in offering?

❖ What else?

Over the past few years I have been very aware of my indebtedness to the interviewees whose stories and insights I have been privileged to ponder and to share. I am very grateful to all of them for giving up their time, for their openness in speaking about their personal experiences, their willingness to engage with some very challenging questions, and for the insights they shared. Again, I would also like to express my heartfelt thanks to my family and friends, my colleagues, and fellow congregation members at Cashmere Presbyterian and St Barnabas Anglican churches, for their support.

Christian faith is shaped and nurtured through our relationships with others, as the stories told within these pages illustrate. It seems appropriate to me, therefore, to conclude this book about midlife and the church with a communal prayer. From the Anglican service of Night Prayer, these lovely words express deep gratitude to God for the past and the present, and commits the future to God's keeping:

> God our Creator, our centre, our friend,
> we thank you for our good life,
> for those who are dear to us,
> for our dead, and for all who have helped
> and influenced us.
> We thank you for the measure of freedom we have,
> and the extent to which we control our lives;
> and most of all we thank you for the faith that is in us,
> for our awareness of you and our hope in you.
> Keep us, we pray you, thankful and hopeful
> and useful until our lives shall end.
>
> Amen.[258]

Appendix — The research process

Some readers may be interested in learning a little more about the research process behind the findings presented this book. Here I would like to provide some background regarding the selection of interviewees, some thoughts about the impact that the research sample had upon what I learned, and a few observations about what I consider to be some of the limitations of this research. Those who would like a more detailed explanation of the research methods employed may wish to refer to my doctoral thesis, which is accessible on-line.[259]

The original interviewees

1. 20 churchgoers between the ages of 40 and 60, drawn from Anglican, Catholic and Presbyterian churches from Auckland, Christchurch and Dunedin
2. Ten ordained clergy from Anglican, Catholic and Presbyterian churches within New Zealand
3. Ten qualified spiritual directors currently working with Christian clients in midlife

Churchgoers in midlife

For my doctoral research, I interviewed 20 women and men aged between 40 and 60. A key priority was to ensure that there was a roughly even spread of interviewees from Anglican, Catholic and Presbyterian churches. I also tried to include people who represented various stages and types of familial life; interviewees included those who were single (including one person who had made religious vows), married, divorced, widowed, had children living at home, children who had left home, and people without children. I made some effort to include participants of different ethnicities, but given the range of other criteria I needed to fulfil I was not as successful in achieving this as I had hoped. Among the middle-aged churchgoers there were some people of Māori/Polynesian, Polynesian, and South African backgrounds, but most interviewees identified as "New Zealand European" (or, equivalently, *Pakeha*).

Anglican, Catholic and Presbyterian churches encompass a range of theology and practice. I was particularly interested in ensuring that diversity of church experience and theological perspective would be expressed. Among the midlife churchgoers I interviewed were those who described themselves or their faith communities as liberal, evangelical, contemporary, charismatic, and contemplative. A number of interviewees attended more than one type of service within their own parish, while others occasionally or regularly attended more than one church. The parishes that the churchgoers came from also varied greatly in size; average Sunday attendances ranged from around 30 to over 1,000.

Table 1: Demographics of participants in midlife

Name	Gender	Age	Denomination	Ethnicity	Familial status
Ian	M	41	Presbyterian	NZ European	Married
Gail	F	41	Anglican	NZ European	Married with children
Nina	F	43	Anglican	NZ-born Cook Island Māori	Married
Murray	M	44	Anglican	NZ European	Married with children
Andrew	M	44	Anglican	South African	Married with children
Keith	M	47	Catholic	NZ European	Married with one child
Raewyn	F	47	Presbyterian	NZ European	Marriedwith children
Richard	M	48	Catholic	NZ European	Single
Simon	M	48	Presbyterian	NZ European	Married with children
Sally	F	49	Catholic	NZ European	Married with children
Debbie	F	51	Catholic	NZ European	Remarried with children
Karen	F	52	Anglican	NZ European	Single
Malcolm	M	52	Anglican	NZ European	Married with one child
Talia	F	53	Presbyterian	Samoan	Divorced with children
Phil	M	53	Catholic	NZ European	Married with children
Grant	M	55	Presbyterian	NZ European	Married with adult child
Michelle	F	58	Catholic	NZ European	Religious Sister
Linda	F	58	Anglican	NZ European	Married with adult children
Alison	F	59	Presbyterian	NZ European	Widowed with adult children
Judith	F	60	Catholic	NZ European	Married with adult children

As I indicated earlier, following the completion of my doctorate I interviewed further churchgoers in midlife. These additional interviewees are described in Table 4.

Clergy

I anticipated that there would be greater similarities of perspective among the clergy than among those in the midlife category, and that interviews with 10 clergy would therefore be sufficient to provide an interesting and useful picture of ways parishes are responding to the needs of those in midlife. Age was not a factor that I considered in the selection of clergy, but it turned out that all but one of the ordained clergy I interviewed were aged between the ages of 52 and 58. The other minister I interviewed was 62. In effect, this increased the sample size of the "midlife churchgoers" category significantly, because all of the ministers reflected on their own experience of midlife as well as speaking about their perceptions of the needs of midlife parishioners.

Clergy came from a range of church sizes and types. The four ministers from Presbyterian churches came from two parishes worshipping in traditional church buildings and two currently worshipping in less conventional venues. The Anglican clergy came from four parishes of varying sizes, each of which offered multiple church services, including weekday services. Notable diversity of liturgy and worship styles was offered within and across their parishes. Both of the Catholic priests I interviewed were responsible for large parishes with associated schools. A third Catholic priest was interviewed in his capacity as a spiritual director, but I also invited him to reflect on matters relating to the experience of midlife churchgoers within the context of parish life. In addition to those listed below, I interviewed two further members of the clergy who fell outside the demographic parameters I had originally set myself, one being from a different denomination, and one who was not working in a parish role. While I did not include any of the comments made by those members of the clergy in my doctoral research, I have incorporated them into this book.

Table 2: Demographics of the participating clergy

Name	Gender	Age	Ethnicity	Denomination	Parish type
Don	M	52	NZ European	Presbyterian	Church with charismatic background offering diverse services in more than one venue
Bernard	M	52	NZ European	Catholic	Very large suburban parish incorporating two churches
Sung-ho	M	53	Korean	Presbyterian	Small multicultural parish
Paul	M	53	Asian New Zealander	Catholic	Large multicultural suburban parish
Liz	F	55	NZ European	Anglican	Small Anglo-Catholic church with an older congregation
Russell	M	56	NZ European	Anglican	Large suburban church offering a range of service styles
Sandra	F	58	NZ European	Anglican	Fairly small suburban parish incorporating two churches and a lower socioeconomic housing area
Yvonne	F	58	NZ European	Presbyterian	Central city parish with a younger well-educated congregation
Patricia	F	58	NZ European	Anglican	Suburban parish in mid-socioeconomic area, with two combined congregations
Greg	M	62	NZ European	Presbyterian	Church offering family-friendly non-traditional services in a venue other than a church
Douglas	M	49	NZ European	Presbyterian	Working in a non-parish role
Hugh	M	52	NZ European	Baptist	Large community-focused church offering multiple services

Spiritual directors

Spiritual directors work one-to-one with directees, often over extended periods of time, and as directees often include those who are in midlife it seemed probable to me that experienced spiritual directors would have considerable understanding of the issues that concern Christians in midlife, as well as insights into the kinds of support or spiritual practices that are found to be helpful by people within that age range. I considered it likely that there would be a degree of similarity of perspective among spiritual directors which would mean that a sample size of ten would be sufficient to provide a representative range of insights and observations about issues affecting Christians in midlife.

I chose to interview spiritual directors who represented different strands in spiritual direction training in New Zealand over the past few years. In New Zealand, spiritual direction training is currently offered through an ecumenical programme provided by Spiritual Growth Ministries (SGM), and through programmes grounded in Ignatian spirituality. A recently-introduced course, *"Te Wairua Mahi*: Forming Spiritual Directors in the Ignatian Tradition"* has replaced the *Arrupé* Programme, an Ignatian formation programme offered through Australia. Spiritual direction training has also been offered in New Zealand, in the past, through the "Spirituality, Energy, Encounter, Direction" programme (SEED), which was a precursor to the *Arrupé* Programme. Some of the directors who were interviewed had received training through that programme. Several of the spiritual directors I interviewed had also trained in spiritual direction through courses offered in a range of locations overseas, often in addition to engaging in training within New Zealand. I hoped that selecting spiritual directors whose training had occurred in different contexts and traditions would add to the breadth of data gathered.

The choice of spiritual directors was not limited to those from Presbyterian, Catholic or Anglican churches (the denominations chosen for the other two categories) for two reasons. First, those advertising themselves as directors sometimes indicate the type of training, qualifications, or experience they have had in spiritual direction, and their interests or emphases in the services they offer, but explicit reference to denomination is rare. Spiritual directors who are members of the Association of Christian Spiritual Directors Aotearoa New Zealand are not identified by denomination on the association's website, although some may be identified as ordained clergy (Reverend or Father) or consecrated to the religious life (Sister). Second, regardless of their own denominational affiliations, it is common for spiritual directors to work with people from a wide range of church backgrounds, and some directors also see clients who have no church affiliation. The "undergirding commitment" of the Association of Christian Spiritual Directors Aotearoa New Zealand is to "an inclusiveness that is ecumenical, theological, and covers gender, sexual orientation, and language; to respectful and ethical practice; to contemplative spirituality; to an openness and hospitality in personal life; and to a willingness to journey into the mystery of life."[260] All of the spiritual directors interviewed were of New Zealand European ethnicity.

Table 3: Demographics of spiritual director participants

Name	Age	Training	Approximate number of directees	Proportion of directees in midlife[261]
Thomas	54	Trained overseas	Up to 20 in the past, but currently only 2 or 3	About half
Tony	56	SGM	25	Half to two thirds are in the 40-60 age range
Maureen	56	SGM	15	About one third, but others are just on the edge of midlife or a little younger
James	57	SGM followed by study in the Ignatian tradition	Up to 15 in the past, but currently fewer	Most in midlife or in their early 60s
Julie	60	SEED followed by further Ignatian studies	16-18	"The overwhelming majority" are in midlife
Matthew	61	SGM	21	About half (6 are younger, 5 older)
Brian	62	SEED followed by further Ignatian studies	25	"Most ... Generally my clientele would be midlife."
Louisa	66	SGM	Not specified	Very few younger than midlife
Carol	66	SEED	5 (at a time)	All have been in midlife or older
Frances	70	SGM followed by study in the Ignatian tradition	20 individuals, in addition to having led extended group programmes	"A lot." And the majority of those involved in group programmes were also in midlife

Table 4: Additional interviewees

Name	Gender	Age	Denomination	Ethnicity	Familial status
Anna	F	41	Catholic	"Kiwi" of Māori and Dutch descent	Married with one child
Bruce	M	49	Presbyterian	NZ European	Married with children
Rosemary	F	51	Catholic	NZ European	Married with adult children
Jane	F	55	Anglican	NZ European	Single
Hamish	M	61	Presbyterian (minister)	NZ European	Married with adult children
Kevin	M	62	Catholic (spiritual director)	NZ European	Married with adult children
Kay	F	62	Catholic	NZ European	Not stated
Christine	F	65	Presbyterian	NZ European	Not stated
Penny	F	71 (68 at time of Moses project)	Presbyterian	NZ European	Married (children not mentioned)
Owen	M	71	Presbyterian	NZ European	Married with adult children
Eleanor	F	71	Presbyterian	NZ European	Married with adult children

Selection of interviewees

I was acquainted with approximately half of the middle-aged churchgoers and with a small number of the spiritual directors and clergy that I interviewed for my doctoral research. Some of these people were well known to me or were connected to people well known by me, whereas others were acquaintances about whom I knew little other than their gender, church affiliation, marital status and approximate age. Among the interviewees I met following the completion of my PhD I knew one person well and I had previously met just one of the other interviewees. Recruitment of people I had met had a number of significant advantages, as reflective Christians from a wide range of church types could be identified and included and requirements relating to diversity of age, gender and familial status could be accommodated. Interviewing acquaintances, as well as people personally recommended by clergy and supervisors, also assisted in establishing rapport and trust, which contributed to the openness of participants and the depth of the interviews. However it is probable that this method of selection restricted the diversity of the sample in some ways. For example, a high proportion of those I interviewed possessed tertiary qualifications. I shall say more about the limitations of the sample shortly.

Academic supervisors, spiritual directors and clergy also suggested potential interviewees. As social scientists Robert Miller and John Brewer observe, "most snowball samples will be biased"[262] because initially accessed respondents make subjective choices about the people they recommend the interviewer approaches. Clergy tended to nominate people who were actively involved in church life, rather than those who were less closely aligned with their church communities.[263] This limitation was, to some extent, balanced by my ability to approach acquaintances I considered likely to broaden the diversity of the sample and potentially provide contrasting perspectives. However, I was aware that the stories of Christians who might consider themselves to be "on the margins" of church were better represented in the insights of spiritual directors who work with them than in the interviews held with midlife churchgoers themselves. It was never my intention to interview Christians who no longer attended church because, as I noted in Chapter 3, within New Zealand this is territory which has been covered by other authors.

Location

All interviewees came from Auckland, Christchurch and Dunedin, mainly for pragmatic reasons. I conducted all interviews face-to-face and I could only travel to a limited number of locations. Regard for interviewees' anonymity means that the cities individuals came from are not identified in the demographic tables which summarise details about interviewees. One point that should be noted is that all of the interviewees from Christchurch had been affected by major earthquakes in the Canterbury region, the first of which occurred on 4 September 2010. Almost all of the participants from Christchurch, at some point in their interviews, mentioned the earthquakes and the resultant stress, financial and physical impacts, or other tangible and intangible consequences for themselves or their families, members of their congregations, or their communities.[264]

The extent and severity of housing issues faced by many people after the earthquakes had an ongoing impact on thousands of families in Canterbury. Some midlife interviewees from Christchurch had been forced to move to suburbs that were far from their original neighbourhoods and parishes; some were travelling long distances to worship with the congregations they had been part of prior to the earthquakes. Several interviewees were attending church services in temporary premises because their church buildings had been seriously damaged or destroyed. Some had also been affected by the closure of their children's schools. These losses were the source of real grief to those affected. Some interviewees from Christchurch also identified positive consequences of the earthquakes, such as lessons they felt they had learned, strengthened relationships,[265] and, in one case, improved business outcomes. For Christchurch residents, dealing with the earthquakes and thousands of aftershocks, and their ongoing consequences at individual and societal level, could not be separated from their "midlife experience."

Clergy from Christchurch were similarly affected, both personally and professionally. Some of the clergy who had been present during and following the earthquakes, and were called on to support others in the immediate aftermath of the February 2011 earthquake, clearly appreciated the opportunity the interview with me afforded them to talk about the unprecedented, multiple, cumulative pressures they had borne during that period. Many clergy in Christchurch were still coping with significant challenges relating to the earthquakes. At the time the interviews were conducted, approximately six years after the 2011 event which caused the most significant damage to the central city, four of the Christchurch clergy I spoke to were holding services of worship in temporary premises. Three of their churches had been destroyed and a fourth was awaiting repairs. In addition, one Anglican priest was serving in a church with a combined congregation because a nearby church building could no longer be used. Only two of the seven interviews with Christchurch clergy took place in offices on church premises. Few of them had permanent private offices from which to work or meet with parishioners. It was hardly surprising that, in this context, clergy and churchgoers from Christchurch placed very high value on close supportive relationships within congregations (and on strategies for fostering these) and on stability and familiarity in forms of liturgy and worship. Like those from Canterbury, interviewees from Dunedin and Auckland prized close connections with other Christians. However, outside Christchurch, a desire for stability and continuity was rarely expressed.

Limitations of the sample

The initial sample size of 40 was adequate to provide a good foundation for addressing the key questions of my doctoral research, but greater diversity among the midlife churchgoers would almost certainly have thrown light upon further challenges and opportunities of midlife that were not raised by the people I interviewed. Inclusion of interviewees whose ages were spread fairly evenly across two decades, who were from three denominations (and who attended different kinds of churches within those denominations), and whose familial circumstances differed, limited the other forms of diversity that could be taken into consideration. For example, among the 20 midlife churchgoers I interviewed first, it was possible to include people who were single, married (with and without children living at home), divorced, remarried, and widowed, but churchgoers with blended families and people living in same-sex relationships were not interviewed.

As I noted earlier, despite making some effort to include a range of ethnicities among the interviewees, people from non-European backgrounds were under-represented because of the priority I placed on other forms of diversity. I was able to include participants from Māori/Polynesian, Polynesian, Asian, and South African backgrounds, but most interviewees identified as New Zealand European (or, equivalently, Pakeha). At the 2013 census 74% of New Zealanders identified as European, Māori made up 14.9% of the population, and 11.8% were Asian.[266] 77.5% of those I interviewed identified as New Zealand European. Among my original interviewees, one identified as being of Māori, Cook Island and European descent. Two members of the clergy (5% of participants) who contributed to my research were born in Asia. Greater cultural diversity within the total sample would have better reflected New Zealand's population and could have raised further interesting questions for exploration.

Greater socioeconomic diversity among participants would almost undoubtedly have thrown up other interesting issues. All the people I interviewed had some form of paid employment. This was not surprising given the low rate of unemployment in New Zealand at the time the interviews were conducted.[267] Even so, the extent of the interviewees' paid employment ranged from a few irregular hours of part-time work per week to full-time work. Two people had only recently returned to paid work, one had just handed in her resignation from work, and one was in the process of reducing work hours significantly. Several mentioned disruption to their working lives which had caused financial hardship in the recent past. Future exploration of the needs and experiences of midlife churchgoers – in discussions held among clergy or within congregations, for example – might seek to redress gaps in the sample diversity.

Cohort effects

A limitation of the research I conducted is that cohort effects are not addressed. A longitudinal study would be necessary to determine the extent to which the experiences and attitudes of the midlife interviewees related to their age and stage of life rather than the cohort to which they belong. It is very likely that the experience of midlife will be different for people born at different points of history. For example, it seems probable that comments made by midlife churchgoers about work, work-life balance, and retirement relate to cohort as well as age. Sterns and Huyck's research relating to the role of work in midlife indicates that "the challenges of the middle years are influenced by cohort" as, at present, middle-aged employees are those most affected by organisations making the transition "from pyramid to more streamlined configurations through downsizing and restructuring."[268] Eriksen, Martinengo and Hill suggest that "longitudinal data are necessary to evaluate how work-family linkages shift over the life course" as "age differences may mask the fact that adults born during the Baby Boom generation may react differently to work conditions than Generation X adults will react when they reach the same age."[269] Given the multitude of types of work that now exist, and the fact that most young people today anticipate working in a series of jobs across their lifespan, Millennials (those born between 1980 and the mid-1990s) will have very different experiences of work from their parents. When they reach midlife, their attitudes to work may be quite different from those who are in midlife today.

The institutional church has also undergone significant changes over the past four or five decades, and, just as churchgoers who are currently in midlife have been shaped by the changes that have occurred during their lifetimes, the faith of churchgoers who are not yet in midlife will undoubtedly be affected by changes occurring now. Edmund Gordon, Secretary for Catholic Education and the Director of Religious Education of the Catholic Diocese of Wilmington, Delaware, describes four different generations of adults within the Catholic Church in the United States at present.[270] Those currently in midlife include some "Vatican II Catholics," born between 1946 and 1964, who are portrayed as having mixed views about authority and institutional commitment but who have, nevertheless, inherited much of their Catholic identity from the pre-Vatican II Catholics so that "the residue of an ethnic Catholic culture persists."[271] Some others in midlife are Generation X adults (born between 1964 and 1980). These church members are sometimes called "Christian Catholics" to emphasize "their lack of a strong Catholic identity" and their much looser connection to the institutional Catholic Church. They have had to create their own Catholic identity "out of bits and pieces they find helpful and meaningful."[272] Those coming of age now, who have "an even more tenuous relationship to the Catholic Church"[273] will, in midlife, have a different relationship with the church than those who are in midlife now.

It is also interesting to consider whether some of the questions relating to spirituality and personal identity which spiritual directors identified as being of import to middle-aged clients will, in the future, concern those whose spirituality is being formed within a societal context which is very different from that which shaped their parents. One spiritual director, Brian (62), spoke to me about the "beautiful spirituality" of some young people who are quite disengaged with church but who are very concerned about such things as the environment and inter-faith connections. They are "not as connected to the ritual" of the church as their predecessors, but questions of "interior integrity" which interested his middle-aged clients were already of concern to these younger people. Brian concluded, "Their midlife might be quite different." There is scope for future research regarding these issues.

As I mentioned earlier, I did not interview middle-aged Christians who do not (or no longer) attend church. Comparing and contrasting their experiences with the experiences of those who do attend church regularly would undoubtedly provide further insights into ways that congregations might support members in midlife.

Bibliography

Aldwin, Carolyn M. and Michael P. Levenson. "Stress, Coping and Health at Midlife: A Developmental Perspective." In *Handbook of Midlife Development*, ed. Margie E. Lachman, 188-214. Hoboken, NJ: John Wiley & Sons Inc, 2001.

Alpha. <http://alpha.org.nz> (3 April 2017).

The Anglican Care Network of Agencies, Parishes and Diocesan Social Services in Aotearoa, New Zealand. <http://www.anglicancarenetwork.org.nz> (10 July 2017).

Anglicans Online: Online Resources. <http://anglicansonline.org/resources/index.html> (31 May 2016).

Ask NT Wright Anything. <https://askntwrightanything.podbean.com/> (11 August 2021).

Aune, Kristin. "Why Women Don't Do Church Any More." *Church Times*, 20 August 2008. <http://test.churchtimes.co.uk/articles/2008/22-august/comment/why-women-don-t-do-church-any-more> (8 June 2017).

Baab, Lynne. *A Renewed Spirituality: Finding Fresh Paths at Midlife*. Downers Grove, Illinois: Inter-Varsity Press, 2002.

_____. "Beating Burnout by Building Teams." *Congregations*, Fall 2003, 6-9. <https://www.lynnebaab.com/articles/beating-burnout-by-building-teams-> (10 June 2021).

_____. *Embracing Midlife: Congregations as Support Systems*. Bethesda, MD: Alban Institute, 1999.

_____. *Sabbath Keeping: Finding Freedom in the Rhythms of Rest*. Downers Grove, Illinois: Inter-Varsity Press, 2005.

Bakke, Jeanette A. *Holy Invitations: Exploring Spiritual Direction*. Grand Rapids Michigan: Baker Books, 2000.

Barry, William A. and William J. Connolly. *The Practice of Spiritual Direction*. 2nd ed. New York: HarperCollins Publishers, 2009.

Benjamin, Maria. *The Middlepause: On Turning Fifty*. Melbourne: Scribe Books, 2016.

Bent, Helen. *Celebration in Times of Grief and Sorrow*. Cambridge: Grove Books, 2018.

_____. *Exploring Worship in Pilgrimage*. Cambridge: Grove Books, 2020.

Bible Study Fellowship. <https://www.bsfinternational.org> (16 May 2016).

Brehony, Kathleen A. *Awakening at Midlife: A Guide to Reviving Your Spirit, Recreating Your Life, and Returning to Your Truest Self.* New York: Riverhead Books, 1996.

Bretherton, Roger, Joanna Collicutt and Jennifer Brickman. *Being Mindful, Being Christian.* Oxford: Monarch Books, 2016.

Brueggemann, Walter. "Psalms and the Life of Faith: A Suggested Typology of Function." *Journal for the Study of the Old Testament* 17 (1980): 3-32.

Buechner, Frederick. *Wishful Thinking: A Seeker's ABC*, 2nd Rev. ed. London: Bloomsbury, 1994.

Buford, Bob. *Half Time: Changing Your Game Plan from Success to Significance.* Grand Rapids, Michigan: Zondervan, 1994.

Capps, Donald. *Life Cycle Theory and Pastoral Care.* Theology and Pastoral Care, ed. Donald S. Browning. Philadelphia: Fortress Press, 1983.

The Catholic Church in Aotearoa New Zealand. "RCIA." <http://www.catholic.org.nz/ms/dsp-default.cfm?loadref=170&pid=C9F2B42F-B3C8-569A-74B5BAAD927FF5F1> (25 October, 2016).

Chittister, Joan D. *Scarred by Struggle, Transformed by Hope.* Grand Rapids, Michigan: Wm B. Eerdmans Publishing, 2003.

The Christian Coaching Centre. "Willow Creek Reveal Study: A Summary," <http://www.christiancoachingcenter.org/index.php/russ-rainey/coachingchurch2/> (25 April 2017).

Christianity Today. "Willow Creek Repents?" <http://www.christianitytoday.com/pastors/2007/october-online-only/willow-creek-repents.html> (25 April 2017).

The Clifton StrengthsFinder.™ <http://www.strengthstest.com/strengths-finder-themes> (14 October, 2016).

Collicutt, Joanna. *The Psychology of Christian Character Formation.* London: SCM Press, 2015.

_____. *Thinking of You: A Resource for the Spiritual Care of People with Dementia.* Oxford: The Bible Reading Fellowship, 2017.

_____. *When You Pray: Daily Bible reflections on the Lord's Prayer.* Oxford: Bible Reading Fellowship, 2019.

Creighton University Retreats. <http://onlineministries.creighton.edu/CollaborativeMinistry/cmo-retreat.html> (27 March 2019)

Droege, Thomas A. "Passages and Patterns of Paschal Faith." <https://scholar.valpo.edu/cgi/viewcontent.cgi?article=1034&context=ils_papers> (20 April 2019)

Dunn, Andrew. "Spiritual Direction." *Candour: News and Views for Ministers* (February 2011): 17-20.

Fischer, Kathleen. *Women at the Well: Feminist Perspectives on Spiritual Direction.* Mahwah, New Jersey: Paulist Press, 1988.

"45 Ways to Encounter God Multilingual Resource." <https://women.salvationarmy.org.nz/resource/45-ways-encounter-god-multilingual-resource> (5 Nov 2021).

Foster, Richard. *Celebration of Discipline.* San Francisco: Harper and Row, 1978.

Fowler, James W. *Faith Development and Pastoral Care.* Theology and Pastoral Care, ed. Donald S. Browning. Philadelphia: Fortress Press, 1987.

_____. "Faith Development Theory and the Postmodern Challenges." *The International Journal for the Psychology of Religion*, 11:3 (2001): 159-172.

_____. *Stages of Faith: The Psychology of Human Development and the Quest for Meaning.* New York: Harper and Row, 1981.

Gallagher, Timothy M., *Meditation and Contemplation: An Ignatian Guide to Praying with Scripture.* New York: Crossroad Publishing, 2008.

Gooley, Laurence L. To *Share in the Life of Christ: Experiencing God in Everyday Life.* St Louis, Missouri: The Institute of Jesuit Sources, 1997.

Gordon, Edmund. "Adult Faith Formation: A Catholic Vision." *Lifelong Faith* 2:3 (Fall 2008): 31-38.

Hagberg, Janet O. and Robert A. Guelich. *The Critical Journey: Stages in the Life of Faith*, 2nd ed. Salem, Wisconsin: Sheffield Publishing, 2005.

Hagerty, Barbara Bradley. *Life Reimagined: The Science, Art and Opportunity of Midlife.* New York: Riverhead Books, 2016.

Harrell, Dawn Duncan. *Ten Ways to Pray: A Short Guide to a Long History of Talking with God.* Stone's Throw, 2012.

Hansen, Gary Neal. *Kneeling with Giants: Learning to Pray with History's Best Teachers.* Downer's Grove, IL: InterVarsity Press, 2012.

Hansen, Michael. *The First Spiritual Exercises: Four Guided Retreats.* Notre Dame, IN: Ave Maria Press, 2013.

Harrell, Dawn Duncan. *Ten Ways to Pray: A Short Guide to a Long History of Talking with God.* Los Angeles: Stone's Throw, 2012.

Hart, Thomas N. *The Art of Christian Listening.* Mahwah, New Jersey: Paulist Press, 1980.

Heywood, D. "Faith Development Theory: A Case for Paradigm Change." *Journal of Beliefs & Values*: 29:3 (2008): 263-272.

Horsfall, Tony. *Facing Midlife: Bible Readings for Special Times.* Abingdon, Oxford: The Bible Reading Fellowship, 2017.

Hope is our Song: New Hymns and Songs from Aotearoa New Zealand. Palmerston North: The New Zealand Hymn Book Trust, 2009.

Hudson, F. M. *The Adult Years: Mastering the Art of Self-Renewal.* San Francisco: Jossey-Bass, 1991.

Hume, Basil. *Basil in Blunderland.* Rev. ed. London: Darton, Longman and Todd, 2005.

Hunt, Gary L. "The Push of Theocracy versus the Pull of Spirituality," July 27, 2012. <https://discernablefutures.wordpress.com/2012/07/27/the-push-of-theocracy-versus-the-pull-of-spirituality/> (1 March 2017).

Hutchinson, Nicholas. *Praying Each Day of the Year: May to August.* Chelmsford: Matthew James Publishing, 1998.

An Ignatian Prayer Adventure. <http://www.ignatianspirituality.com/ignatian-prayer/the-spiritual-exercises/an-ignatian-prayer-adventure/> (7 June 2017).

IgnatianSpirituality.com. <http://www.ignatianspirituality.com> (12 June 2021).

Jamieson, Alan. "AJ's Blog." South West Baptist Church. <https://www.swbc.org.nz/ajs-blog/some-questions-and-answers/> (17 May 2017).

_____. *Called Again: In and Beyond the Deserts of Faith.* Wellington: Philip Garside Publishing, 2004.

_____. *A Churchless Faith: Faith Journeys Beyond Evangelical, Pentecostal and Charismatic Churches.* Wellington: Philip Garside Publishing, 2000.

_____. "Construction – Deconstruction – Reconstruction." Spirited Exchanges. <http://www.spiritedexchanges.org.nz/store/doc/Article_construction%20etc.pdf> (14 February, 2017).

_____. "Off-road Faith." Spirited Exchanges, 2005. <http://www.spiritedexchanges.org.nz/store/doc/issue%2036.pdf> (6 August, 2021).

Jamieson, Alan and Jenny McIntosh and Adrienne Thompson. *Five Years On: Continuing Faith Journeys of those who left the Church.* Wellington: Portland Research Trust, 2006.

Johnstone, Carlton. "Understanding the Practice of Church Two-Timing." *International Journal For The Study Of The Christian Church* 9:1 (2009): 17-31. <http://www.tandfonline.com/doi/abs/10.1080/14742250802577382> (3 November 2016).

Joshua Catholic Men's Fellowship. <http://joshua.org.nz> (6 March 2016).

Karp, D. "A Decade of Reminders: Age Consciousness between Fifty and Sixty Years Old." *Gerontologist* 28:6 (1988): 727-738.

Keller, Timothy. *Every Good Endeavour: Connecting Your Work to God's Plan for the World*. London: Hodder and Stoughton, 2014.

Lachman, Margie E. "Development in Midlife." *Annual Review of Psychology*, Vol. 55 (February 2004): 305-331.

Lachman, M. E., C. Lewkowicz, A. Marcus, & Y. Peng. "Images of Midlife Development among Young, Middle-aged, and Older Adults." *Journal of Adult Development* 1: 201-211.

Levinson, Daniel. *The Seasons of a Man's Life*. New York: Ballantine Books, 1978.

MacArthur Foundation. The John D. and Catherine T. MacArthur Foundation Research Network on Successful Midlife Development. <http://midmac.med.harvard.edu> (16 September 2015).

Maccaulay, Martin. "Take it Personally – Discipleship as Personal Interaction rather than Programme." *Candour: News and Views for Ministers* (April 2011): 10-11. <http://presbyterian.org.nz/sites/default/files/publications/candour/Candour_Apr_2011_lo-res.pdf> (28 May 2017).

Mackenzie, Alistair and Wayne Kirkland. *Where's God on Monday? Integrating Faith and Work Every Day of the Week*. Colorado Springs: NavPress, 2003.

McLeod, Frederick G. "Apophatic or Kataphatic Prayer?" <http://opcentral.org/resources/2015/01/13/frederick-g-mcleod-apophatic-or-kataphatic-prayer/> (29 February 2016).

Manney, Jim. *A Simple Life-Changing Prayer: Discovering the Power of St. Ignatius Loyola's Examen*. Chicago: Loyola Press, 2011.

The Marriage Course. <http://alphausa.org/the-marriage-course> (7 November 2016).

Martin, James and Jeremy Langford (eds). *Professions of Faith: Living and Working as a Catholic*. Kansas City: Rowman and Littlefield, 2002.

Martin, James, S.J. *The Jesuit Guide to (Almost) Everything: A Spirituality for Real Life*. New York: HarperCollins, 2010.

_____. *Learning to Pray: A Guide for Everyone*. London: William Collins, 2021.

Mayne, Michael. *Prayer*. London: Darton, Longman and Todd, 2013.

_____. *This Sunrise of Wonder: Letters for the Journey*. London: Fount, 1995.

_____. *To Trust and to Love: Sermons and Addresses*. London: Darton, Longman and Todd, 2010.

The Men's Series. <http://www.olivetreemedia.com.au/mens-series/> (11 August 2017).

Messy Church NZ. <http://messychurch.nz> (11 October, 2016).

Miller, Robert L. and Brewer, John D. *The A-Z of Social Research: A Dictionary of Key Social Science Research Concepts*. London: Sage Publications, 2003.

Moss, Sarah. "Unpacking the Dimensions of Our Healthy Church Model." *The Anglican*, November 2018, 4. <http://www.auckanglican.org.nz/ Anglican/media/Images/The%20Anglican/The-Anglican-November-2018-WEB.pdf> (March 14, 2014).

Myers, Jane E. and Melanie C. Harper. "Midlife Concerns and Caregiving Experiences: Intersecting Life Issues Affecting Mental Health." In *The Challenges of Mental Health Caregiving: Research. Practice. Policy*, ed. Benjamin G. Druss, Gregory Fricchione and Ronda C. Talley, 123-142. New York: Springer, 2014.

New Zealand Attitudes and Values Study. <https://www.psych.auckland. ac.nz/en/about/our-research/research-groups/new-zealand-attitudes-and-values-study.html> (27 July 2017).

"New Zealand Families Today." Ministry of Social Development, 2004. <https://www.msd.govt.nz/documents/about-msd-and-our-work/ publications-resources/research/nz-families-today/nz-families-today.pdf> (21 June 2016).

A New Zealand Prayer Book: He Karakia Mihinare o Aotearoa. The Anglican Church in Aotearoa, New Zealand and Polynesia. San Francisco: HarperSan Francisco, 1997.

Nouwen, Henri. *Bread for the Journey: A Daybook of Wisdom and Faith*. New York: Harper One, 2006.

Nouwen, Henri and Donald McNeill and Douglas Morrison. *Compassion*. London: Darton, Longman and Todd, 1982.

O'Brien, Kevin, S.J. *The Ignatian Adventure: Experiencing the Spiritual Exercises of Saint Ignatius in Daily Life*. Chicago, Ill.: Loyola Press, 2011.

O'Collins, Gerald. *The Second Journey*. New York: Paulist Press, 1978.

O'Connor, Dennis J. and Donald M. Wolfe. "On Managing Transitions in Career and Family." *Human Relations* 40 (1987): 799-816.

Palmer, Parker J. *Let Your Life Speak: Listening for the Voice of Vocation*. San Francisco: Jossey-Bass, 2000.

Papalia, Diane E., Sally Wendkos Olds and Ruth Duskin Feldman. *Human Development.* 7th ed. Boston, Mass: McGraw Hill, 1998.

Passionist Family Group Movement. <http://www.passionistfamily.org.nz> (27 January 2016).

The Perennial Gen: Growing Deeper Roots in the Dirt and Light of Midlife. <http://theperennialgen.com> (11 August 2021).

Peterson, Eugene. *Practise Resurrection: A Conversation on Growing up in Christ.* London: Hodder and Stoughton, 2010.

Philippe, Jacques. *Interior Freedom.* Translated by Helena Scott. New York: Scepter Publishers, 2007.

Phillips, Susan S. *Candlelight: Illuminating the Art of Spiritual Direction.* Harrisburg: Morehouse Publishing, 2008.

_____. *The Cultivated Life: From Ceaseless Striving to Receiving Joy.* Downers Grove, IL: InterVarsity Press, 2015.

Pickering, Sue. *Listening and Spiritual Conversation: Singing God's Songs in a Noisy World.* Norwich: Canterbury Press, 2017.

_____. *Spiritual Direction: A Practical Introduction.* London: Canterbury Press Norwich, 2008.

Pontifical Council for Justice and Peace. *Compendium of the Social Doctrine of the Church.* London: Continuum International Publishing Group, 2004.

Pope Francis. *The Church of Mercy: A Vision for the Church.* London: Darton, Longman and Todd, 2014.

_____. *Evangelii Gaudium: The Joy of the Gospel.* London: The Incorporated Catholic Truth Society, 2013.

Pritchard, Andrew. "Fowler, Faith and Fallout." *Reality Magazine* 33 (June/July 1999): 22-30. <http://www.reality.org.nz/articles/33/33-pritchard.html> (5 July 2021).

_____. "Your Church's Personality." *Reality Magazine* 45 (June/July 2001): 17-22. <https://www.reality.org.nz/articles/45/45-pritchard.php> (5 July 2021)

Pritchard, Sheila. *The Lost Art of Meditation: Deepening Your Prayer Life.* Queensway, Bletchley; Scripture Union, 2003.

Putney, Norella M. and Vern L. Bengtson. "Families, Intergenerational Relationships, and Kinkeeping in Midlife." *In Handbook of Midlife Development,* ed. Margie E. Lachman, 528-570. Hoboken, NJ: John Wiley & Sons Inc, 2001.

Rauch, Jonathan. *The Happiness Curve: Why Life Gets Better after 50.* New York: Thomas Dunne Books, 2018.

Robinson, Oliver. *Development Through Adulthood: An Integrative Sourcebook*. Basingstoke: Palgrave Macmillan, 2013.

_____. "The Mid-Life Crisis ... It's Real." Interview by Kathryn Ryan. *Nine to Noon*, Radio New Zealand. 9 May 2016. <http://www.radionz.co.nz/national/programmes/ninetonoon/audio/201799963/the-mid-life-crisis-it's-real> (9 May 2016).

Ruffing, Janet. "Personality Sciences." *The Blackwell Companion to Christian Spirituality*, ed. Arthur Holder, 308-324. Oxford: Blackwell Publishing, 2005.

_____. "Spiritual Identity and Narrative: Fragmentation, Coherence, and Transformation." *Spiritus* 12 (2012): 63-74.

Rushton, Kathleen P. *The Cry of the Earth and the Cry of the Poor: Hearing Justice in John's Gospel*. London: SCM Press, 2020.

Sampson, Barbara. *Encountering God*. Rev. ed. Wellington: The Salvation Army, New Zealand, Fiji, Tonga and Samoa Territory, 2019.

Schweitzer, Friedrich L. *The Postmodern Life Cycle: Challenges for Church and Theology*. St Louis, Missouri: Chalice Press, 2004.

Shave, Anne. *Your Strength in Our Hearts: New Zealand Churchgoers in Midlife*. <https://ourarchive.otago.ac.nz/bitstream/handle/10523/7820/ShaveAnneE2017PhD.pdf?sequence=1&isAllowed=y> (8 May 2019).

Sheehy, Gail. *Passages: Predictable Crises of Adult Life*. New York: E.P Dutton, 1976.

Spirited Exchanges. <http://www.spiritedexchanges.org.nz> (11 August 2017).

Spiritual Growth Ministries. <http://www.sgm.org.nz> (1 June 2017).

_____. "2013 Census QuickStats about Families and Households." <http://www.stats.govt.nz/Census/2013-census/profile-and-summary-reports/qstats-families-households/households.aspx> (28 July 2016).

Staudinger, Ursula M. and Susan Bluck. "A View of Midlife Development from Life-Span Theory." In *Handbook of Midlife Development*, ed. Margie E. Lachman, 3-39. Hoboken, NJ: John Wiley & Sons Inc, 2001.

Sterns, Harvey L. and Margaret Hellie Huyck. "The Role of Work in Midlife." In *Handbook of Midlife Development*, ed. Margie E. Lachman, 447-486. Hoboken, NJ: John Wiley & Sons Inc, 2001.

Streib, Heinz. "Faith Development Theory Revisited: The Religious Styles Perspective." *The International Journal for the Psychology of Religion*, 11:3 (2001):143-158.

Studzinski, Raymond. *Spiritual Direction and Midlife Development.* Loyola University Press, Chicago, 1985.

"Theology at Work." Carey Baptist College. <http://carey.ac.nz/course/theology-at-work/> (16 November 2016).

Tozer, A.W. *The Pursuit of God.* 15th ed. Chicago: Moody Publishers, 2015.

Tripp, Paul David. *Lost in the Middle: Midlife and the Grace of God.* Wapwallopen, Pennsylvania: Shepherd Press, 2004.

Troughton, Geoffrey, Joseph Bulbulia and Chris G. Sibley. "Strength of Religion and the Future of the Churches." *Stimulus* 22 (2014): 26-34.

Vaillant, George E. *Aging Well: Surprising Guideposts to a Happier Life from the Landmark Study of Adult Development.* New York: Little, Brown and Company, 2002.

Van Loon, Michelle. *Becoming Sage: Cultivating Meaning, Purpose, and Spirituality in Midlife.* Chicago: Moody Publishers, 2020.

_____. "Why Friends Disappear When You Reach Midlife." <http://theperennialgen.com/why-friends-disappear-when-you-reach-midlife/> (30 April 2020).

Walters, Laura. "Kiwis Suffering from Disconnect." 15 May 2015. <http://www.stuff.co.nz/life-style/well-good/68591123/kiwis-suffering-from-disconnect> (5 April 2017).

Ward, Kevin. "Is New Zealand's Future Churchless?" *Stimulus* vol. 12, no. 2 (May 2004): 2-12.

_____. *Losing our Religion: Changing Patterns of Believing and Belonging in Secular Western Societies.* Eugene, Oregon: Wipf & Stock, 2013.

Welch, Sally. *Walking the Labyrinth: A Spiritual and Practical Guide.* London: Canterbury Press, 2010.

Wethington, Elaine, and Ronald C. Kesseler, and Joy E. Pixley. "Turning Points in Adulthood." In *How Healthy Are We? A National Study of Well-Being at Midlife*, ed. Orville Gilbert Brim, et al., 586-613. Chicago: University of Chicago Press, 2004.

"What do Single Christians say about Church." *Single Friendly Church.* <http://www.singlefriendlychurch.com/what-do-single-christians-say-about-church/what-do-single-christians-say-about-church> (4 July 2017).

Williams, Rowan. *Being Human: Bodies, Minds, Persons.* London: SPCK, 2018.

Yancey, Philip. *What Good is God? In Search of a Faith that Matters.* New York: Little, Brown and Company, 2013.

Endnotes

Introduction

1 Michael Mayne, *To Trust and to Love: Sermons and Addresses* (London: Darton, Longman and Todd, 2010), 164.

2 Throughout this book the word "Roman" will be omitted when references to the Catholic Church are made, for ease of reading, and also because the Catholic Church in New Zealand describes itself as the Catholic Church (or its Māori equivalent, *te Hāhi Katorika ki Aotearoa*). <http://www.catholic.org.nz> (8 August 2020). The word "church" will not be capitalised unless the definite article is used prior to refer to a whole denomination. Again, this is for ease of reading.

3 Anne Shave, *Your Strength in Our Hearts: New Zealand Churchgoers in Midlife.* <https://ourarchive.otago.ac.nz/bitstream/handle/10523/7820/ShaveAnneE2017PhD.pdf?sequence=1&isAllowed=y> (8 May 2019).

4 Research regarding the "churchlessness" of New Zealanders has been described in the following studies: Alan Jamieson, *A Churchless Faith: Faith Journeys Beyond Evangelical, Pentecostal and Charismatic Churches* (Wellington: Philip Garside Publishing, 2000) and Alan Jamieson, Alan and Jenny McIntosh and Adrienne Thompson, *Five Years On: Continuing Faith Journeys of those who left the Church* (Wellington: Portland Research Trust, 2006). Troughton, Geoffrey, Joseph Bulbulia and Chris G. Sibley. "Strength of Religion and the Future of the Churches." *Stimulus* 22 (2014): 26-34. Kevin Ward, "Is New Zealand's Future Churchless?" Stimulus vol. 12, no. 2, (May 2004): 2-12.

5 Kathleen Fischer, *Women at the Well: Feminist Perspectives on Spiritual Direction* (Mahwah, NJ: Paulist Press, 1988), 3.

6 The John D. and Catherine T. MacArthur Foundation, Research Network on Successful Midlife Development, <http://midmac.med.harvard.edu> (September 16, 2015).

7 The John D. and Catherine T. MacArthur Foundation, Research Network on Successful Midlife Development, <http://midmac.med.harvard.edu> (16 September 2015).

1 — Counting our days

8 Ursula M. Staudinger and Susan Bluck, "A View of Midlife Development from Life-Span Theory," in *Handbook of Midlife Development*, ed. Margie E. Lachman. Wiley series on Adulthood and Aging (Hoboken, NJ, US: John Wiley & Sons Inc), 6.

9 "New Zealand General Social Survey: 2012," <http://www.stats.govt.nz/browse_for_stats/people_and_ communities/Households/nzgss_HOTP2012/Definitions.aspx> (7 January, 2015).

10 "As life expectancy has increased, each life phase has changed. In 1950 people moved into midlife at about 35 and claimed a government pension at 60, which signalled the start of older age. In the 2000s midlife started at about 45 and superannuation was claimed at 65 – typically signifying the end of the midlife period." Alison Gray, "Midlife Adults - Middle Age and Midlife," Te Ara - the Encyclopedia of New Zealand, <www.TeAra.govt.nz/en/midlife-adults/page-1> (8 January 2015).

11 "Midlife New Zealanders Aged 40-64 in 2008: Enhancing Wellbeing in an Ageing Society" (2010) ed. C. Waldegrave and P. Koopman-Boyden (Population Studies Centre, The University of Waikato and The Family Centre Social Policy Research Unit), <http://www.ewas.net.nz> (8 January 2015).

12 Judith A. Davey, "Human Capital Issues in an Ageing Workforce," *Social Policy Journal of New Zealand*: Issue 20 (June 2003), <https://www.msd.govt.nz/documents/about-msd-and-our-work/publications- resources/journals-and-magazines/social-policy-journal/spj20/20-pages156-172.pdf> (27 July 2017), 163.

13 Shona Thompson, Bevan Grant and A Dharmalingam, "Leisure time in Midlife: What are the Odds?," Leisure Studies 21 (2002): 125-143, <http://funlibre.org/biblioteca2/docs_digitales/ocio_edad/tiempo_de_ocio_en_la_mitad_de_la_vida.pdf> (8 January 15).

14 Marc Greenhill, "Quake Stress Creates the 'New Vulnerable'," *The Christchurch Press*, 19 March 2014. One on-line reader, responding to another's comment that people in their 30s were too young to be described as middle aged, replied: "According to this we have become middle aged while we've been waiting for EQC/insurance. We were young when all this started!" <http://www.stuff.co.nz/the-press/news/christchurch-earthquake-2011/9842518/Quake-stress-creates-the-new-vulnerable> (21 January, 2015).

15 The Western concept of midlife is not meaningful in certain societies where life expectancy is extremely low. In 22 countries, all of them in sub-Saharan Africa, newborns have life expectancy of less than 60 years. World Health Organisation <http://www.who.int/mediacentre/news/releases/2016/health-inequalities- persist/en/> (23 May 2016).

16 Margie E. Lachman, "Development in Midlife." *Annual Review of Psychology*, Vol. 55 (February 2004), 306.

17 Ibid., 310-11.

18 M.E Lachman, C. Lewkowicz, A Marcus, & Y. Peng, "Images of Midlife Development among Young, Middle-aged, and Older Adults," *Journal of Adult Development* 1: 201-211.

19 Oliver Robinson, *Development Through Adulthood: An Integrative Sourcebook* (Basingstoke: Palgrave Macmillan, 2013), 154.

20 Robinson, *Development Through Adulthood*, 142-3. Lachman agrees that this division can be helpful when exploring the experiences of people

in midlife. She writes, "Given the expanding period of midlife, it may be useful to think about early and late midlife, as the experiences, roles, and health are likely to be vastly different for those who are 30 to 40 and those who are 50 to 60 and beyond." "Development in Midlife," 311.

21 Gerald O'Collins, *The Second Journey* (New York: Paulist Press, 1978).

22 Tony Horsfall, *Facing Midlife: Bible Readings for Special Times* (Abingdon: Bible Reading Fellowship, 2017), 6.

23 Elaine Wethington, Ronald C. Kesseler and Joy E. Pixley, "Turning Points in Adulthood," in *How Healthy Are We? A National Study of Well-Being at Midlife*, ed. Orville Gilbert Brim, et al. (Chicago: University of Chicago Press, 2004), 598. Chapter available on-line.

24 Elliott Jaques, "Death and the Midlife Crisis," *International Journal of Psychoanalysis*, 1965.

25 One such influential book in the 1970s was Gail Sheehy's *Passages: Predictable Crises of Adult Life* (New York: E.P Dutton, 1976).

26 O'Connor and Wolfe, "On Managing Midlife Transitions in Career and Family."

27 Paul David Tripp, *Lost in the Middle: Midlife and the Grace of God* (Wapwollopen: Shepherd Press, 2004), 38-42.

28 Joanna Collicutt, *The Psychology of Christian Character Formation*, 6.

29 Raymond Studzinski, *Spiritual Direction and Midlife Development* (Chicago: Loyola University Press, 1985), 57.

30 Oliver Robinson was interviewed by Kathryn Ryan on RNZ (Radio New Zealand) on 9 May 2016, and the interview was reported on the programme's website under the heading, "The Mid-Life Crisis ... It's Real." <http://www.radionz.co.nz/national/programmes/ninetonoon/audio/201799963/the-mid-life-crisis- it's-real> (9 May 2016).

31 Robinson, *Development Through Adulthood*, 145.

32 Carolyn M. Aldwin and Michael R. Levenson, "Stress, Coping, and Health at Midlife: A Developmental Perspective," in *Handbook of Midlife Development*, ed. Margie E. Lachman (Hoboken, NJ: John Wiley & Sons Inc, 2001), 188.

33 Barbara Bradley Hagerty, *Life Reimagined: The Science, Art and Opportunity of Midlife* (New York, Riverhead Books, 2016), 5.

34 In *A Renewed Spirituality: Finding Fresh Paths at Midlife*, 13, Lynne Baab draws on this image used by Bob Buford throughout his book, *Half Time: Changing Your Game Plan from Success to Significance* (Grand Rapids, MI: Zondervan, 1994).

35 Tony Horsfall, *Facing Midlife*, 8.

36 Jonathan Rauch, *The Happiness Curve: Why Life Gets Better after 50* (New York: Thomas Dunne Books, 2010).

37 Robinson, *Development Through Adulthood*, 86-87. Robinson summaries findings from A. A. Stone, J. E. Broderick, and A. Deaton, "A snapshot of the age distribution of psychological well-being in the United States," *Proceedings of the National Academy of Sciences of the United States of America*, 107, 9985-9990.

38 Carolyn M. Aldwin and Michael R. Levenson, "Stress, Coping, and Health at Midlife: A Developmental Perspective," in *Handbook of Midlife Development*, ed. Margie E. Lachman (Hoboken, NJ: John Wiley & Sons Inc, 2001), 189.

39 Lachman, "Development in Midlife," 320-321.

40 Ursula M. Staudinger and Susan Bluck, "A View of Midlife Development from Life-Span Theory," in *Handbook of Midlife Development*, ed. Margie E. Lachman. Wiley series on Adulthood and Aging (Hoboken, NJ, US: John Wiley & Sons Inc), 15.

41 Jane E. Myers and Melanie C. Harper, "Midlife Concerns and Caregiving Experiences: Intersecting Life Issues Affecting Mental Health," in *The Challenges of Mental Health Caregiving: Research. Practice. Policy*, ed. Benjamin G. Druss, Gregory Fricchione and Ronda C. Talley (New York: Springer, 2014), 129.

42 Vaillant builds on Erik Erikson's stages of psychosocial development, which identifies a critical antithesis in adulthood between "generativity" and "stagnation." Erik H. Erikson, *The Life Cycle Completed: A Review* (New York: W.W Norton & Company, 1985), 67.

43 George E. Vaillant, *Aging Well: Surprising Guideposts to a Happier Life from the Landmark Study of Adult Development* (New York: Little, Brown and Company, 2002), 141-158.

44 Ursula M. Staudinger and Susan Bluck, "A View of Midlife Development from Life-Span Theory," in *Handbook of Midlife Development*, ed. Margie E. Lachman (Hoboken, NJ: John Wiley & Sons Inc, 2001), 14.

45 Studzinski, *Spiritual Direction and Midlife Development*, 40-47.

46 Lynne Baab, *Embracing Midlife: Congregations as Support Systems* (Bethesda, MD: Alban Institute, 1999), 38.

47 Ibid., xiii.

48 Collicutt, *The Psychology of Christian Character Formation*, 202.

49 Ibid., 208.

50 Ibid., xiii.

51 Ibid., 22.

52 Sterns and Huyck, "The Role of Work in Midlife," 466.

53 Sterns and Huyck refer to the work of Richard A. Shweder and Usha Menon as they highlight the need to consider cultural contexts when building models of adult development. "The Role of Work in Midlife," 469. Menon and Shweder's work considers different points of transition that

occur in "traditional cultures." Usha Menon and Richard A. Shweder, "The Return of the White Man's Burden: The Moral Discourse of Anthropology and the Domestic life of Hindu Women," in R. A. Shweder, ed., *Welcome to Middle Age!* 139-186 (Chicago: University of Chicago Press, 1998).

54 Lachman writes, "Presumably, there is still just as much time left as has gone by. Of course with life one doesn't know the endpoint, so the timing of the middle is an estimate. Whether one thinks midlife signifies that life is half over or half is still remaining could lead to different outcomes, as optimism research suggests." "Development in Midlife," 310.

55 Ibid.

56 Kathleen Brehony, *Awakening at Midlife: A Guide to Reviving Your Spirit, Recreating Your Life, and Returning to Your Truest Self* (New York: Riverhead Books, 1996), 11.

57 Interview with author, San Francisco, 19 June 2015.

58 D. Karp, "A Decade of Reminders: Age Consciousness between Fifty and Sixty Years Old," *Gerontologist* 28:6 (1988): 736.

59 Ibid.

60 Ibid.

61 Carolyn M. Aldwin and Michael P. Levenson, "Stress, Coping and Health at Midlife: A Developmental Perspective," in *Handbook of Midlife Development*, ed. Margie E. Lachman (Hoboken, NJ: John Wiley & Sons Inc, 2001), 205.

62 Oliver Robinson summarises a number of models of wisdom, including the "Berlin wisdom paradigm," Sternberg's "Balance theory of wisdom," and Ardelt's "Three dimensional wisdom scale," in *Development Through Adulthood*, 214-228.

63 Monika Ardelt, "Empirical Assessment of a Three-Dimensional Wisdom Scale," *Research on Aging* 25:3 (May 2003): 275-324. <http://users.clas.ufl.edu/ardelt/empirical%20assessment%20of%20the%203d-ws.pdf> (22 July 2017).

64 Hagerty, *Life Reimagined*, 31.

65 Hagerty, *Life Reimagined*, 44.

66 Ibid., 326.

2 — Faith development and midlife

67 Excerpt from "We thank you for the Heritage," *Hope is our Song: New Hymns and Songs from Aotearoa New Zealand* (Palmerston North: The New Zealand Hymn Book Trust, 2009), 290.

68 JB Phillips, *Your God is Too Small* (London: Epworth Press, 1952).

69 Ken Wilber, *Integral Spirituality: A Startling New Role for Religion in the Modern and Postmodern World* (Boston: Integral Books, 2007).

70   Sheila Pritchard. Adapted from the keynote address at the Spiritual Directors' Refresher Day Auckland 12/2/11. *Refresh: Journal of Contemplative Spirituality*, Volume 11 Number 1 Summer 2012, 40.

71   Kevin Ward, "Is New Zealand's Future Churchless?" *Stimulus* vol. 12, no. 2, (May 2004): 2-12.

72   Helen Bent, *Exploring Worship in Pilgrimage* (Cambridge: Grove Books, 2020).

73   Pope Francis, Address to the Clergy in the Cathedral of San Rufino in Assisi, Italy, 4 October 2013. *The Church of Mercy: A Vision for the Church* (London: Darton, Longman and Todd, 2014), 75.

74   The opening line of the classic hymn "Trust and Obey," by John Henry Sammis. Published in many hymnals including *With One Voice* (Auckland: William Collins, 1982).

75   Walter Brueggemann, "Psalms and the Life of Faith: A Suggested Typology of Function," *Journal for the Study of the Old Testament* 17 (1980): 6-9.

76   Frederic. M. Hudson, *The Adult Years: Mastering the Art of Self-Renewal* (San Francisco: Jossey-Bass, 1991), 38.

77   Ibid., 120.

78   Joanna Collicutt, *The Psychology of Christian Character Formation*, 80.

79   Sally Welch, *Walking the Labyrinth: A Spiritual and Practical Guide* (London: Canterbury Press, 2010).

80   Daniel Levinson, *The Seasons of a Man's Life* (New York: Ballantine Books, 1978), 6-7.

81   Erik H. Erikson, *The Life Cycle Completed: A Review* (New York: W.W Norton & Company, 1985), 67.

82   Levinson, *The Seasons of a Man's Life*, 51.

83   Parker J. Palmer. *Let Your Life Speak: Listening for the Voice of Vocation* (San Francisco: Jossey-Bass, 2000), 96.

84   Jacques Philippe, *Interior Freedom*, trans. by Helena Scott (New York: Scepter Publishers, 2007), 29.

85   Susan S. Phillips, *Candlelight: Illuminating the Art of Spiritual Direction* (Harrisburg: Morehouse Publishing, 2008), 166-7.

86   Ibid., 96.

87   Collicutt, *The Psychology of Christian Character Formation*, 13.

88   Ibid., 14.

89   Susan S. Phillips, *The Cultivated Life: From Ceaseless Striving to Receiving Joy* (Downers Grove, IL: InterVarsity Press, 2015), 32.

90   Ibid., 34.

91   Ibid., 34-35.

92 James W. Fowler, *Stages of Faith: The Psychology of Human Development and the Quest for Meaning* (New York: Harper and Row, 1981).

93 James W. Fowler, *Faith Development and Pastoral Care. Theology and Pastoral Care*, ed. Donald S. Browning (Philadelphia: Fortress Press, 1987), 101.

94 See, for example, Thomas A. Droege, *Faith Passage and Patterns* (Philadelphia, PA: Fortress Press, 1983). Janet O. Hagberg and Robert A. Guelich, *The Critical Journey: Stages in the Life of Faith*, 2nd ed (Salem, WI: Sheffield Publishing, 2005). Alan Jamieson, *Called Again: In and Beyond the Deserts of Faith* (Wellington: Philip Garside Publishing, 2004) and "Construction – Deconstruction – Reconstruction." *Spirited Exchanges.* Andrew Pritchard, "Fowler, Faith and Fallout." Reality Magazine 33 (1999): 22-30.

95 Jamieson, *Called Again*, 112.

96 Fowler, *Stages of Faith*, 164.

97 Fowler, *Stages of Faith*, 186.

98 Ibid., 198.

99 Jamieson, *Called Again*, 114.

100 Ron Rolheiser, "The Major Imperatives within Mature Discipleship" <https://ronrolheiser.com/the-major-imperatives-within-mature-discipleship/#.YHvhsJMzbL8> (18 April 2021).

101 Heinz Streib, "Faith Development Theory Revisited: The Religious Styles Perspective," *The International Journal for the Psychology of Religion* 11:3 (2001).

102 Alan Jamieson, "Off-road Faith," *Spirited Exchanges*, 2005. <http://www.spiritedexchanges.org.nz/store/doc/issue%2036.pdf> (6 August 2021), 3.

103 Fowler, *Stages of Faith*, 274.

104 Alan Jamieson, *A Churchless Faith: Faith Journeys Beyond Evangelical, Pentecostal and Charismatic Churches* (Wellington: Philip Garside Publishing, 2000).

105 Janet O. Hagberg and Robert A. Guelich, *The Critical Journey: Stages in the Life of Faith* 2nd ed. (Salem, WI: Sheffield Publishing, 2005).

106 Adrienne Thompson, "Spiritual Direction through Faith Stage and Cross Cultural Transitions," *Spiritual Growth Ministries*, 2003, 8. <http://www.sgm.org.nz/Research%20Papers/Spiritual%20Direction%20through%20Faith%20Stage%20and%20Cross%20Cultur.pdf> (17 February 2013).

107 Ibid.

108 For Christians, a sense of God's distance or inexplicable absence during times of disequilibrium may compound their anxieties. Janet Ruffing, then Professor of Spirituality and Spiritual Direction at Fordham University in New York (now at Yale Divinity School) notes that during times of

spiritual struggle and change prayer "may be one of life's stressors rather than a stress-reducer." Janet Ruffing, "Personality Sciences," *The Blackwell Companion to Christian Spirituality*, ed Arthur Holder (Oxford: Blackwell Publishing, 2005), 322.

109   Lynne Baab, *Embracing Midlife: Congregations as Support Systems* (Bethesda, MD: Alban Institute, 1999), 4.

110   Fowler, *Stages of Faith*, 296.

111   Matthew's reference is to *The Alpha Course* which a number of churches in New Zealand, as well as throughout the world, offer as an introduction to the basics of the Christian faith. <http://alpha.org.nz> (3 April 2017).

112   Jamieson, *A Churchless Faith*.

113   Alan Jamieson, "Construction – Deconstruction – Reconstruction," *Spirited Exchanges*, <http://www.spiritedexchanges.org.nz/store/doc/ Article_construction%20etc.pdf> (14 February, 2017), 1.

114   Andrew Pritchard, "Fowler, Faith and Fallout," *Reality Magazine*, Issue 33 (1999): 29. <http://www.reality.org.nz/articles/33/33-pritchard. html> (18 March 2014).

115   Ibid., 22-30.

116   "Spirited Exchanges" is a New Zealand website which provides "resources, support and connection with like-minded others for people who sense their faith is changing and their relationship with church is being renegotiated." New material is no longer being added to this site, but existing resources and links are still accessible. <http://www. spiritedexchanges.org.nz/page/3/whoweare.boss> (18 May 2017).

3 — Part of the Family

117   Hymn by James K. Manley, "Part of the Family," in *Songs for a Gospel People*, ed. R Gerald Hobbs (Winfield, British Columbia: Wood Lake Books, 1987).

118   "The Anglican," November 2018, 4. <https://aucklandanglican.org.nz/ Anglican/media/Images/The%20Anglican/The-Anglican-November-2018-WEB.pdf> (22 June 2020)

119   The study was carried out by AUT University's Human Potential Centre and insurance company Sovereign in 2015. "Only 36 per cent of those surveyed said they felt appreciated by people close to them. New Zealand ranked last in this category compared to other countries surveyed. Denmark was ranked first, with 83 per cent." Laura Walters, "Kiwis Suffering from Disconnect," 15 May 2015 <http://www.stuff.co.nz/life-style/well-good/68591123/kiwis-suffering-from-disconnect> (5 April 2017).

120   Oliver Robinson, *Development Through Adulthood: An Integrative Sourcebook* (Basingstoke: Palgrave Macmillan, 2013), 300. See also

Michelle Van Loon. "Why Friends Disappear When You Reach Midlife." http://theperennialgen.com/why-friends-disappear-when-you-reach-midlife/ (12 June 2017).

121   The results of one survey, published in 2006, found that the loneliest people in the United States are aged between 45 and 65. "Loneliness Among Older Adults: A National Survey of Adults 45+," *AARP The Magazine*, September 2010. Cited in Barbara Bradley Hagerty, *Life Reimagined: The Science, Art and Opportunity of Midlife* (New York: Riverhead Books, 2016), 107-108. Since the coronavirus pandemic even more people are working from home.

122   According to data from the 2013 Census, 23.5% of New Zealanders live in one-person households. In 2013, the median age of people living alone was 62 years. "2013 Census QuickStats about Families and Households," Statistics New Zealand, 2013 Census Data, <http://archive.stats.govt.nz/Census/2013-census/profile-and-summary-reports/qstats-families-households/households.aspx#gsc.tab=0> (1 July 2020)

123   Laura Walters, "Kiwis Suffering from Disconnect," 15 May 2015 <http://www.stuff.co.nz/life-style/well-good/68591123/kiwis-suffering-from-disconnect> (5 April 2017).

124   Pope Francis, *Evangelii Gaudium: The Joy of the Gospel* (London: The Incorporated Catholic Truth Society, 2013).

125   Passionist Family Group Movement, <http://www.passionistfamily.org.nz> (1 July 2020).

126   Vaillant, *Aging Well*, 47-48.

127   Janet K Ruffing, "Spiritual Identity and Narrative: Fragmentation, Coherence, and Transformation," *Spiritus* 12 (2012): 63, 68-9.

128   The Men's Series, <http://www.olivetreemedia.com.au/mens-series/> (1 July 2020). This DVD series was one of the few resources specifically relating to midlife that was identified by midlife churchgoers.

129   Claire Dalpra of The Sheffield Centre, UK, defines Messy church as "an all-age fresh expression of church that offers counter-cultural transformation of family life through families coming together to be, to make, to eat and to celebrate God." Messy Church NZ, <http://messychurch.nz> (11 October, 2016).

130   Phil made reference to the Joshua Catholic Men's Fellowship (New Zealand) which exists "to build up and encourage men in their growth and discipleship in the Lord Jesus to help form men of strength, vision, compassion, hope and joy, to be fully alive as husbands, fathers work mates and friends to those whose lives they touch." <http://joshua.org.nz> (6 March 2016).

131   Frederick Buechner suggests, "The kind of work God usually calls you to is the kind of work (a) that you most need to do and (b) that the world most needs to be done. ... The place God calls you to is the place where

your deep gladness and the world's deep hunger meet." *Wishful Thinking: A Seeker's ABC*, 2nd rev. ed. (London: Bloomsbury, 1994), 118-119.

132   Collicutt, *The Psychology of Christian Character Formation*, 156-157.

133   At the time of his interview Peter was using a book called *Rediscover Jesus* (New York: Beacon Publishing, 2015) by Matthew Kelly.

134   Nicholas Hutchinson, *Praying Each Day of the Year: May to August* (Chelmsford: Matthew James Publishing, 1998), 113.

135   Joanna Collicutt, *When You Pray: Daily Bible Readings for Lent and Easter on the Lord's Prayer* (Abingdon, UK: Bible Reading Fellowship, 2012), 23.

136   Five of the 40 people I interviewed for my PhD had changed denomination around midlife. All three groups of interviewees – of midlife churchgoers, clergy, and spiritual directors – included at least one person who had changed denomination. In addition to these five people who had changed from one denomination to another, two of the midlife churchgoers had made a formal commitment to join a denomination, one after many years of participation in a parish, and one for whom regular church attendance was a fairly new practice.

137   Eugene Peterson, *Practise Resurrection: A Conversation on Growing up in Christ* (London: Hodder and Stoughton, 2010), 17.

138   Rowan Williams, *Being Human* (London: SPCK, 2018), 100-101.

4 — Challenges

139   Bruce Gilberd, Prayer for April 28th in *Two Prayers for Today*, 2018. <https://handleybaptist.com/reading/two-prayers-for-today/> (29 October 2021).

140   Geoffrey Troughton, Joseph Bulbulia and Chris G. Sibley, "Strength of Religion and the Future of the Churches," *Stimulus: The New Zealand Journal of Christian Thought and Practice*, 21:2 (August 2014): 27.

141   "The New Zealand Attitudes and Values Study" (NZAVS) is a longitudinal social survey endeavouring to track repeat responses from 12,000 participants, between 2009 and 2029. "New Zealand Attitudes and Values Study" <https://www.psych.auckland.ac.nz/en/about/our-research/research-groups/new-zealand-attitudes-and-values-study.html> (27 July 2017).

142   Troughton, Bulbulia and Sibley note that there is currently insufficient data to determine whether these findings represent "an age effect" or "a generation effect." "Strength of Religion and the Future of the Churches," 32.

143   A follow-up study to *A Churchless Faith* was published by Alan Jamieson, Jenny McIntosh and Adrienne Thompson, *Five Years On: Continuing Faith Journeys of those who left the Church* (Wellington: Portland Research Trust, 2006). Jamieson explores similar themes

in *Called Again: In and Beyond the Deserts of Faith* (Wellington, Philip Garside Publishing, 2004).

144 Margie E. Lachman, "Development in Midlife," *Annual Review of Psychology*, Vol. 55 (February 2004): 306.

145 Ibid, 306-307.

146 Ibid, 325-6.

147 Alan Jamieson, "AJ's Blog," South West Baptist Church, <http://www.swbc.org.nz/ajs-blog/some-questions-and-answers/> (17 May 2017).

148 Philip Yancey. *What Good is God? In Search of a Faith that Matters* (New York: Little, Brown and Company, 2013).

149 In order to preserve this interviewee's anonymity I have chosen not to identify the denomination to which she was referring. Her comments could apply to quite a few!

150 "Longer lives have meant a dramatic increase in the numbers of midlife adults who have surviving parents. An increasing proportion of those parents will survive to very old ages, although not without serious impairments." Diane E. Papalia, Sally Wendkos Olds and Ruth Duskin Feldman, *Human Development*, 7th ed. (Boston, MA: McGraw Hill, 1998), 524.

151 Norella M. Putney and Vern L. Bengtson. "Familes, Intergenerational Relationships and Kinkeeping in Midlife." *Handbook of Midlife Development*, ed. Margie E. Lachman (Hoboken, NJ: John Wiley and Sons Inc, 2001), 530.

152 Ibid.

153 In New Zealand, there is a rise in the number of older people who are supported by the state, whether in hospitals or rest homes, or by home-based services, rather than being cared for solely by family members. "New Zealand Families Today," a briefing prepared for the Families' Commission by the Ministry of Social Development, 2004, 6, <https://www.msd.govt.nz/documents/about-msd-and-our-work/publications-resources/research/nz-families-today/nz-families-today.pdf> (21 June 2016). The few participants in this project who mentioned accessing these forms of eldercare continued to feel a deep sense of responsibility for their parents' wellbeing.

154 Putney and Bengtson, "Families, Intergenerational Relationships, and Kinkeeping in Midlife," 560. "Prolonged parenthood – when children remain home longer than expected, or don't leave, or return to the "empty nest" not because of their parents' needs but because of their own economic needs – has become a significant challenge in intergenerational relations at midlife." Ibid., 535.

155 Anglicans Online: Online Resources, <http://anglicansonline.org/resources/index.html> (31 May 2016).

156 Joanna Collicutt. *Thinking of You: A Resource for the Spiritual Care of People with Dementia* (Oxford: The Bible Reading Fellowship, 2017). This is one resource which I would recommend to people caring for the elderly. The author is not only a lecturer in Psychology and Spirituality and an ordained priest, but the Oxford Diocesan Advisor for the Spiritual Care of Older People. This is an accessible book which includes practical suggestions for families, caregivers and congregations.

157 Carolyn M. Aldwin and Michael R. Levenson, "Stress, Coping, and Health at Midlife: A Developmental Perspective," in *Handbook of Midlife Development*, ed. Margie E. Lachman (Hoboken, NJ: John Wiley & Sons Inc, 2001), 194.

158 Ibid., 195. American spelling retained from the original.

159 Kathleen A. Brehony dedicates a chapter to "Losses and Confronting Death," in *Awakening at Midlife: A Guide to Reviving Your Spirit, Recreating Your Life, and Returning to Your Truest Self* (New York: Riverhead Books, 1996), 100.

160 Helen Bent, *Celebration in Times of Grief and Sorrow* (Cambridge: Grove Books, 2018), 5.

161 *A New Zealand Prayer Book: He Karakia Mihinare o Aotearoa*. The Anglican Church in Aotearoa, New Zealand and Polynesia. San Francisco: HarperSan Francisco, 1997), 195.

162 Bent, *Celebration in Times of Grief and Sorrow*, 8.

163 Some churches offer special services for people who are bereaved or coping with other significant challenges. Reflective and gentle "Blue Christmas" services, for example, create "sacred space for people living through dark times." The United Methodist Church, "Blue Christmas/ Longest Night Worship With Those Who Mourn." <https://www.umcdiscipleship.org/resources/blue-christmaslongest-night-worship-with-those-who-mourn> (20 May 2019). Although the symbolism associated with the winter solstice is lost when these services are held in the Southern Hemisphere, they are nonetheless valued when they are offered in New Zealand. St Margaret's Anglican Church, Hillsborough, Auckland, offers a Blue Christmas service. It is described in the parish's 2018 annual report <https://stmags.org.nz/wp-content/uploads/2019/03/St-Mags-Report-2018-final-web.pdf> (20 May 2019), 9.

164 Harvey L. Sterns and Margaret Hellie Huyck, "The Role of Work in Midlife," in *Handbook of Midlife Development*, ed. Margie E. Lachman, 3-39 (Hoboken, NJ: John Wiley & Sons Inc, 2001), 447.

165 Sterns and Huyck, "The Role of Work in Midlife," 469.

166 In 2016 Carey Baptist College advertised a course entitled "Theology at Work" which is described as follows: "How do we live Christianly from Monday to Saturday, in locations other than home or church? This course explores a theology of work, work ethics, career choice, the notion of

laity and the way in which 'church' becomes a far wider concept when it encounters the marketplace." <http://carey.ac.nz/course/theology-at-work/> (16 November 2016).

167 *Pontifical Council for Justice and Peace's Compendium of the Social Doctrine of the Church* (London: Continuum International Publishing Group, 2004), 134-164.

168 Theology of Work <www.theologyofwork.org> (5 September 2021).

169 James Martin and Jeremy Langford (eds), *Professions of Faith: Living and Working as a Catholic* (Kansas City: Rowman and Littlefield, 2002).

170 Lynne Baab, *Sabbath Keeping: Finding Freedom in the Rhythms of Rest* (Downers Grove, IL: Inter-Varsity Press, 2005).

171 "Through the kumara wireless" is a colloquial expression with some equivalence to the phrase "on the grape vine." (In New Zealand sweet potatoes are called kumara.)

172 Interview by author, Christchurch, 30th November 2015.

173 *A whakataukī* (Māori proverb).

174 The Marriage Course, <http://alphausa.org/the-marriage-course> (7 November 2016).

5 — Something more

175 *A New Zealand Prayer Book: He Karakia Mihinare o Aotearoa*, 605.

176 A. W. Tozer, *The Pursuit of God*. 15th ed. (Chicago: Moody Publishers, 72015), 17.

177 The Catholic Church in Aotearoa New Zealand, "RCIA," <http://www. catholic.org.nz/ms/dsp-default.cfm?loadref=170&pid=C9F2B42F-B3C8-569A-74B5BAAD927FF5F1> (25 October, 2016).

178 Bible Study Fellowship, <https://www.bsfinternational.org> (16 May 2016). The website describes the aims of the Bible Study Fellowship, which is an international organisation, and outlines all the courses that are offered.

179 I was grateful that one middle-aged churchgoer recommended NT Wright's podcast, "Ask NT Wright Anything" <https:// askntwrightanything.podbean.com/> (11 August 2021).

180 See, for example, the *My Catholic Life!* series of 24 studies. <https:// mycatholic.life/rcia/> (2 September 2019). Another popular resource used by some New Zealand congregations is an Australian book, *At Home with God's People* (Faith and Life, Archdiocese of Brisbane, Adult Faith Education 1990, revised edition 2011).

181 "Lord Jesus Christ, Son of God, have mercy on me, a sinner."

182 *A New Zealand Prayer Book: He Karakia Mihinare o Aotearoa* (The Anglican Church in Aotearoa, New Zealand and Polynesia. San Francisco: HarperSan Francisco, 1997).

183 In an engaging article entitled "Prayer by the Book," Anglican priest Tish Harrison Warren explores this concept. She argues that while self-expression in prayer has an important place, using "other people's words" in prayer can be considered "a kind of craft or exercise that shapes us." Tish Harrison Warren, "Prayer by the Book," *Comment: Public Theology for the Common Good*. Winter 2016, Vol 34, Issue 4, 44-49. <https://www.cardus.ca/comment/article/4982/by-the-book/> (24 April 2020).

184 Jeanette A. Bakke, *Holy Invitations: Exploring Spiritual Direction* (Grand Rapids, MI: Baker Books, 2000), 195.

185 In the kataphatic tradition, words and images are used in prayer, whereas the apophatic tradition is a way of prayer, of being present with God, without images or words. Frederick G. McLeod, "Apophatic or Kataphatic Prayer?" <http://opcentral.org/resources/2015/01/13/frederick-g-mcleod-apophatic-or-kataphatic-prayer/> (29 February 2016).

186 Michael Mayne, *This Sunrise of Wonder: Letters for the Journey* (London: Fount, 1995).

187 Michael Leunig, "Prayer of Gratitude," <http://www.leunig.com.au> (6 April 2020)

188 "45 Ways to Encounter God Multilingual Resource." <https://women.salvationarmy.org.nz/resource/45-ways-encounter-god-multilingual-resource> (5 Nov 2021).

189 "Praying with Martin Luther: The Lord's Prayer," in *Praying with Giants: Learning to Pray with History's Best Teachers* (Downer's Grove, IL: InterVarsity Press, 2012), 36-52.

190 This is a point developed by Joanna Collicutt in the introduction to her book, *When You Pray: Daily Bible Reflections on the Lord's Prayer* (Oxford: Bible Reading Fellowship, 2019).

191 Kathleen P. Rushton, *The Cry of the Earth and the Cry of the Poor: Hearing Justice in John's Gospel* (London: SCM Press, 2020), xvii.

192 James Martin, *The Jesuit Guide to Almost Everything: A Spirituality for Real Life* (New York: HarperCollins, 2010), 159.

193 Jim Manney, *A Simple Life-Changing Prayer: Discovering the Power of St. Ignatius Loyola's Examen* (Chicago: Loyola Press, 2011).

194 Collicutt, *The Psychology of Christian Character Formation*, 157.

195 See, for example, many resources on the IgnatianSpirituality.com website. <http://www.ignatianspirituality.com> (7 June 2017). James Martin, S.J. *The Jesuit Guide to (Almost) Everything: A Spirituality for Real Life* (New York: Harper Collins, 2010). Kevin O'Brien, S.J. *The Ignatian Adventure: Experiencing the Spiritual Exercises of Saint Ignatius in Daily Life* (Chicago: Loyola Press, 2011).

196 An Ignatian Prayer Adventure, <http://www.ignatianspirituality.com/ignatian-prayer/the-spiritual- exercises/an-ignatian-prayer-adventure/> (7 June 2017).

197 Gary Neal Hansen, *Kneeling with Giants: Learning to Pray with History's Best Teachers* (Downer's Grove, IL: InterVarsity Press, 2012).

198 Dawn Duncan Harrell, *Ten Ways to Pray: A Short Guide to a Long History of Talking with God* (Los Angeles: Stone's Throw, 2012).

199 Sheila Pritchard, *The Lost Art of Meditation: Deepening Your Prayer Life* (UK: Scripture Union Publishing, 2003).

200 Barbara Sampson, *Encountering God*, rev. ed. (Wellington: The Salvation Army, New Zealand, Fiji, Tonga and Samoa Territory, 2019)

201 Barbara Sampson, *Encountering God* <https://www.salvationarmy.org.nz/resource/knowing-god> (15 Sept 2021). This is the earlier edition of the book but most changes are stylistic. The content differs little.

202 "The Ho-hum Hymn," in *Hope is Our Song: New Hymns and Songs from Aotearoa New Zealand* (Palmerston North: The New Zealand Hymn Book Trust, 2009).

203 William Shakespeare, *Hamlet* (I,ii,133).

204 C.S Lewis, "On the Reading of Old Books," in *God in the Dock: Essays on Theology and Ethics* (Wm B. Eerdmans Publishing, 2014), 217-25. Originally published 1970 by the Trustees of the Estate of C.S Lewis.

205 In this context Hugh referred to the "flow model" of Mihály Csíkszentmihályi. Achieving flow is often colloquially referred to as being "in the zone." <https://en.wikipedia.org/wiki/Flow_(psychology)> (27 April 2019).

206 *A New Zealand Prayer Book: He Karakia Mihinare o Aotearoa* (The Anglican Church in Aotearoa, New Zealand and Polynesia. San Francisco: HarperSan Francisco, 1997), 464. Italics mine.

207 <http://epistle.us/inspiration/franciscanbenediction.html> (26 October 2020).

208 Pope Francis, Address to a General Audience, 27 March 2013. *The Church of Mercy: A Vision for the Church* (London: Darton, Longman and Todd, 2014), 72-3.

209 Henri Nouwen, Donald McNeill and Douglas Morrison. *Compassion* (London: Darton, Longman and Todd, 1982), 122.

210 Cardinal Basil Hume describes waiting as "a purifying process, as we come to rely less – or if at all – on our own resources and have to abandon ourselves into God's hands." Basil Hume, *Basil in Blunderland* rev. ed. (London: Darton, Longman and Todd, 2005), 67.

211 Michael Mayne speaks of this clergyman in a talk delivered on 11 July 2002 at the Mustard Seed Christian Bookshop, Marlborough. *To Trust and To Love: Sermons and Addresses* (London: Dartman, Longman and Todd, 2010), 163.

6 — Addressing the Discipleship Gap

212 The Christian Coaching Centre, "Willow Creek Reveal Study: A Summary," <http://www.christiancoachingcenter.org/index.php/russ-rainey/coachingchurch2/> (27 May 2020)

213 Christianity Today, "Willow Creek Repents?" <http://www.christianitytoday.com/pastors/2007/october-online-only/willow-creek-repents.html> (27 May 2020).

214 The Christian Coaching Centre, "Willow Creek Reveal Study: A Summary," <http://www.christiancoachingcenter.org/index.php/russ-rainey/coachingchurch2/> (27 May 2020)

215 Michelle Van Loon, "Middle-Aged Women Face a Crisis of Discipleship," <http://www.christianitytoday.com/women/2017/june/middle-aged-women-face-crisis-discipleship.html> (27 May 2020).

216 Ibid., 1.

217 Ibid., 2.

218 "Pray as You Go" is an aural daily prayer guide provided by the Society of Jesus (the Jesuits) in Britain. It is available on-line, <https://pray-as-you-go.org> (3 July 2019), and as a phone app.

219 Andrew Pritchard, "Fowler, Faith and Fallout." *Reality Magazine* 33 (1999): 22-30.

220 Janet K. Ruffing, "Spiritual Identity and Narrative," 69.

221 Ibid.

222 Andrew Pritchard, "Your Church's Personality," *Reality Magazine*, Issue 45 (2001) <https://www.reality.org.nz/articles/45/45-pritchard.php> (28 May, 2021).

223 A plea from a Presbyterian elder, cited in Hamish Galloway, "Hope Springs – Empowering the Next Generation." (2015). <https://knoxcentre.ac.nz/wp-content/uploads/2012/11/2015-Jun-Galloway-H-Hope-Springs.pdf> (18 May 2020). This interesting article includes some reflection on the positive impact of mentoring and guidance for younger adults.

224 The Peer Support Programme: *Te Aka Tautoko Akonga* <http://www.peersupport.org.nz/> (19 May 2020).

225 Hamish Galloway, "Hope Springs".

226 Donald Capps, *Life Cycle Theory and Pastoral Care, Theology and Pastoral Care*, ed. Donald S. Browning (Philadelphia: Fortress Press, 1983), 28.

227 Daniel Levinson, *The Seasons of a Man's Life* (New York: Ballantine Books, 1978), 254.

228 *The Clifton StrengthsFinder*™ measures the presence of 34 talents/ themes/strengths. <http://www.strengthstest.com/strengths-finder-themes> (14 October, 2016).

229 *Renovaré* is an organisation that was founded in 1988 by Richard J. Foster, author of *Celebration of Discipline* (San Francisco: Harper and Row, 1978), among other titles. <https://renovare.org/groups> (13 June 2017).

230 Anglican Cursillo New Zealand <http://cursillo.org.nz/> (26 May 2021).

231 Emmaus Fourth Day Reunion Groups <http://www.etownemmaus.org/download/servicesheet.pdf> (26 May 2021).

232 Baptist minister, interview with author, 28th October 2015.

233 Louisa (spiritual director).

234 Raymond Studzinski, *Spiritual Direction and Midlife Development* (Chicago: Loyola University Press, 1985), 96.

235 Susan Phillips, *Candlelight: Illuminating the Art of Spiritual Direction* (Harrisburg: Morehouse Publishing, 2008), 38.

236 Andrew Dunn, "Spiritual Direction," *Candour: News and Views for Ministers* (February 2011): 18.

237 When looking for a spiritual director many people find it helpful to begin by speaking to a priest or minister or someone they know who attends spiritual direction. That person may be able to suggest a spiritual director. People may also find a spiritual director by searching diocesan websites, such as <https://chchcatholic.nz/pastoral/spiritual-direction/>. The website of "The Association of Christian Spiritual Directors in Aotearoa New Zealand" provides a list of spiritual directors by location <http://www.acsd.org.nz>.

238 Thomas N. Hart, *The Art of Christian Listening* (New York: Paulist Press, 1980), 1.

239 "The Story of My Days," an address given at The Mustard Seed Christian Bookshop, 11 July 2002. *To Trust and To Love*, (London: Darton, Longman and Todd, 2010), 160-171.

240 Henri Nouwen, "Listening as Spiritual Hospitality," reading for 11th March, *Bread for the Journey: A Daybook of Wisdom and Faith* (New York: Harper One, 2006).

7 — Two case studies

241 Address of His Holiness Pope Francis to participants in the plenary assembly of the Pontifical Council for the Laity, 17 June 2016. <http://w2.vatican.va/content/francesco/en/speeches/2016/june/documents/papa-francesco_20160617_plenaria-pc-laici.html> (9 August 2018).

242 See Chapter 6.

243 *The Clifton StrengthsFinder*™ measures the presence of 34 talents/themes/strengths. <http://www.strengthstest.com/strengths-finder-themes> (14 October, 2016).

244 Michael Hansen, *The First Spiritual Exercises: Four Guided Retreats* (Notre Dame, IN: Ave Maria Press, 2013). Although Hansen's prayer suggestions had been adapted for the retreats, several of the leaders and participants felt that the material should be further modified. Kevin is finding that very simple, less wordy, resources are often the most helpful. It is my own belief that the most effective retreats within parishes are likely to use "home grown" resources which are of relevance to a particular community at a given point in time.

245 "Christian Life Communities" are present in more than 55 countries. These groups follow the spirituality of St Ignatius Loyola, with its three main elements of prayer, community and mission. <https://clc.org.nz> (7 November 2018)

246 One introductory text used by these groups was Laurence Gooley's *To Share in the Life of Christ: Experiencing God in Everyday Life* (St Louis, Missouri: The Institute of Jesuit Sources, 1997).

247 On-line retreats of 34 weeks are offered through Creighton University, a Jesuit Catholic university in the United States of America. These can be completed by individuals or used as a resource for groups. <http://onlineministries.creighton.edu/CollaborativeMinistry/cmo-retreat.html> (27 March 2019).

248 Retreats of this type are offered from centres throughout the world. I enjoyed an online retreat offered by the Ignation Spirituality Centre Glasgow <https://www.iscglasgow.co.uk> which was led by a spiritual director in Malaysia.

249 Parker J. Palmer, *Let Your Life Speak: Listening for the Voice of Vocation* (San Francisco: Jossey-Bass, 2000), 91-92.

250 Ibid, 92. Italics retained from the original.

251 Interestingly, it is the observation of some people who offer these and similar programmes that when participants are asked to pay a fee to attend (even if it is a small sum) they seem more committed to attending and more appreciative of what they receive.

252 William A. Barry and William J. Connolly, *The Practice of Spiritual Direction*, 2nd ed. (New York: HarperCollins Publishers, 2009), 22.

8 — Observations and next steps

253 Published in many hymnals including *With One Voice* (Auckland: William Collins, 1982).

254 A large body of existing research into the connections between spirituality or religion and psychological wellbeing exists. Within

New Zealand, these connections are explored by "The Spirituality and Well-being Strategy Group." Members include Dr Richard Egan, Lecturer, University of Otago; Dr Chris Perkins, Director Selwyn Centre for Ageing and Spirituality; Simon Cayley, CEO Bishop's Action Foundation; Charles Waldegrave, Family Centre Social Policy Research Unit, Dr Tess Moeke-Maxwell, and Dr Anna Holmes, Clinical Senior Lecturer, Department of General Practice, University of Otago. See "Spirituality and Well-being: Discussion Paper," July 2013. <https://spiritualityandwellbeing.co.nz> (25 April 2017).

255   Parker J. Palmer, *Let Your Life Speak: Listening for the Voice of Vocation* (San Francisco: Jossey-Bass, 2000), 37.

256   Pope Francis, Address to the Participants at the International Congress on Catechesis, 27 September 2013. *The Church of Mercy: A Vision for the Church* (London: Darton, Longman and Todd, 2014), 16. Italics retained from the original.

257   William A. Barry and William J. Connolly, *The Practice of Spiritual Direction*, 2nd ed. (New York: HarperCollins Publishers, 2009), 22.

Appendix: The research process

258   *A New Zealand Prayer Book: He Karakia Mihinare o Aotearoa.* The Anglican Church in Aotearoa, New Zealand and Polynesia, 183. <https://anglicanprayerbook.nz/167.html> (12 June 2021).

259   Anne Shave, *Your Strength in Our Hearts: New Zealand Churchgoers in Midlife.* <https://ourarchive.otago.ac.nz/bitstream/handle/10523/7820/ShaveAnneE2017PhD.pdf?sequence=1&isAllowed=y> (8 May 2019).

260   Peter Ball, *Anglican Spiritual Direction* (Harrisburg, PA: Morehouse Publishing, 2007), 107.

261   I asked the spiritual directors approximately what proportion of their clients were in midlife. The table includes the words directors used in response to this question. Their perceptions of the age range of midlife differed from one another, as other comments in each interview revealed, but the spiritual directors were all aware I was interviewing churchgoers between the ages of 40 and 60 when they answered this question.

262   Robert L. Miller and John D. Brewer, *The A-Z of Social Research: A Dictionary of Key Social Science Research Concepts* (London: Sage Publications, 2003), 279.

263   It is possible that ministers and academic supervisors may also have been inclined to nominate people whose academic backgrounds were similar to their own, but this was certainly not always the case.

264   "'While research showed the third year post-disaster as the worst for mental illness, Canterbury was different because of the number of aftershocks and indirect issues like insurance problems. In this instance, it was more akin to the effects of a war,' Child, Adolescent and Family (CAF) clinical director Dr Harith Swadi said." Ashleigh Stewart,

"Canterbury residents 'most vulnerable' five years after the quakes." *The Christchurch Press*, 7 November 2015.

265 Data relating to Physical and Mental Health and Well-being, released in April 2017 by "All Right?" – a Healthy Christchurch initiative led by the Canterbury District Health Board and the Mental Health Foundation of New Zealand – revealed that four fifths of respondents "agreed" that they valued others more now than before the earthquakes (81% in 2016, 83% in 2012). Over four fifths of respondents reported having a better sense of what is important to them now, compared with before the earthquakes (82% in 2016, 83% in 2012). More respondents reported that their faith, religion or spirituality had helped them to deal with the last few years (42% in 2016, 34% in 2012). <https://allright.org.nz/media/documents/2017_Research_Summary_FINAL.pdf> (7 June 2017).

266 According to the 2013 census, "Nearly three-quarters of the population (74.0 percent) identified themselves as being of European ethnicity, which was an increase from 67.6 percent in 2006. This increase seems to be partly due to fewer people identifying themselves as 'New Zealander'. In 2013, 65,973 people identified as 'New Zealander' on their census form, compared with 429,429 people in 2006. There was a media campaign in 2006 that encouraged people to give the response 'New Zealander'." Statistics New Zealand, <http://www.stats.govt.nz/Census/2013-census/profile-and-summary-reports/quickstats-about-national-highlights/cultural-diversity.aspx> (11 May 2017).

267 The New Zealand unemployment rate across the first three months of 2016, during which period the majority of the participants were interviewed, was 5.7%. New Zealand Unemployment Rate, <http://www.tradingeconomics.com/new-zealand/unemployment-rate> (23 May 2016).

268 Harvey L. Sterns and Margaret Hellie Huyck, "The Role of Work in Midlife," in *Handbook of Midlife Development*, ed. Margie E. Lachman (Hoboken, NJ: John Wiley & Sons Inc, 2001), 463-4.

269 Jenet Jacob Erikson, Giuseppe Martinengo and E. Jeffrey Hill, "Putting Work and Family Experiences in Context: Differences by Family Life Stage," *Human Relations* 63:7 (2010): 976.

270 Edmund Gordon, "Adult Faith Formation: A Catholic Vision," *Lifelong Faith* vol 2.3 (Fall 2008), 31-38.

271 Ibid., 32.

272 Ibid., 33. It seems probable that Gordon's comments, based on the situation in the United States of America, also apply within the New Zealand context. It is worth considering the influence that immigration has had on the Catholic Church in New Zealand, however. The "Catholic culture" of a significant proportion of those worshipping in Catholic parishes is shaped by their ethnicity. Again, there is scope for further exploration here.

273 Ibid.

About the Author

Anne Shave graduated with her doctorate in Theology through the University of Otago in 2018. Her research explored the experiences of Christians in midlife, within Catholic, Anglican and Presbyterian congregations in New Zealand.

In 2019 Anne was a scholar in residence at Vaughan Park Anglican Retreat Centre in Auckland, and also completed a short course in retreat direction and spiritual guidance at St Beuno's Jesuit Spirituality Centre in Wales.

Formerly a secondary-school English teacher, Anne is now employed part-time within the Presbyterian Church of Aotearoa New Zealand and also works as a tutor at disability support and service provider Hōhepa Canterbury.